SPIDER-MAN

Plot: Stan Lee & Steve Ditko
Script: Daniel Quantz
Art: Mark Brooks & Jonboy Meyers
with Pat Davidson
Colors: UDON's Danimation with Simon Yeung
& Larry Molinar
Udon Chief: Erik Ko
Letters: Randy Gentile & Dave Sharpe

Assistant Editors: MacKenzie Cadenhead & Nick Lowe
Editor: C.B. Cebulski
Consulting Editor: Ralph Macchio

Collections Editor: Jeff Youngquist
Assistant Editor: Jennifer Grünwald
Book Designer: Jeof Vita

Editor in Chief: Joe Quesada
Publisher: Dan Buckley

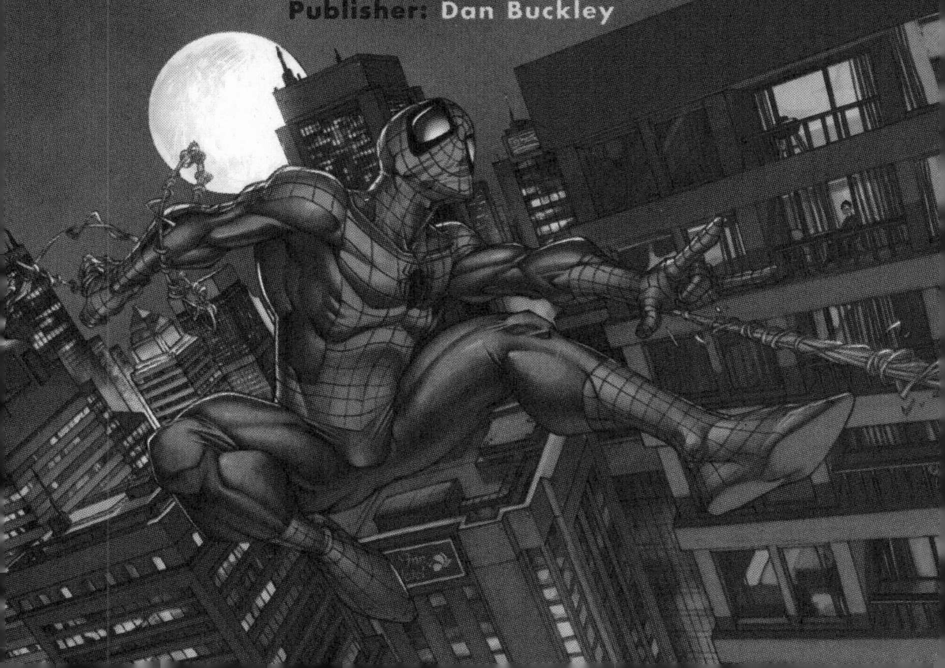

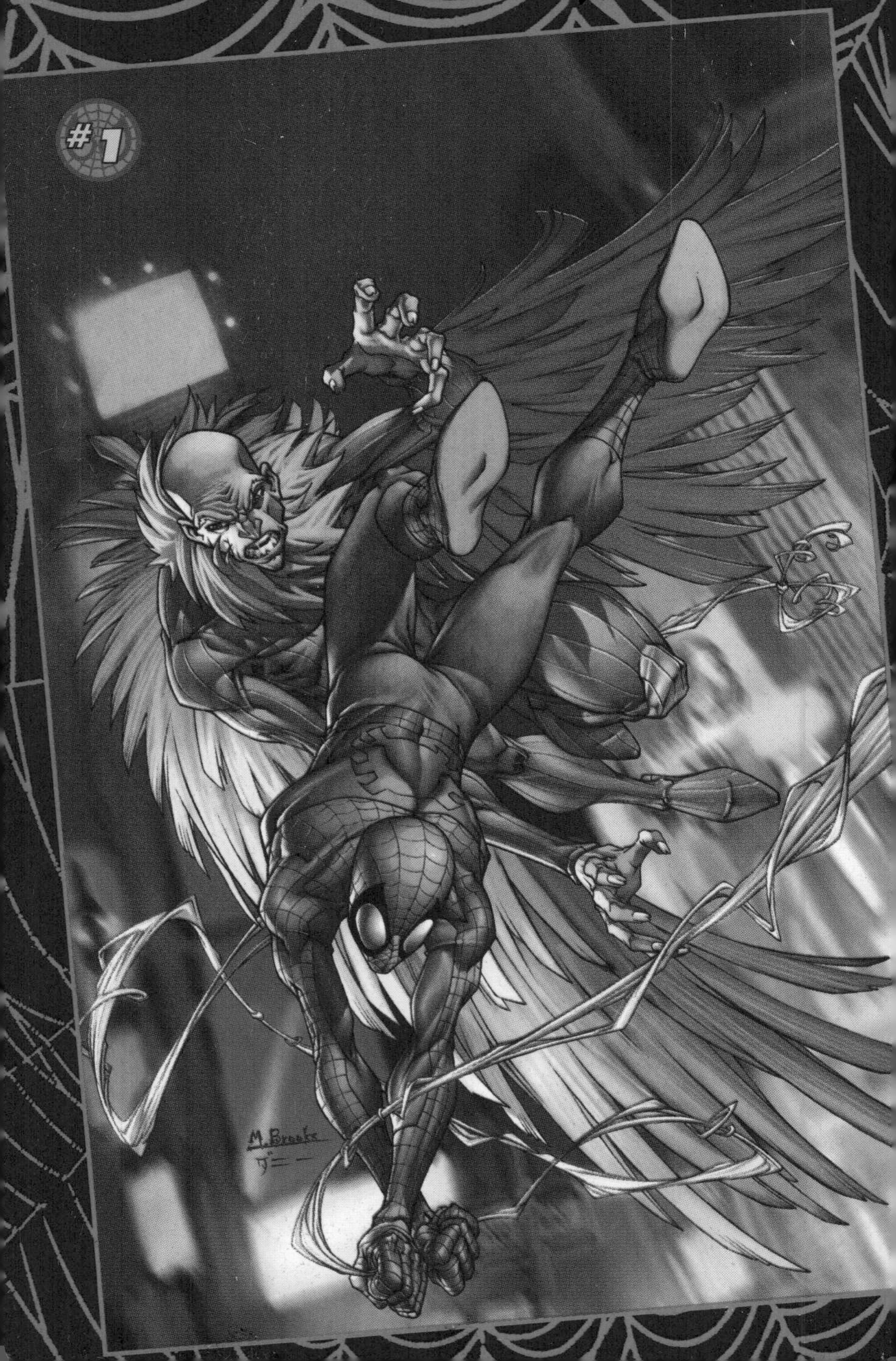
#1

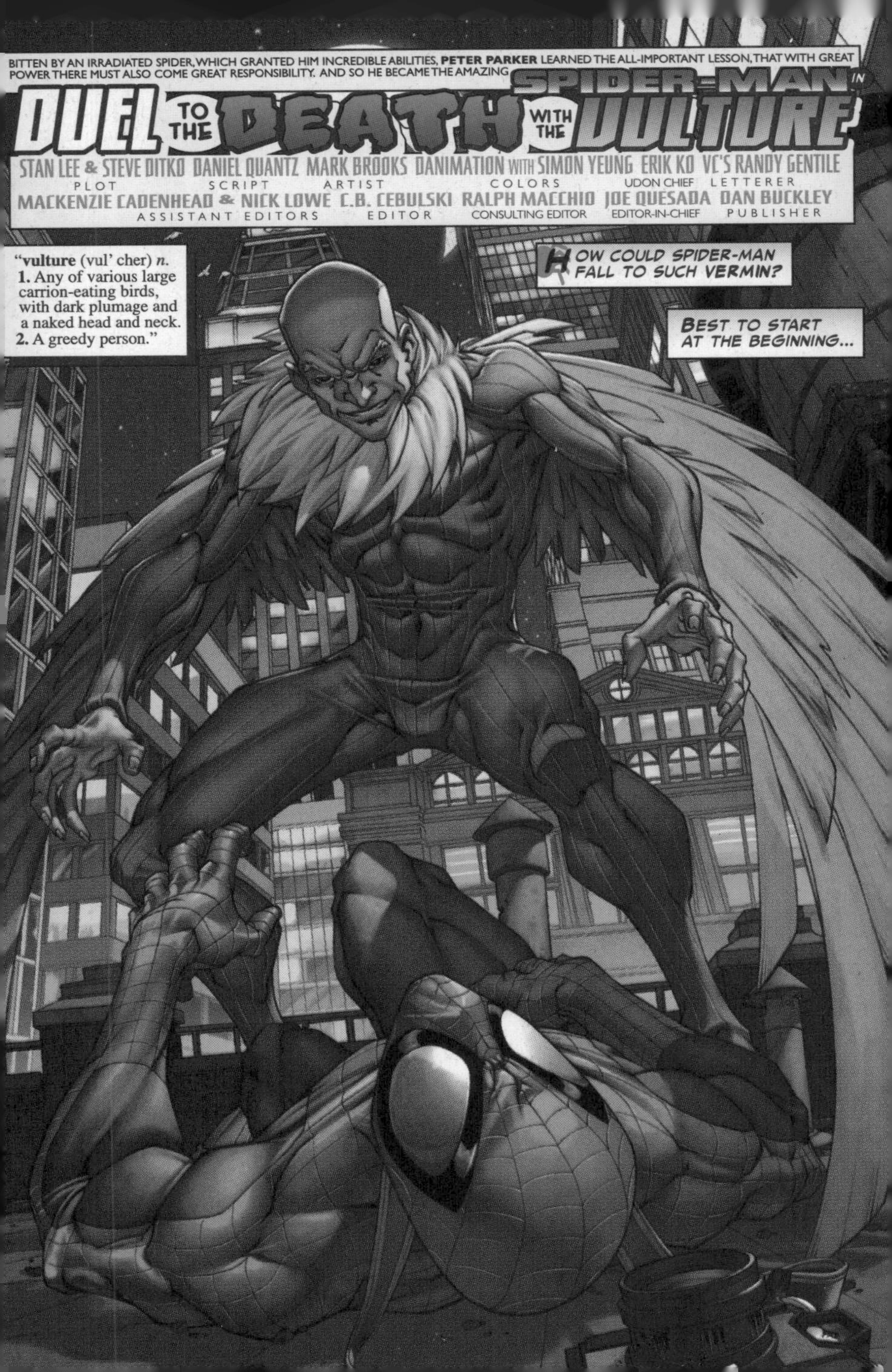

BITTEN BY AN IRRADIATED SPIDER, WHICH GRANTED HIM INCREDIBLE ABILITIES, PETER PARKER LEARNED THE ALL-IMPORTANT LESSON, THAT WITH GREAT POWER THERE MUST ALSO COME GREAT RESPONSIBILITY. AND SO HE BECAME THE AMAZING
SPIDER-MAN IN
DUEL TO THE DEATH WITH THE VULTURE
STAN LEE & STEVE DITKO PLOT
DANIEL QUANTZ SCRIPT
MARK BROOKS ARTIST
DANIMATION WITH SIMON YEUNG COLORS
ERIK KO UDON CHIEF
VC'S RANDY GENTILE LETTERER
MACKENZIE CADENHEAD & NICK LOWE ASSISTANT EDITORS
C.B. CEBULSKI EDITOR
RALPH MACCHIO CONSULTING EDITOR
JOE QUESADA EDITOR-IN-CHIEF
DAN BUCKLEY PUBLISHER
"vulture (vul' cher) n. 1. Any of various large carrion-eating birds, with dark plumage and a naked head and neck. 2. A greedy person."
HOW COULD SPIDER-MAN FALL TO SUCH VERMIN?
BEST TO START AT THE BEGINNING...

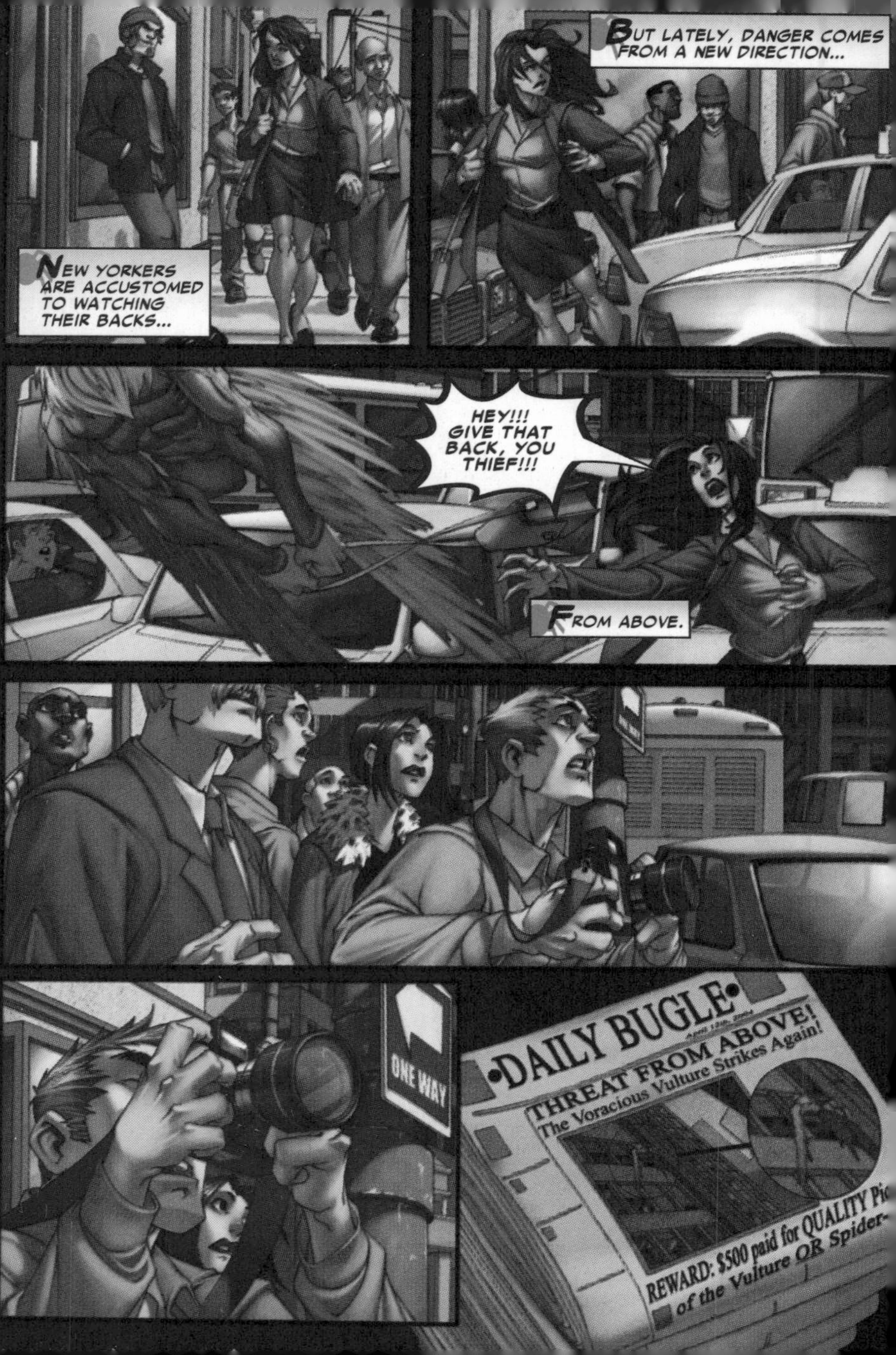
NEW YORKERS ARE ACCUSTOMED TO WATCHING THEIR BACKS...
BUT LATELY, DANGER COMES FROM A NEW DIRECTION...
HEY!!! GIVE THAT BACK, YOU THIEF!!!
FROM ABOVE.
ONE WAY
DAILY BUGLE
THREAT FROM ABOVE!
The Voracious Vulture Strikes Again!
REWARD: $500 paid for QUALITY Pic
of the Vulture OR Spider-

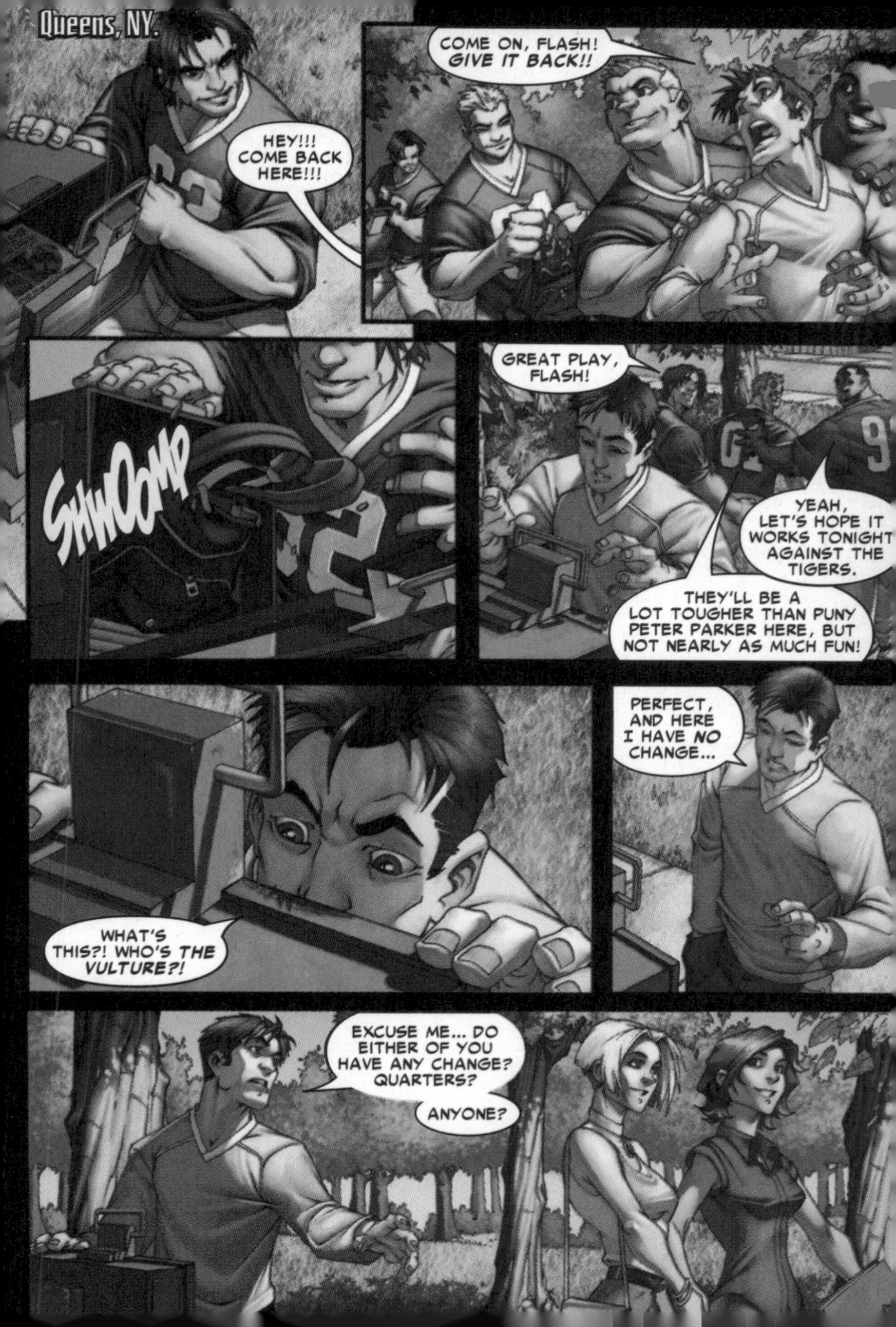
Queens, NY.
HEY!!! COME BACK HERE!!!
COME ON, FLASH! GIVE IT BACK!!
SHWOOMP
GREAT PLAY, FLASH!
YEAH, LET'S HOPE IT WORKS TONIGHT AGAINST THE TIGERS.
THEY'LL BE A LOT TOUGHER THAN PUNY PETER PARKER HERE, BUT NOT NEARLY AS MUCH FUN!
WHAT'S THIS?! WHO'S THE VULTURE?!
PERFECT, AND HERE I HAVE NO CHANGE...
EXCUSE ME... DO EITHER OF YOU HAVE ANY CHANGE? QUARTERS?
ANYONE?

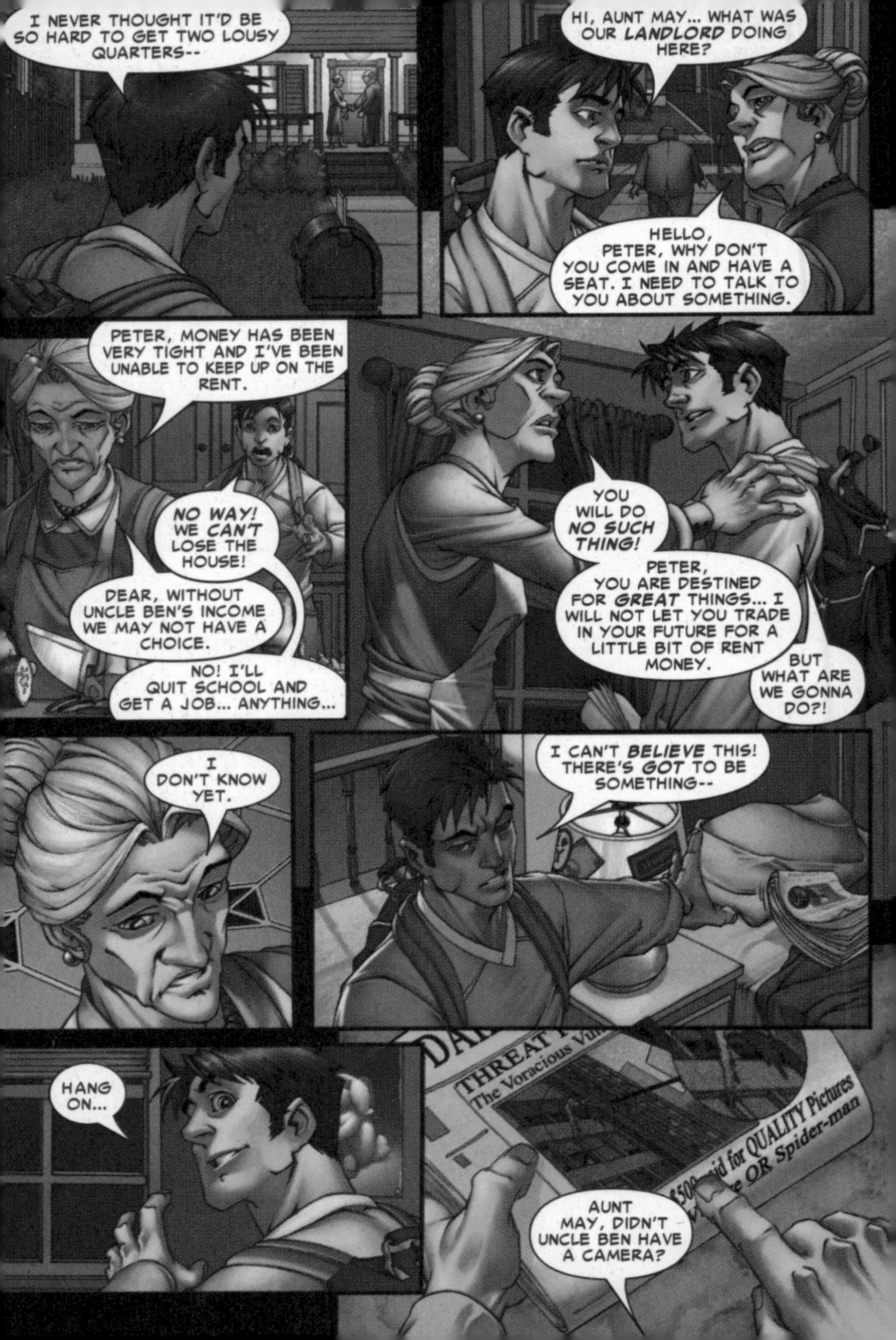

I NEVER THOUGHT IT'D BE SO HARD TO GET TWO LOUSY QUARTERS--
HI, AUNT MAY... WHAT WAS OUR *LANDLORD* DOING HERE?
HELLO, PETER, WHY DON'T YOU COME IN AND HAVE A SEAT. I NEED TO TALK TO YOU ABOUT SOMETHING.
PETER, MONEY HAS BEEN VERY TIGHT AND I'VE BEEN UNABLE TO KEEP UP ON THE RENT.
NO WAY! WE *CAN'T* LOSE THE HOUSE!
DEAR, WITHOUT UNCLE BEN'S INCOME WE MAY NOT HAVE A CHOICE.
NO! I'LL QUIT SCHOOL AND GET A JOB... ANYTHING...
YOU WILL DO *NO SUCH THING!*
PETER, YOU ARE DESTINED FOR *GREAT* THINGS... I WILL NOT LET YOU TRADE IN YOUR FUTURE FOR A LITTLE BIT OF RENT MONEY.
BUT WHAT ARE WE GONNA DO?!
I DON'T KNOW YET.
I CAN'T *BELIEVE* THIS! THERE'S *GOT* TO BE SOMETHING--
HANG ON...
THREAT
The Voracious
paid for QUALITY Pictures
OR Spider-man
AUNT MAY, DIDN'T UNCLE BEN HAVE A CAMERA?

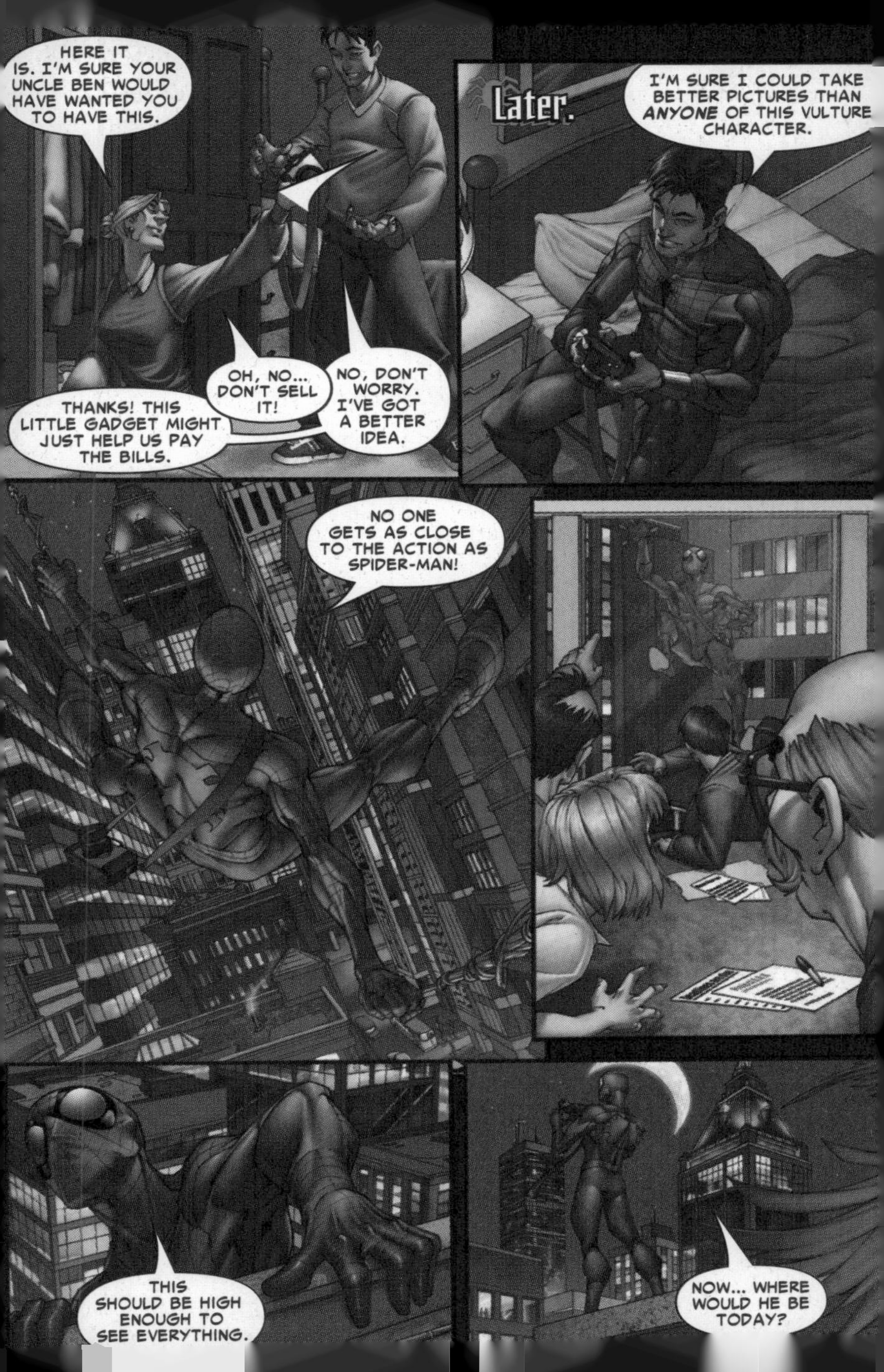
HERE IT IS. I'M SURE YOUR UNCLE BEN WOULD HAVE WANTED YOU TO HAVE THIS.
THANKS! THIS LITTLE GADGET MIGHT JUST HELP US PAY THE BILLS.
OH, NO... DON'T SELL IT!
NO, DON'T WORRY. I'VE GOT A BETTER IDEA.
Later.
I'M SURE I COULD TAKE BETTER PICTURES THAN *ANYONE* OF THIS VULTURE CHARACTER.
NO ONE GETS AS CLOSE TO THE ACTION AS SPIDER-MAN!
THIS SHOULD BE HIGH ENOUGH TO SEE EVERYTHING.
NOW... WHERE WOULD HE BE TODAY?

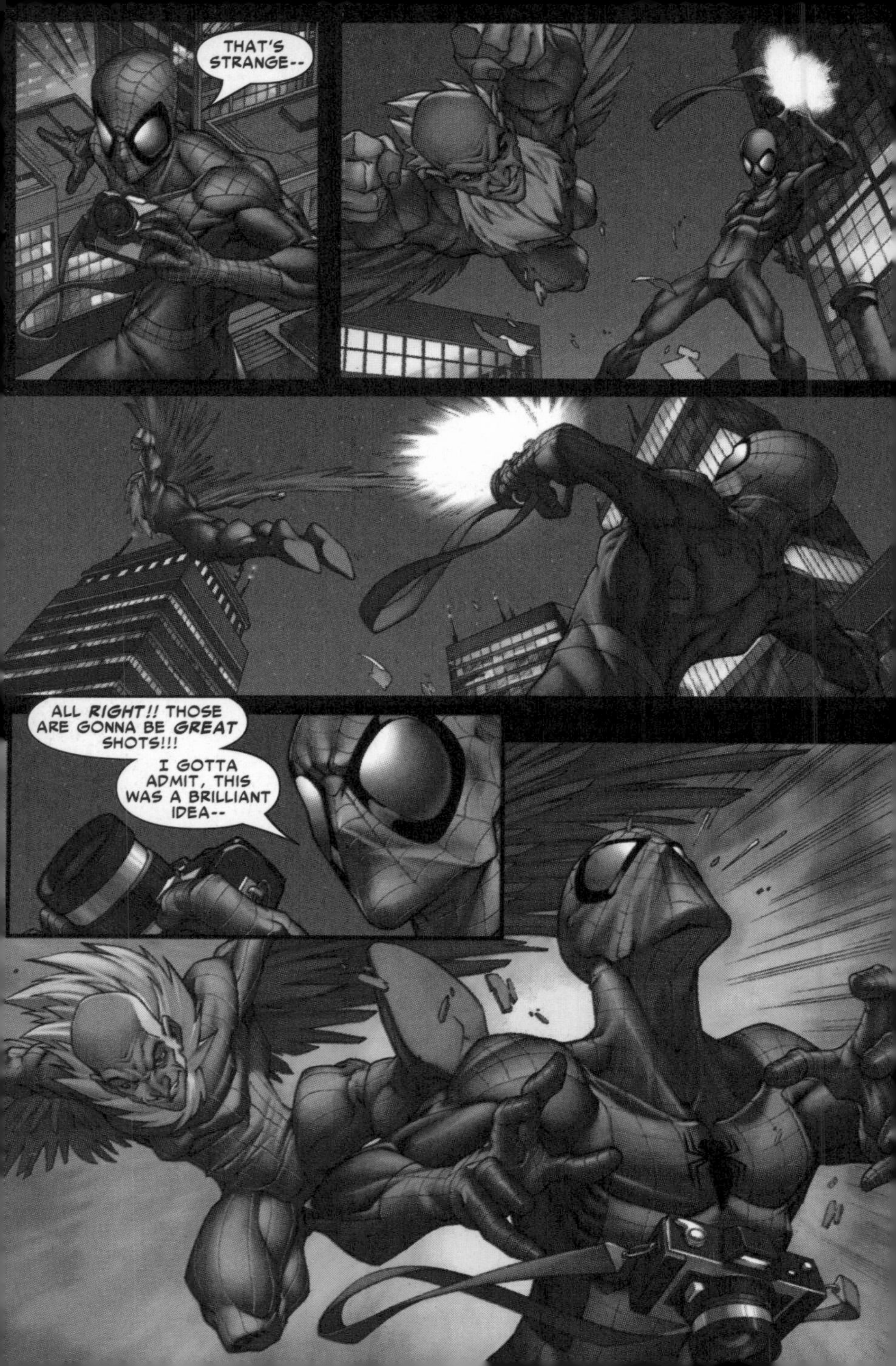
THAT'S STRANGE--
ALL RIGHT!! THOSE ARE GONNA BE GREAT SHOTS!!!
I GOTTA ADMIT, THIS WAS A BRILLIANT IDEA--

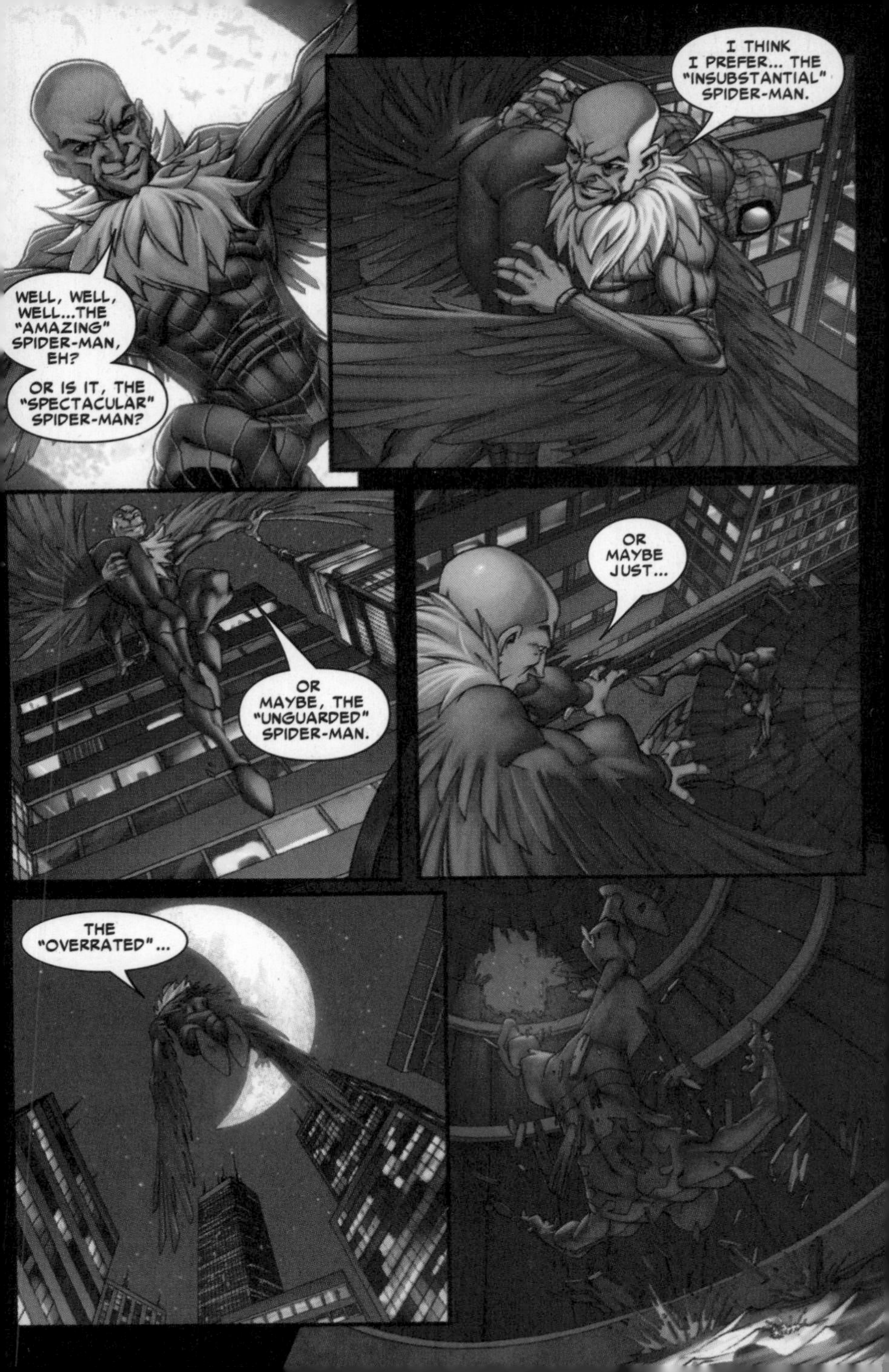
WELL, WELL, WELL...THE "AMAZING" SPIDER-MAN, EH?
OR IS IT, THE "SPECTACULAR" SPIDER-MAN?
I THINK I PREFER... THE "INSUBSTANTIAL" SPIDER-MAN.
OR MAYBE, THE "UNGUARDED" SPIDER-MAN.
OR MAYBE JUST...
THE "OVERRATED"...

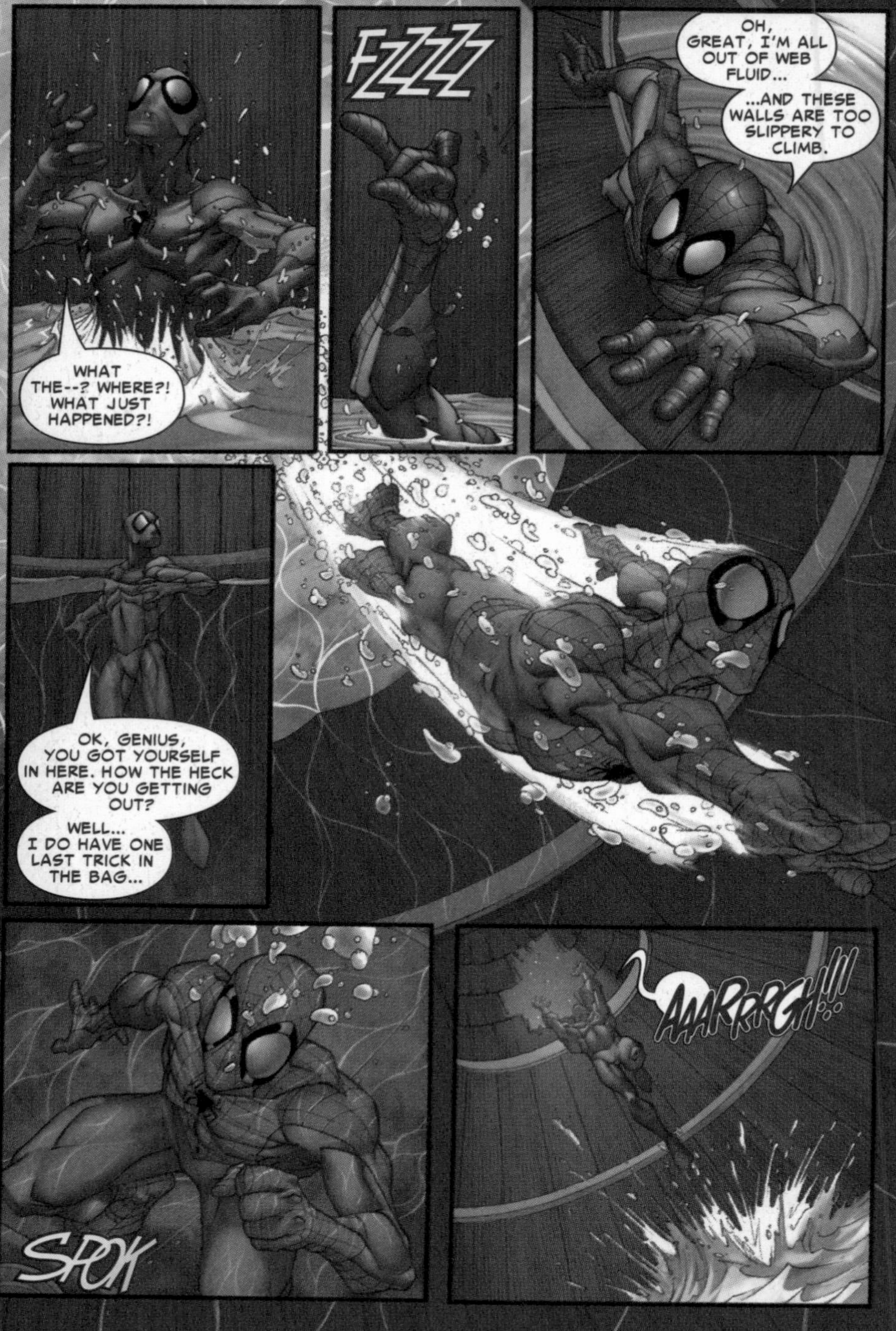
WHAT THE--? WHERE?! WHAT JUST HAPPENED?!
FZZZZ
OH, GREAT, I'M ALL OUT OF WEB FLUID...
...AND THESE WALLS ARE TOO SLIPPERY TO CLIMB.
OK, GENIUS, YOU GOT YOURSELF IN HERE. HOW THE HECK ARE YOU GETTING OUT?
WELL... I DO HAVE ONE LAST TRICK IN THE BAG...
SPOK
AAARRRGH!!!

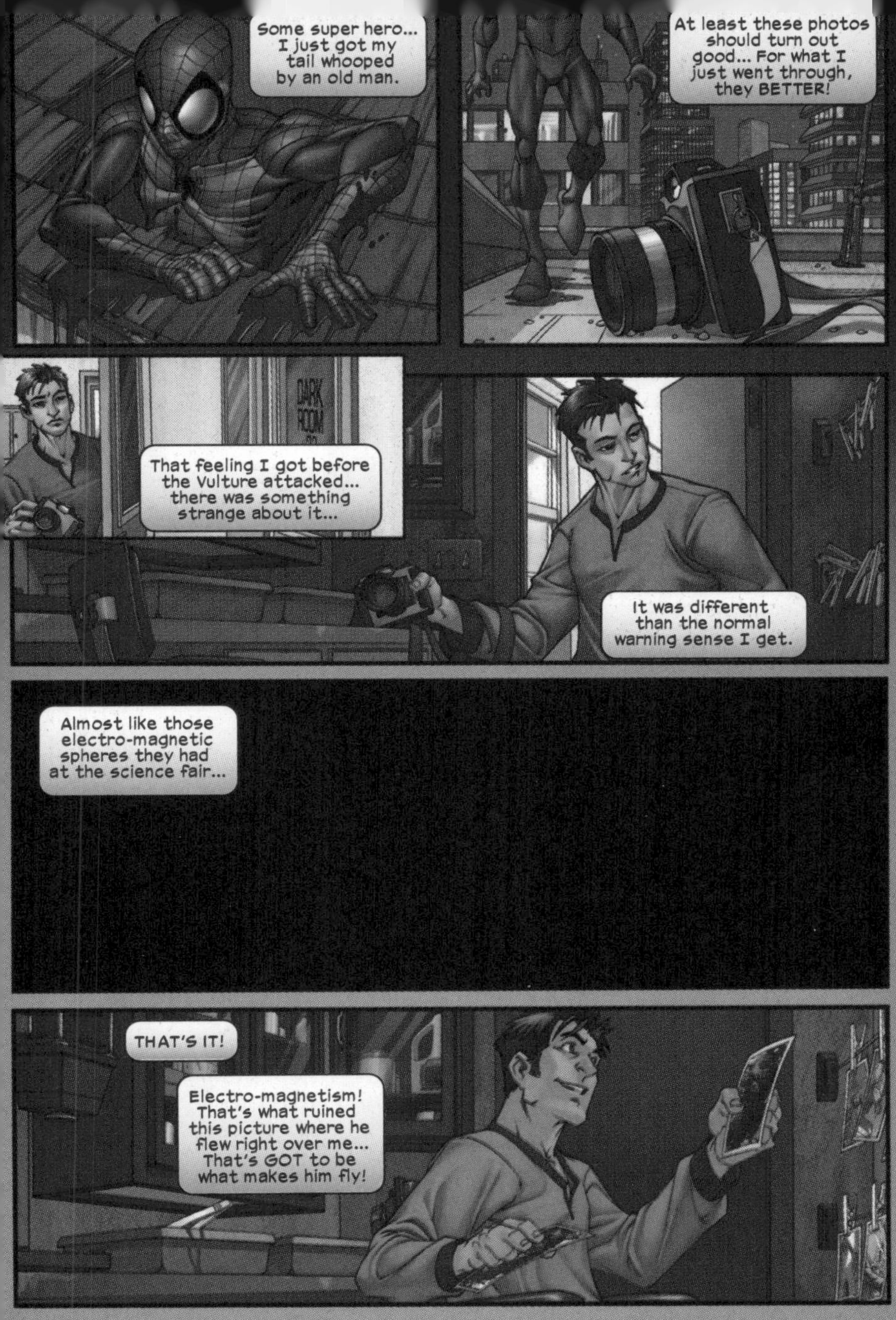
Some super hero... I just got my tail whooped by an old man.
At least these photos should turn out good... For what I just went through, they BETTER!
DARK ROOM
That feeling I got before the Vulture attacked... there was something strange about it...
It was different than the normal warning sense I get.
Almost like those electro-magnetic spheres they had at the science fair...
THAT'S IT!
Electro-magnetism! That's what ruined this picture where he flew right over me... That's GOT to be what makes him fly!

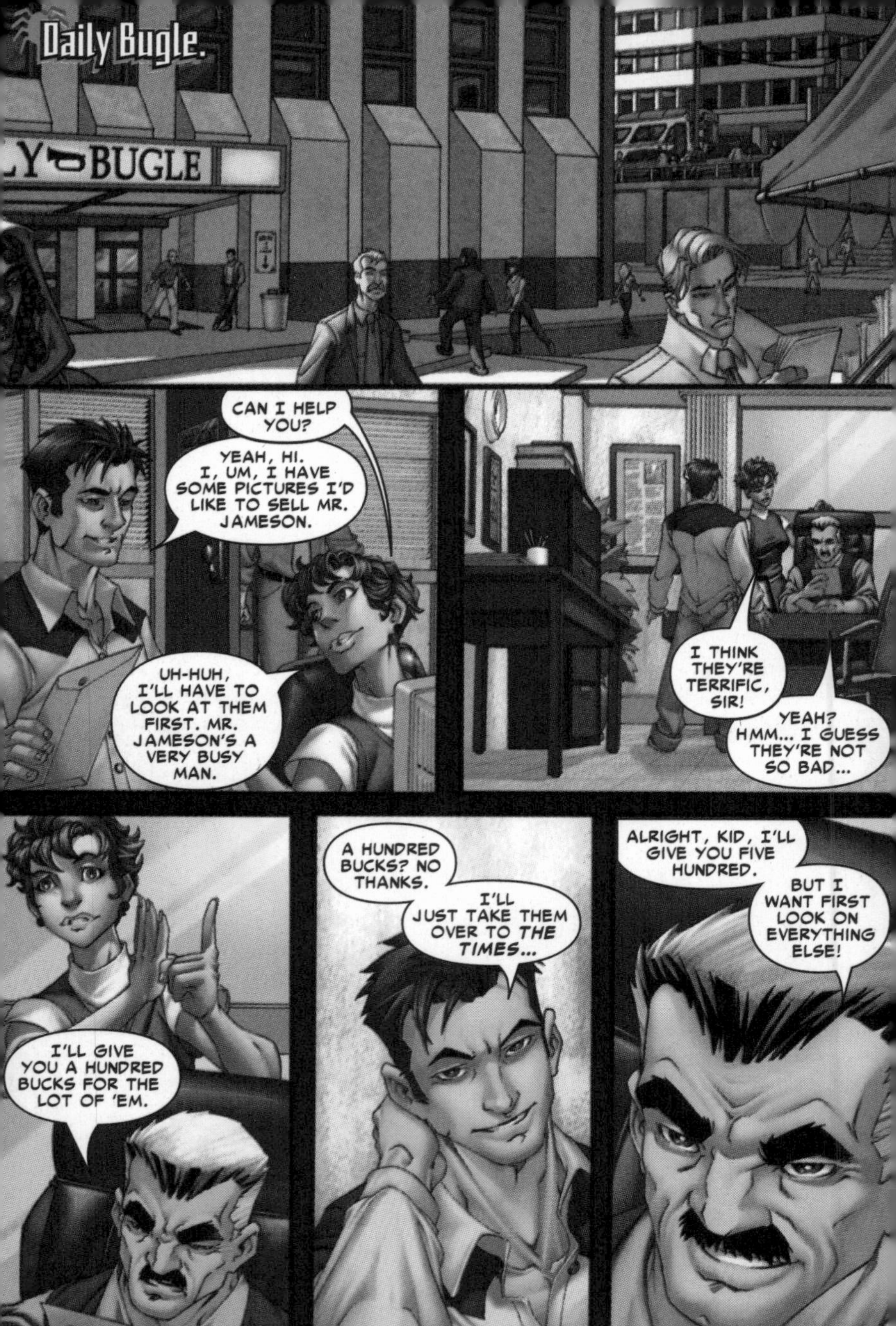
Daily Bugle.
DAILY BUGLE
CAN I HELP YOU?
YEAH, HI. I, UM, I HAVE SOME PICTURES I'D LIKE TO SELL MR. JAMESON.
UH-HUH, I'LL HAVE TO LOOK AT THEM FIRST. MR. JAMESON'S A VERY BUSY MAN.
I THINK THEY'RE TERRIFIC, SIR!
YEAH? HMM... I GUESS THEY'RE NOT SO BAD...
I'LL GIVE YOU A HUNDRED BUCKS FOR THE LOT OF 'EM.
A HUNDRED BUCKS? NO THANKS.
I'LL JUST TAKE THEM OVER TO *THE TIMES*...
ALRIGHT, KID, I'LL GIVE YOU FIVE HUNDRED.
BUT I WANT FIRST LOOK ON EVERYTHING ELSE!

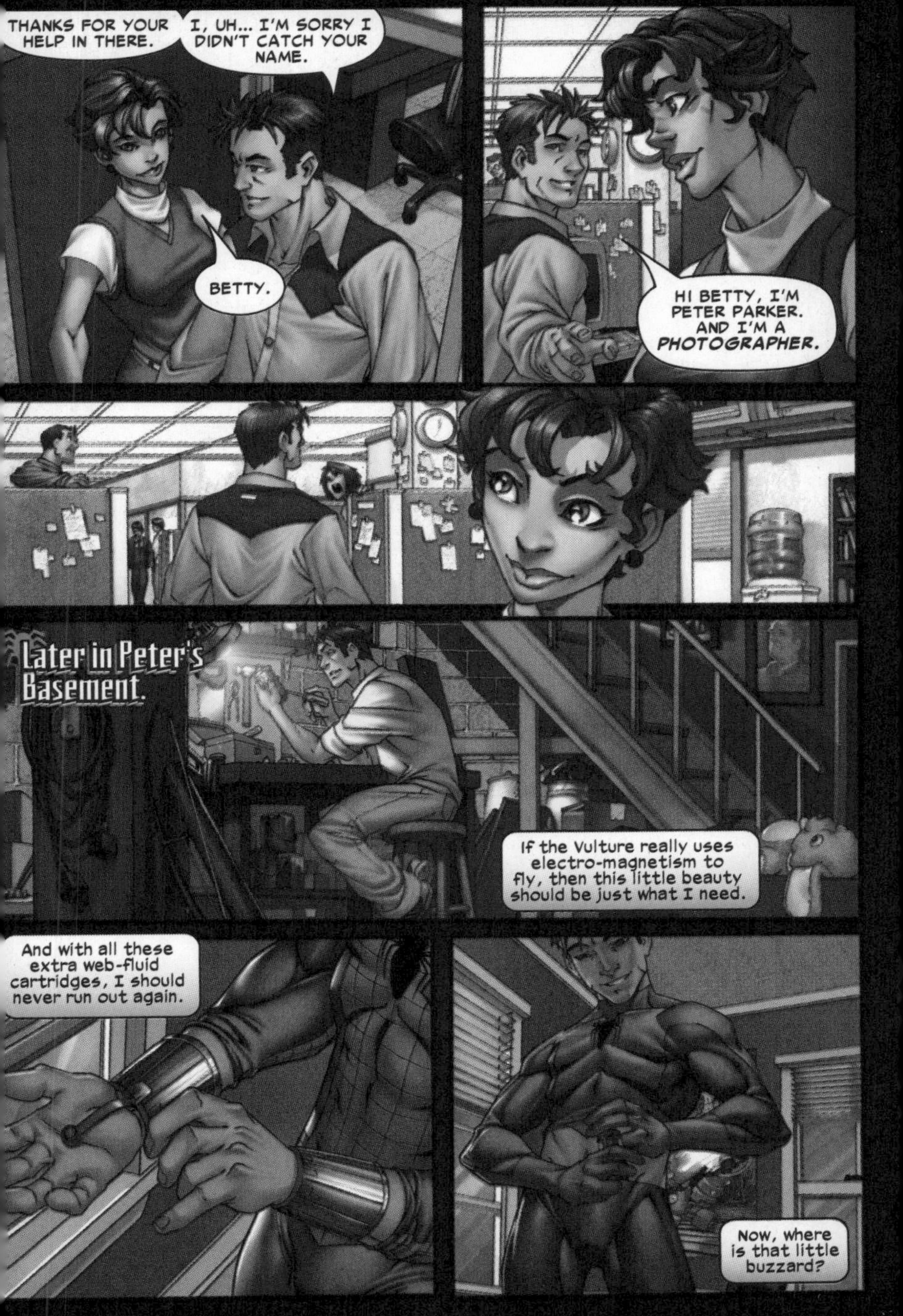
THANKS FOR YOUR HELP IN THERE.
I, UH... I'M SORRY I DIDN'T CATCH YOUR NAME.
BETTY.
HI BETTY, I'M PETER PARKER. AND I'M A PHOTOGRAPHER.
Later in Peter's Basement.
If the Vulture really uses electro-magnetism to fly, then this little beauty should be just what I need.
And with all these extra web-fluid cartridges, I should never run out again.
Now, where is that little buzzard?

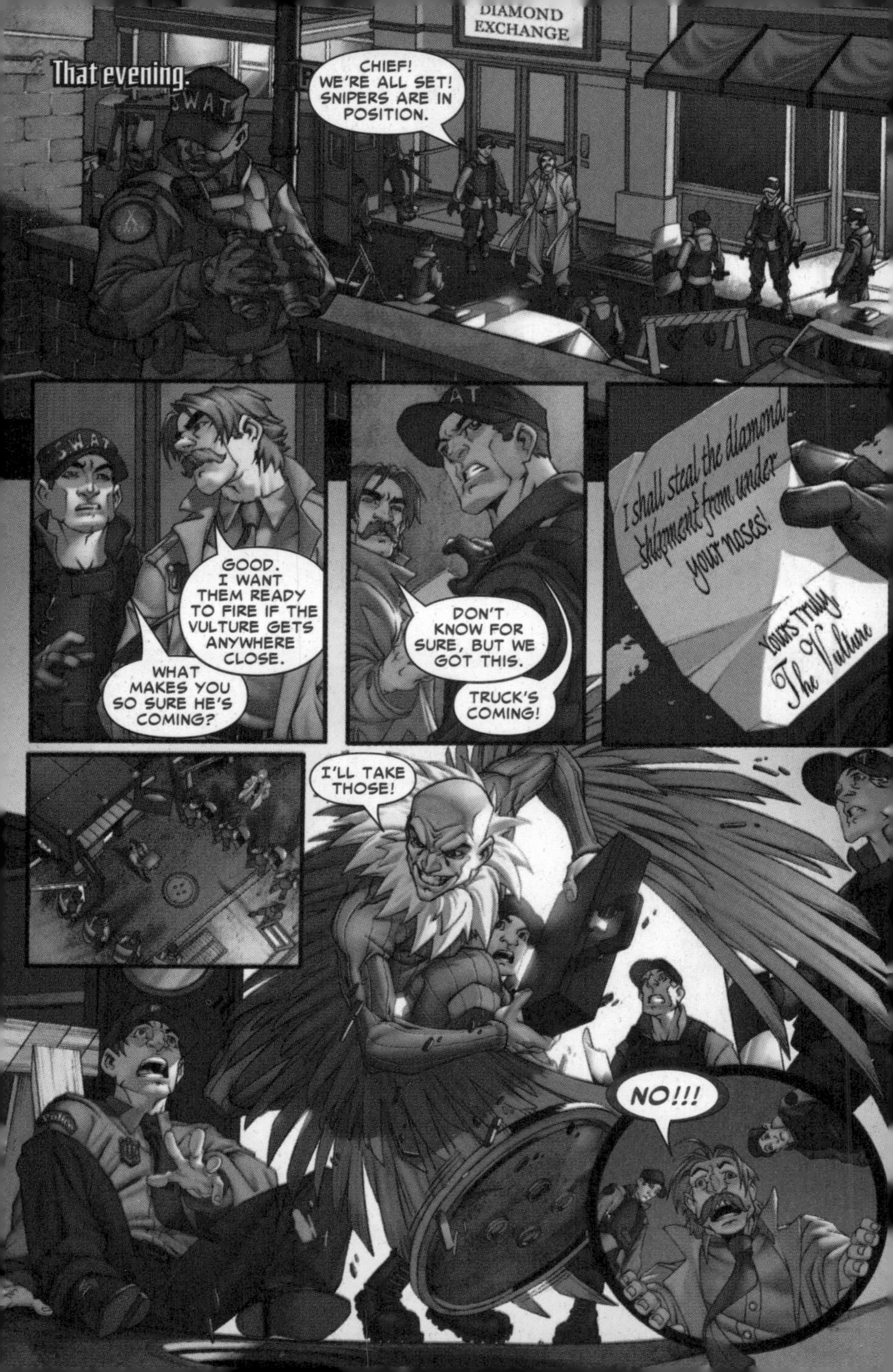
That evening.
DIAMOND EXCHANGE
CHIEF! WE'RE ALL SET! SNIPERS ARE IN POSITION.
GOOD. I WANT THEM READY TO FIRE IF THE VULTURE GETS ANYWHERE CLOSE.
WHAT MAKES YOU SO SURE HE'S COMING?
DON'T KNOW FOR SURE, BUT WE GOT THIS.
TRUCK'S COMING!
I shall steal the diamond shipment from under your noses!
Yours Truly The Vulture
I'LL TAKE THOSE!
NO!!!

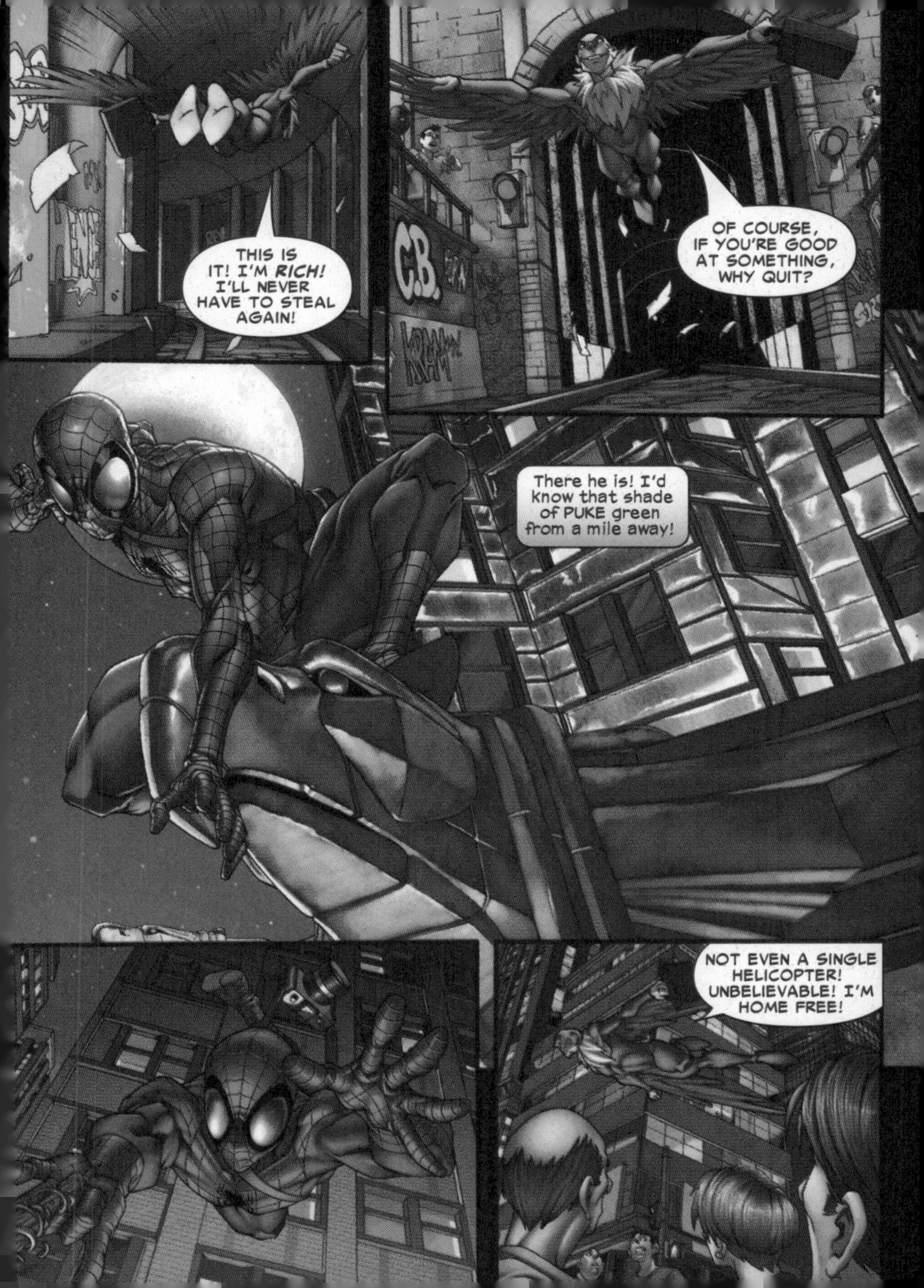
THIS IS IT! I'M *RICH!* I'LL NEVER HAVE TO STEAL AGAIN!
OF COURSE, IF YOU'RE GOOD AT SOMETHING, WHY QUIT?
C.B.
There he is! I'd know that shade of PUKE green from a mile away!
NOT EVEN A SINGLE HELICOPTER! UNBELIEVABLE! I'M HOME FREE!

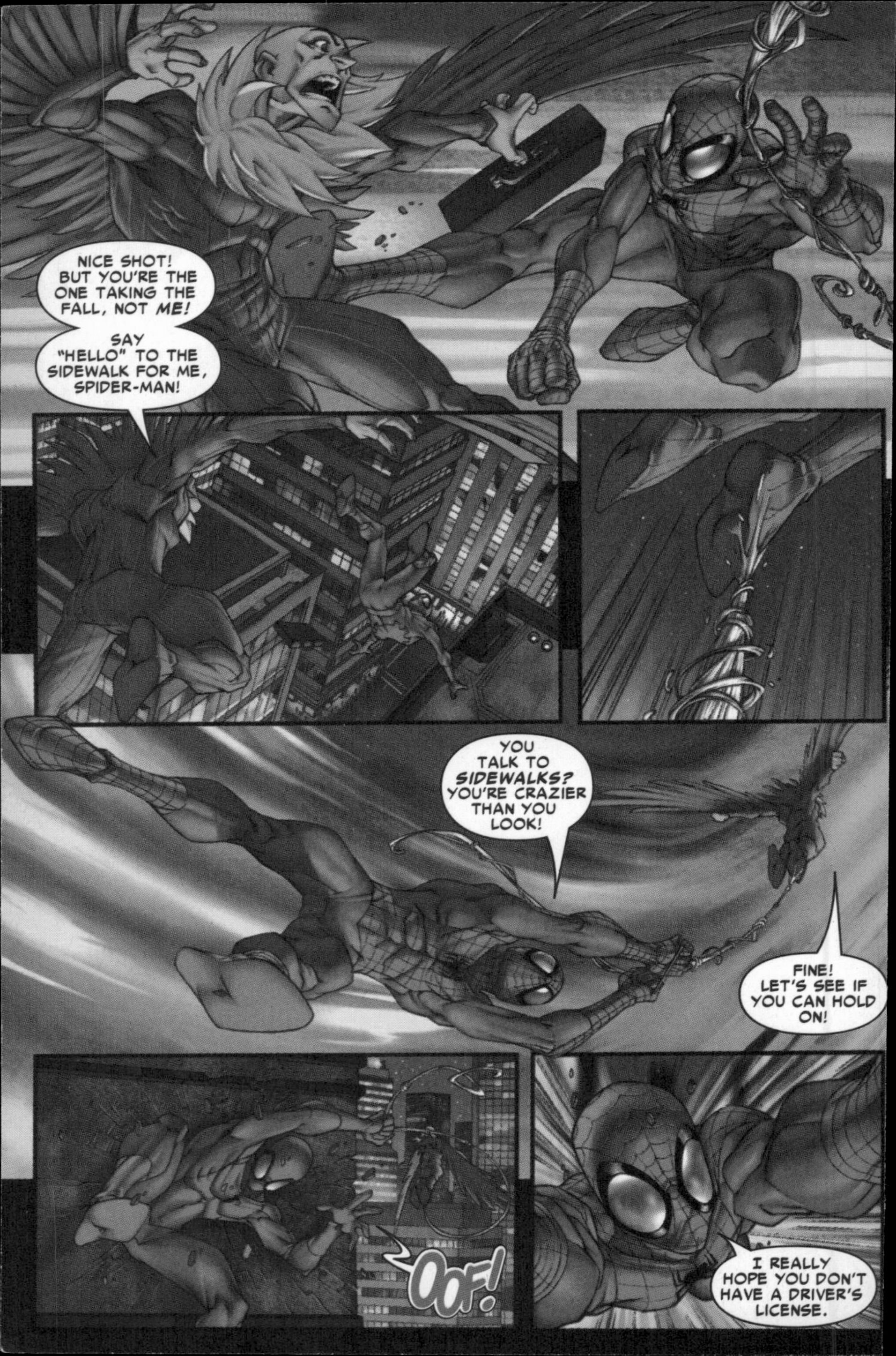
NICE SHOT! BUT YOU'RE THE ONE TAKING THE FALL, NOT ME!
SAY "HELLO" TO THE SIDEWALK FOR ME, SPIDER-MAN!
YOU TALK TO SIDEWALKS? YOU'RE CRAZIER THAN YOU LOOK!
FINE! LET'S SEE IF YOU CAN HOLD ON!
OOF!
I REALLY HOPE YOU DON'T HAVE A DRIVER'S LICENSE.

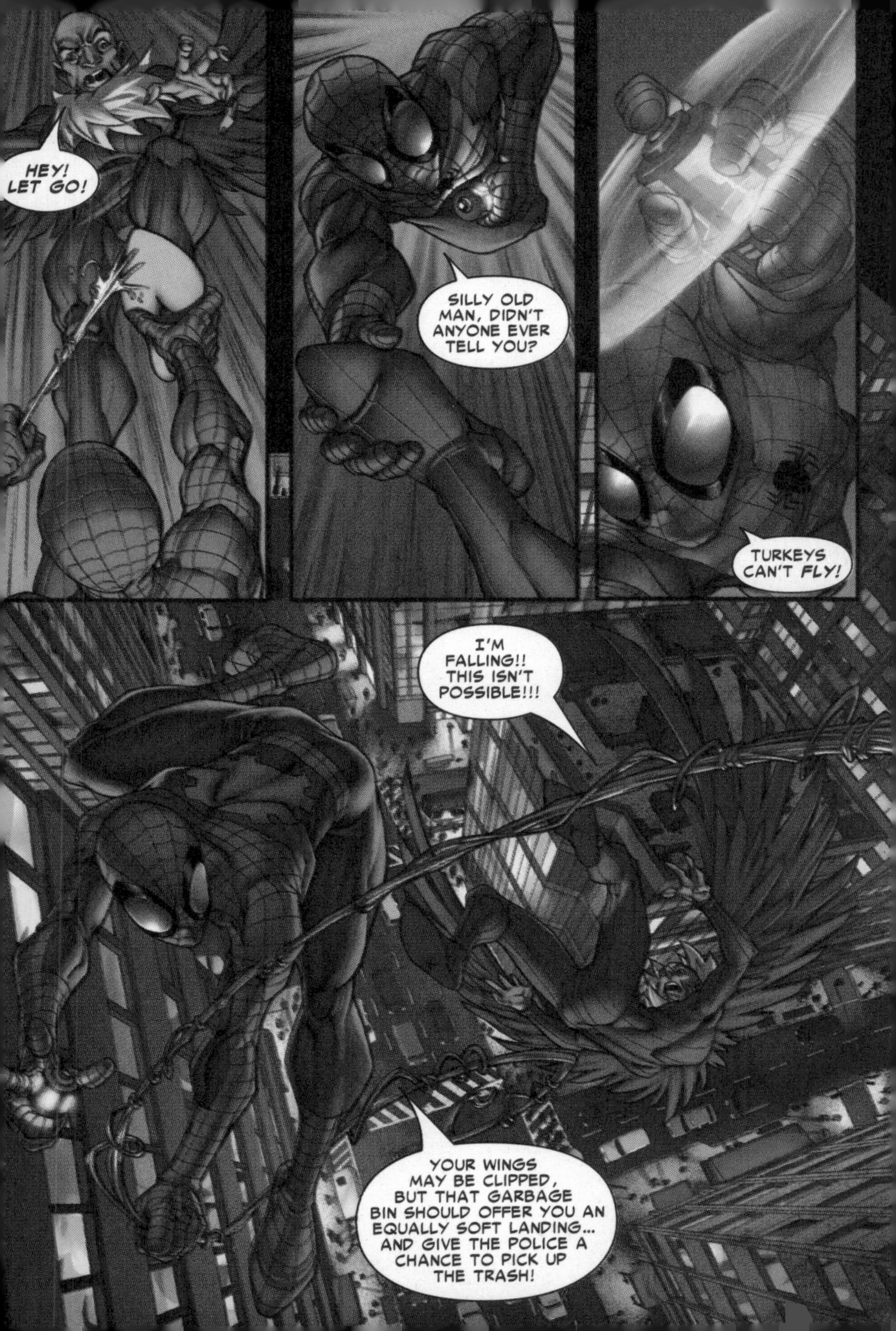
HEY! LET GO!
SILLY OLD MAN, DIDN'T ANYONE EVER TELL YOU?
TURKEYS CAN'T FLY!
I'M FALLING!! THIS ISN'T POSSIBLE!!!
YOUR WINGS MAY BE CLIPPED, BUT THAT GARBAGE BIN SHOULD OFFER YOU AN EQUALLY SOFT LANDING... AND GIVE THE POLICE A CHANCE TO PICK UP THE TRASH!

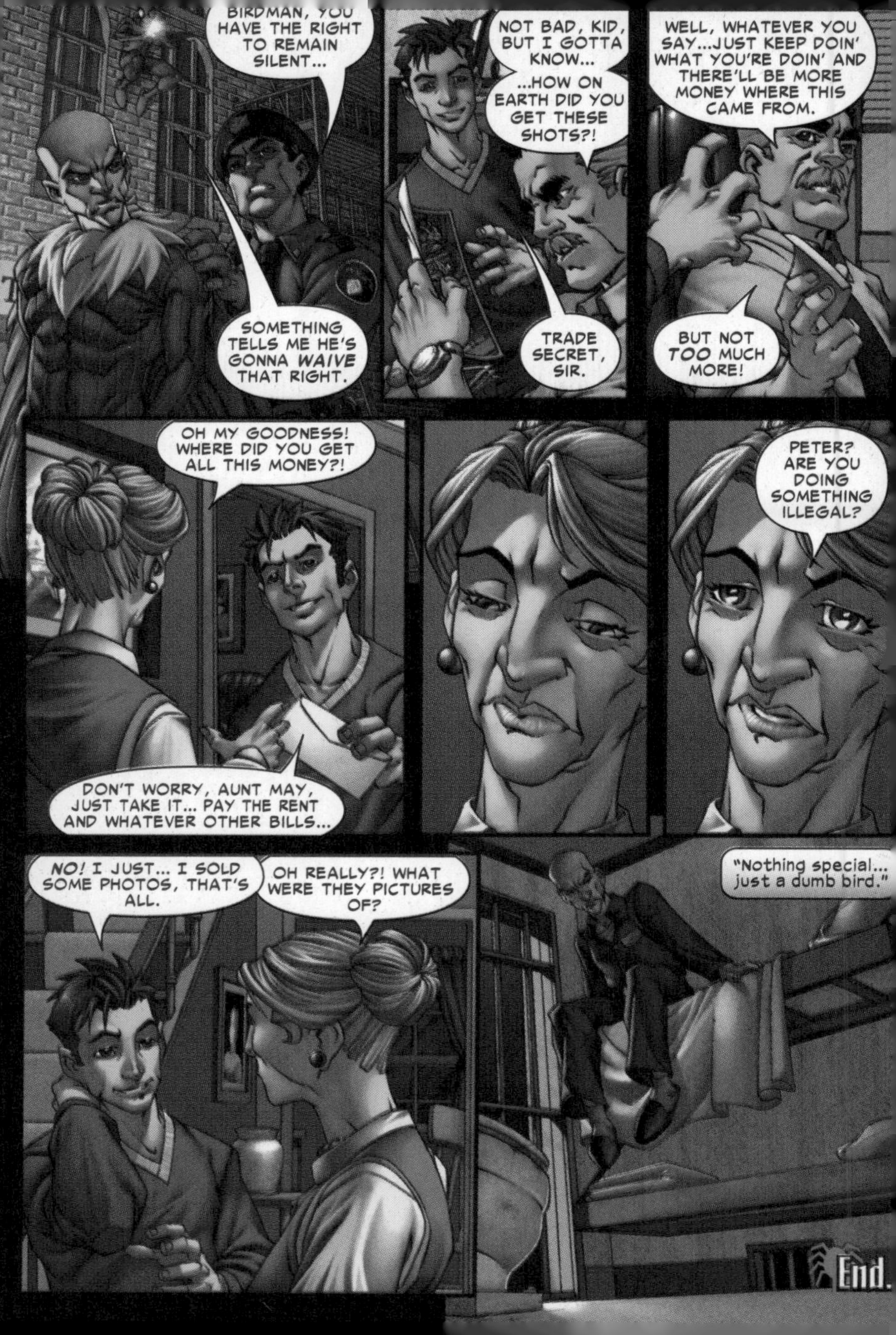
BIRDMAN, YOU HAVE THE RIGHT TO REMAIN SILENT...
SOMETHING TELLS ME HE'S GONNA *WAIVE* THAT RIGHT.
NOT BAD, KID, BUT I GOTTA KNOW...
...HOW ON EARTH DID YOU GET THESE SHOTS?!
TRADE SECRET, SIR.
WELL, WHATEVER YOU SAY...JUST KEEP DOIN' WHAT YOU'RE DOIN' AND THERE'LL BE MORE MONEY WHERE THIS CAME FROM.
BUT NOT *TOO* MUCH MORE!
OH MY GOODNESS! WHERE DID YOU GET ALL THIS MONEY?!
DON'T WORRY, AUNT MAY, JUST TAKE IT... PAY THE RENT AND WHATEVER OTHER BILLS...
PETER? ARE YOU DOING SOMETHING ILLEGAL?
NO! I JUST... I SOLD SOME PHOTOS, THAT'S ALL.
OH REALLY?! WHAT WERE THEY PICTURES OF?
"Nothing special... just a dumb bird."
End.

BITTEN BY AN IRRADIATED SPIDER, WHICH GRANTED HIM INCREDIBLE ABILITIES, **PETER PARKER** LEARNED THE ALL-IMPORTANT LESSON, THAT WITH GREAT POWER THERE MUST ALSO COME GREAT RESPONSIBILITY. AND SO HE BECAME THE AMAZING SPIDER-MAN!

The Uncanny Threat of the Terrible Tinkerer!

STAN LEE & STEVE DITKO — PLOT
DANIEL QUANTZ — SCRIPT
JONBOY MEYERS — PENCILS
PAT DAVIDSON — INKS
UDON'S LARRY MOLINAR — COLORS
ERIK KO — UDON CHIEF
VC'S RANDY GENTILE — LETTERER
MACKENZIE CADENHEAD & NICK LOWE — ASSISTANT EDITORS
C.B. CEBULSKI — EDITOR
RALPH MACCHIO — CONSULTING EDITOR
JOE QUESADA — EDITOR-IN-CHIEF
DAN BUCKLEY — PUBLISHER

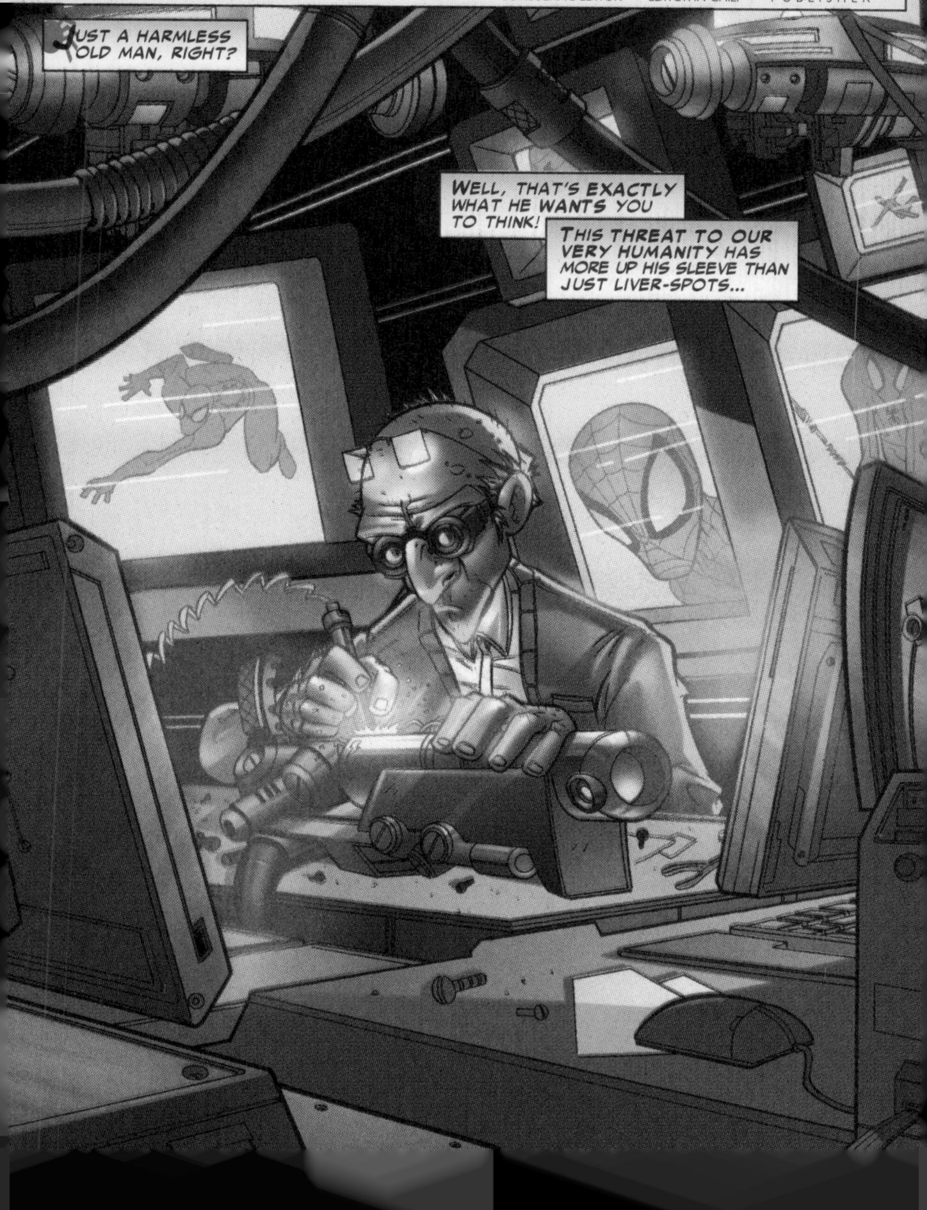

JUST A HARMLESS OLD MAN, RIGHT?
WELL, THAT'S EXACTLY WHAT HE WANTS YOU TO THINK!
THIS THREAT TO OUR VERY HUMANITY HAS MORE UP HIS SLEEVE THAN JUST LIVER-SPOTS...

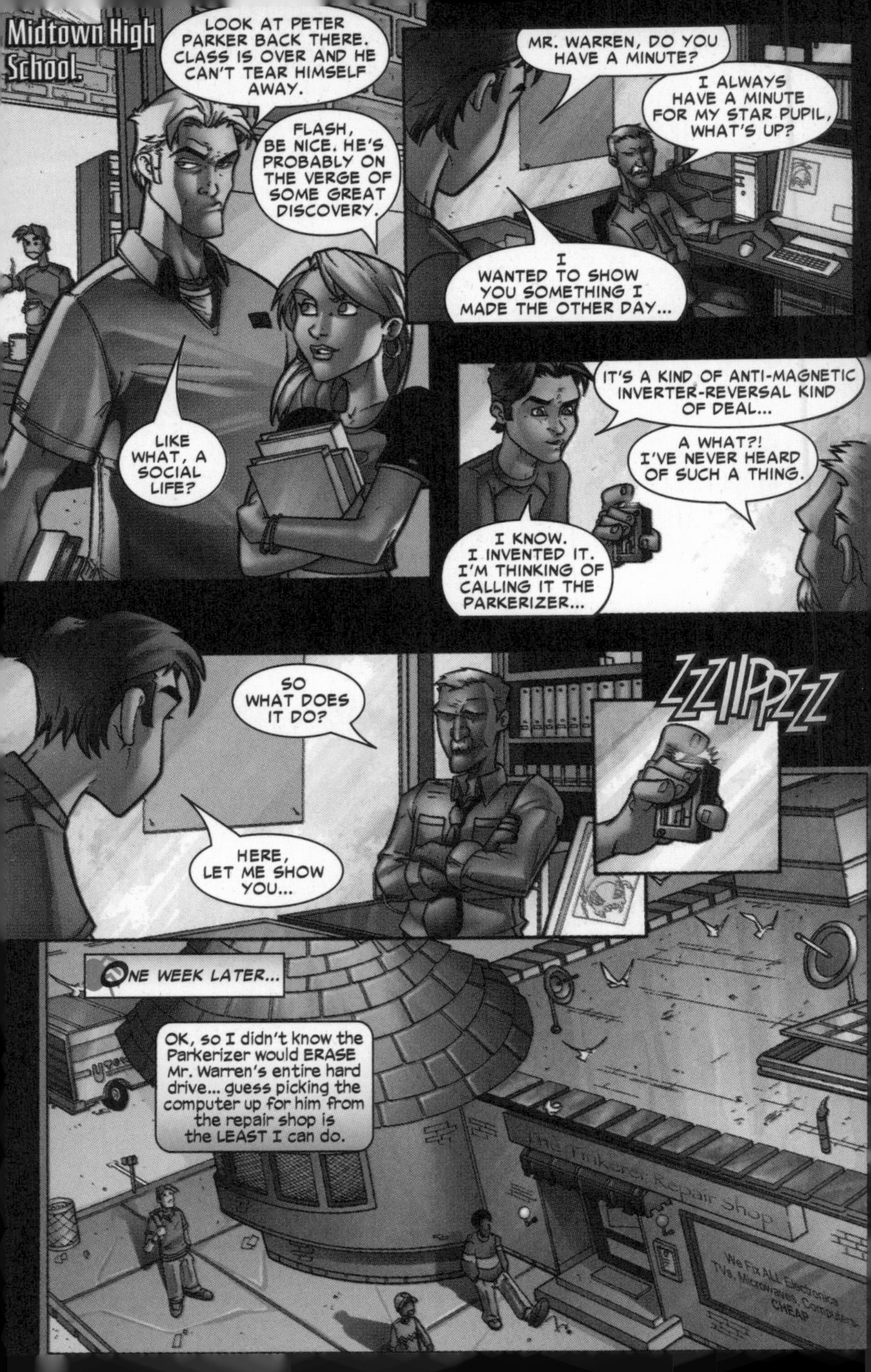
Midtown High School.
LOOK AT PETER PARKER BACK THERE. CLASS IS OVER AND HE CAN'T TEAR HIMSELF AWAY.
FLASH, BE NICE. HE'S PROBABLY ON THE VERGE OF SOME GREAT DISCOVERY.
LIKE WHAT, A SOCIAL LIFE?
MR. WARREN, DO YOU HAVE A MINUTE?
I ALWAYS HAVE A MINUTE FOR MY STAR PUPIL, WHAT'S UP?
I WANTED TO SHOW YOU SOMETHING I MADE THE OTHER DAY...
IT'S A KIND OF ANTI-MAGNETIC INVERTER-REVERSAL KIND OF DEAL...
A WHAT?! I'VE NEVER HEARD OF SUCH A THING.
I KNOW. I INVENTED IT. I'M THINKING OF CALLING IT THE PARKERIZER...
SO WHAT DOES IT DO?
HERE, LET ME SHOW YOU...
ZZZIIPPZZZ
ONE WEEK LATER...
OK, so I didn't know the Parkerizer would ERASE Mr. Warren's entire hard drive... guess picking the computer up for him from the repair shop is the LEAST I can do.
Repair Shop
We Fix ALL Electronics
TVs, Microwaves, Computers
CHEAP

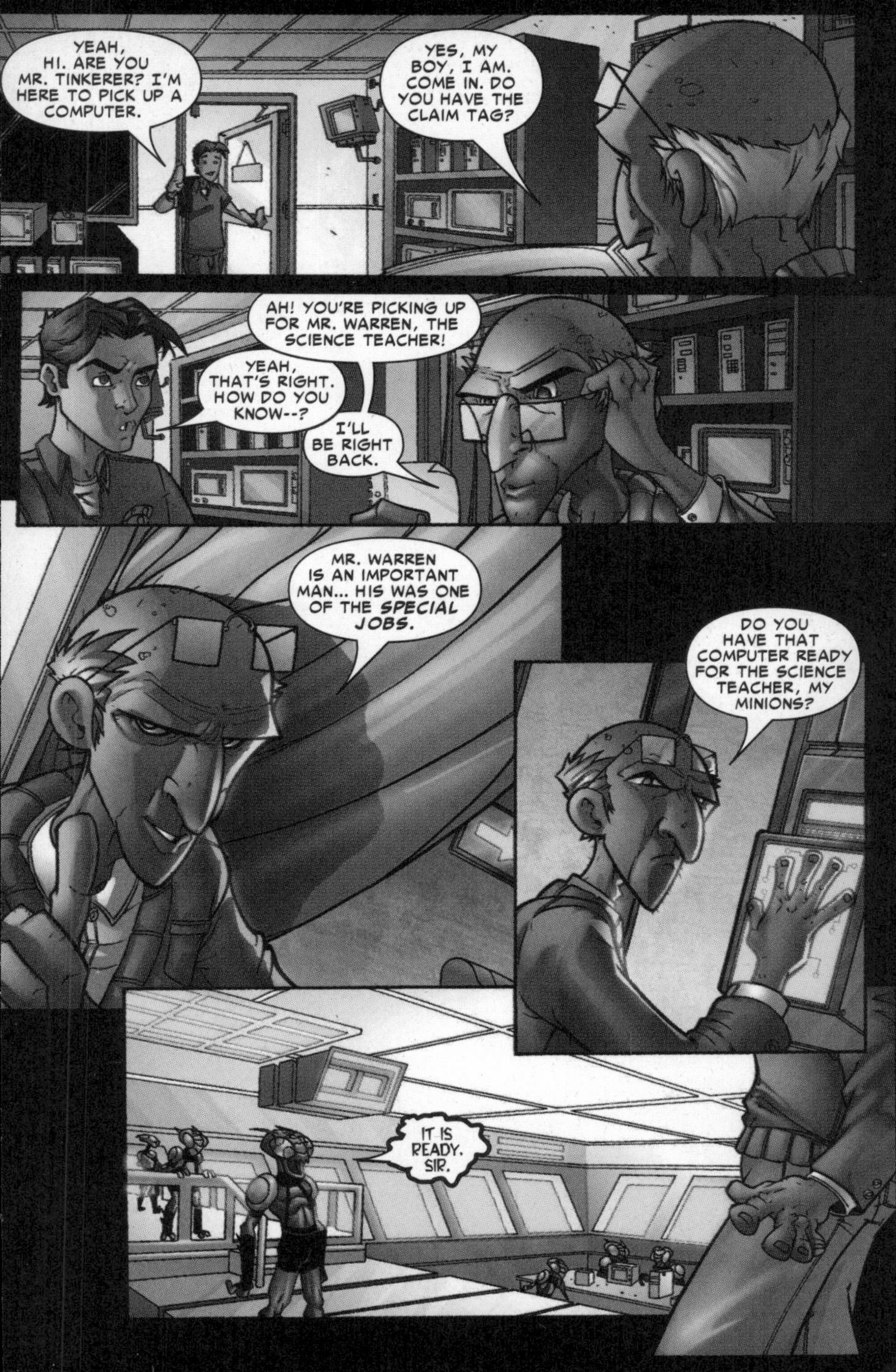
YEAH, HI. ARE YOU MR. TINKERER? I'M HERE TO PICK UP A COMPUTER.
YES, MY BOY, I AM. COME IN. DO YOU HAVE THE CLAIM TAG?
AH! YOU'RE PICKING UP FOR MR. WARREN, THE SCIENCE TEACHER!
YEAH, THAT'S RIGHT. HOW DO YOU KNOW--?
I'LL BE RIGHT BACK.
MR. WARREN IS AN IMPORTANT MAN... HIS WAS ONE OF THE SPECIAL JOBS.
DO YOU HAVE THAT COMPUTER READY FOR THE SCIENCE TEACHER, MY MINIONS?
IT IS READY. SIR.

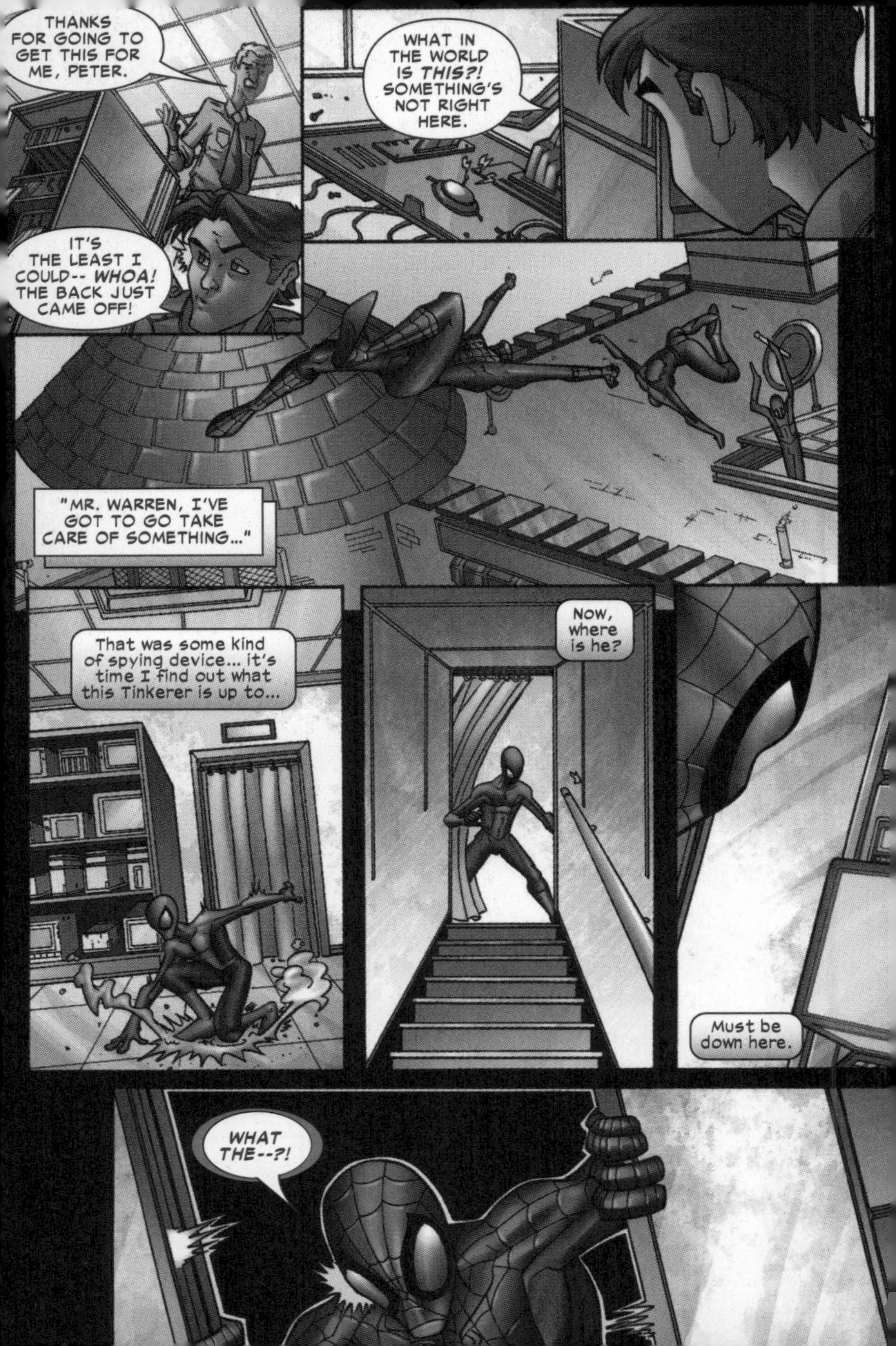
THANKS FOR GOING TO GET THIS FOR ME, PETER.
IT'S THE LEAST I COULD-- WHOA! THE BACK JUST CAME OFF!
WHAT IN THE WORLD IS THIS?! SOMETHING'S NOT RIGHT HERE.
"MR. WARREN, I'VE GOT TO GO TAKE CARE OF SOMETHING..."
That was some kind of spying device... it's time I find out what this Tinkerer is up to...
Now, where is he?
Must be down here.
WHAT THE--?!

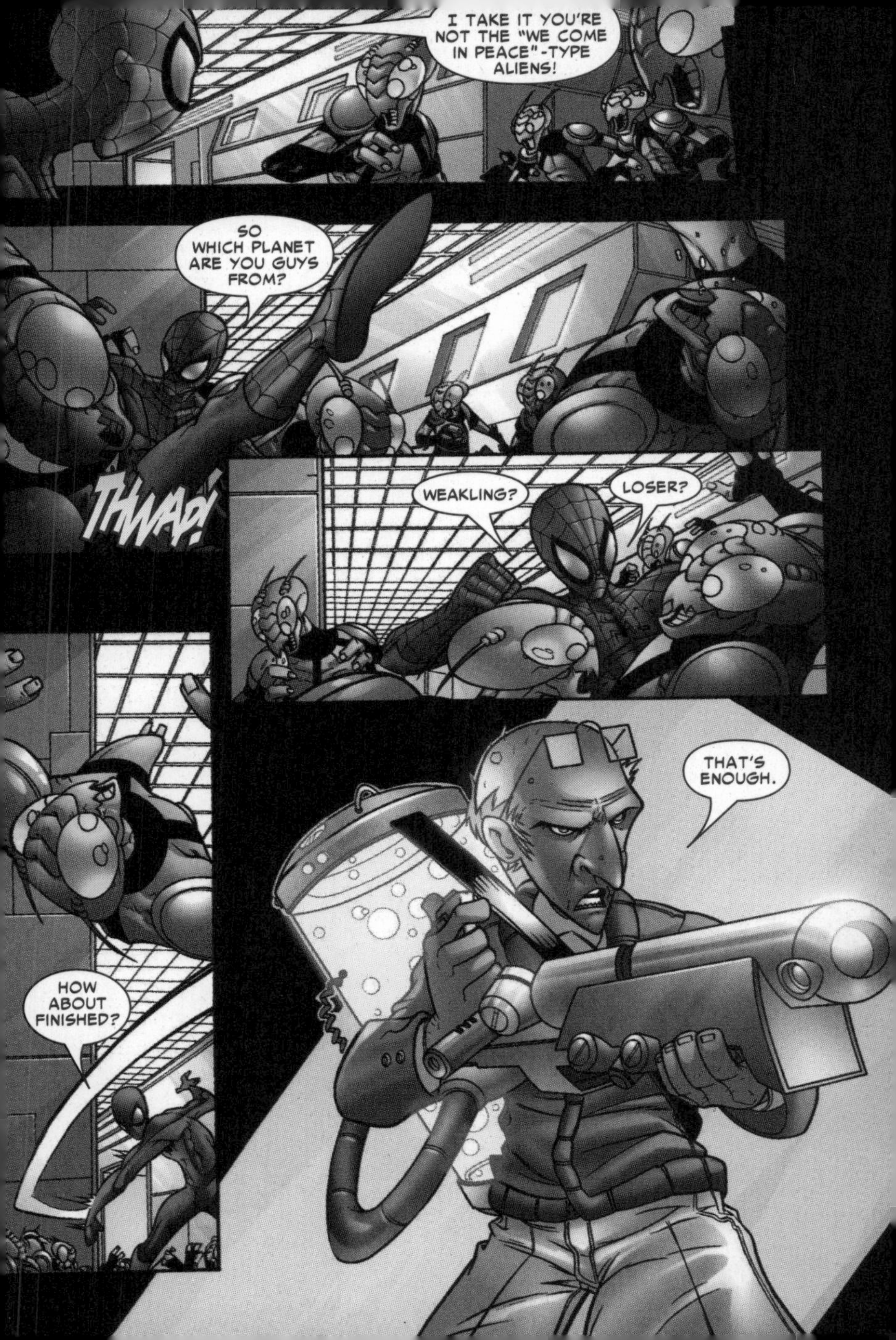

I TAKE IT YOU'RE NOT THE "WE COME IN PEACE"-TYPE ALIENS!
SO WHICH PLANET ARE YOU GUYS FROM?
THWAP!
WEAKLING?
LOSER?
HOW ABOUT FINISHED?
THAT'S ENOUGH.

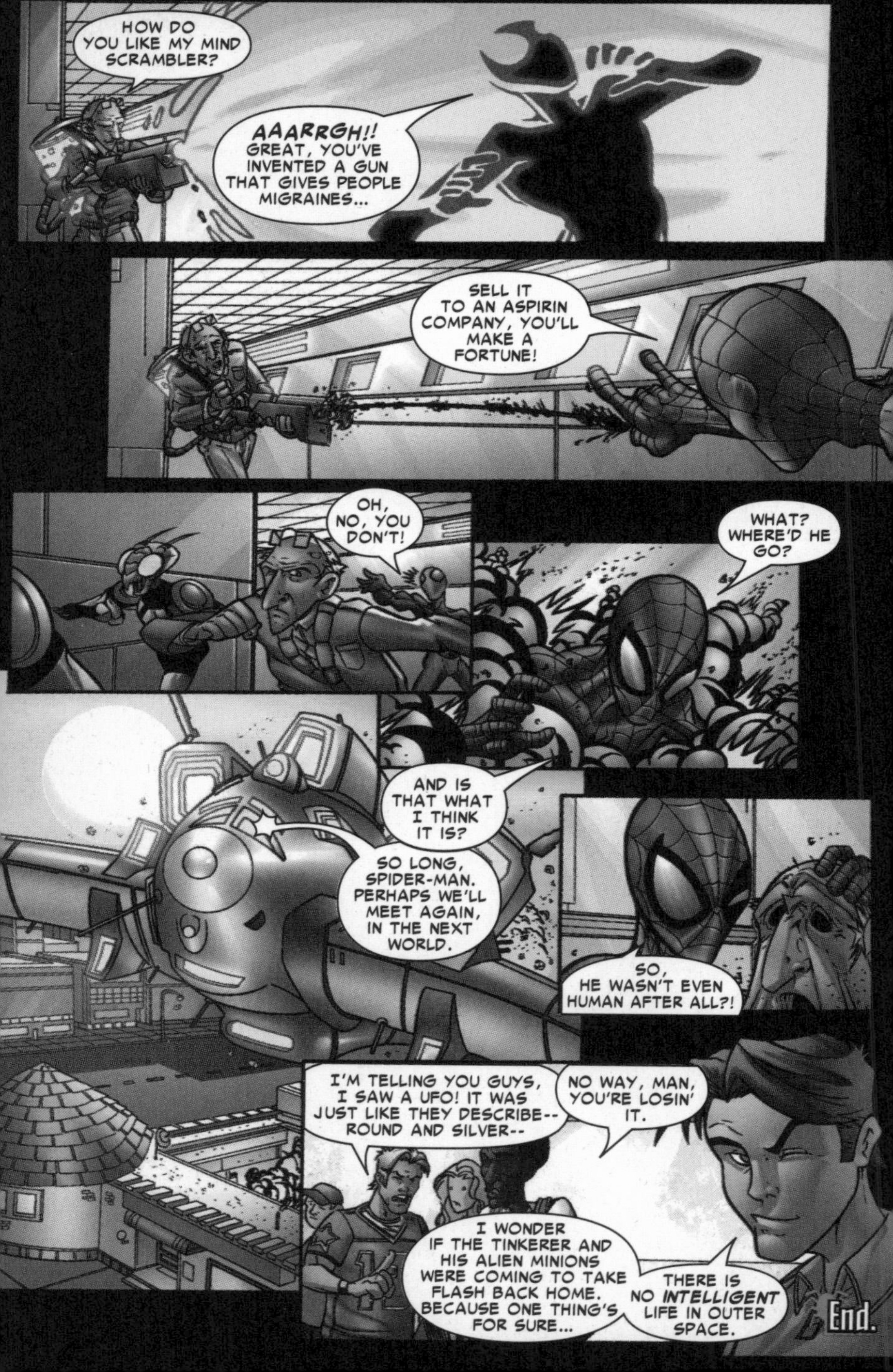
HOW DO YOU LIKE MY MIND SCRAMBLER?
AAARRGH!! GREAT, YOU'VE INVENTED A GUN THAT GIVES PEOPLE MIGRAINES...
SELL IT TO AN ASPIRIN COMPANY, YOU'LL MAKE A FORTUNE!
OH, NO, YOU DON'T!
WHAT? WHERE'D HE GO?
AND IS THAT WHAT I THINK IT IS?
SO LONG, SPIDER-MAN. PERHAPS WE'LL MEET AGAIN, IN THE NEXT WORLD.
SO, HE WASN'T EVEN HUMAN AFTER ALL?!
I'M TELLING YOU GUYS, I SAW A UFO! IT WAS JUST LIKE THEY DESCRIBE-- ROUND AND SILVER--
NO WAY, MAN, YOU'RE LOSIN' IT.
I WONDER IF THE TINKERER AND HIS ALIEN MINIONS WERE COMING TO TAKE FLASH BACK HOME. BECAUSE ONE THING'S FOR SURE...
THERE IS NO INTELLIGENT LIFE IN OUTER SPACE.
End.

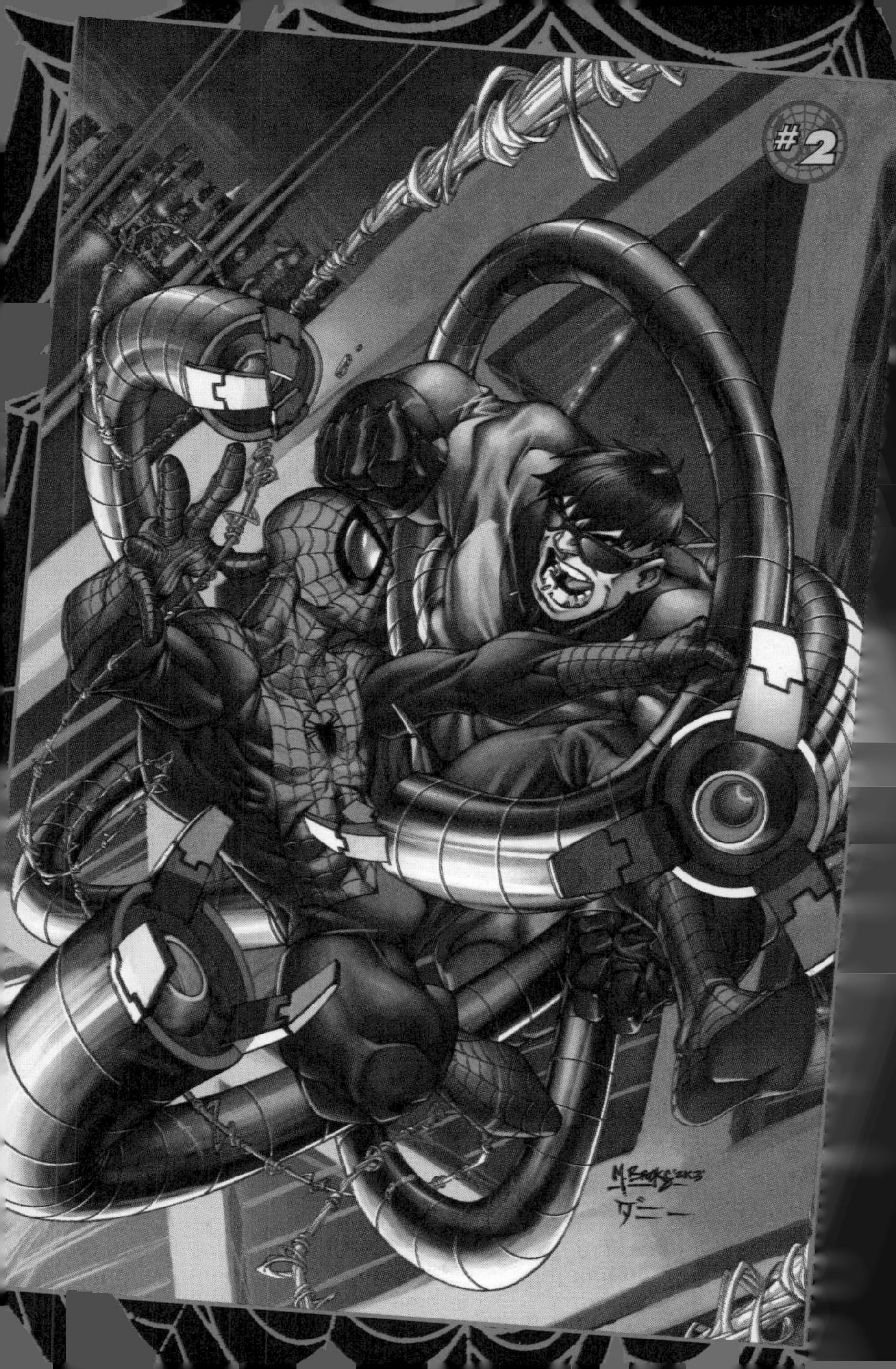
#2

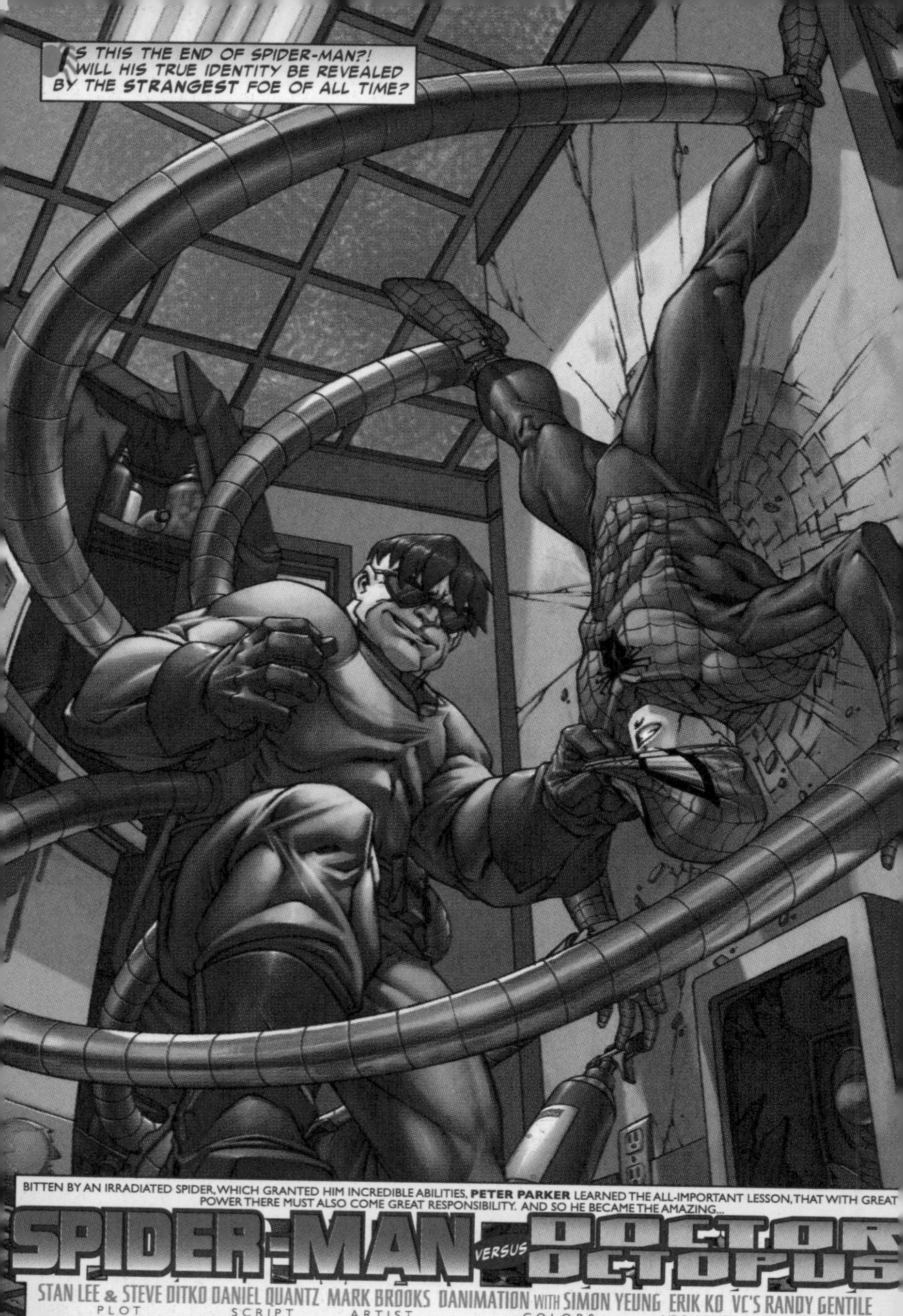
IS THIS THE END OF SPIDER-MAN?! WILL HIS TRUE IDENTITY BE REVEALED BY THE STRANGEST FOE OF ALL TIME?

BITTEN BY AN IRRADIATED SPIDER, WHICH GRANTED HIM INCREDIBLE ABILITIES, **PETER PARKER** LEARNED THE ALL-IMPORTANT LESSON, THAT WITH GREAT POWER THERE MUST ALSO COME GREAT RESPONSIBILITY. AND SO HE BECAME THE AMAZING...

SPIDER-MAN VERSUS DOCTOR OCTOPUS

STAN LEE & STEVE DITKO PLOT
DANIEL QUANTZ SCRIPT
MARK BROOKS ARTIST
DANIMATION WITH SIMON YEUNG COLORS
ERIK KO UDON CHIEF
VC'S RANDY GENTILE LETTERER
MACKENZIE CADENHEAD & NICK LOWE ASSISTANT EDITORS
C.B. CEBULSKI EDITOR
RALPH MACCHIO CONSULTING EDITOR
JOE QUESADA EDITOR-IN-CHIEF
DAN BUCKLEY PUBLISHER

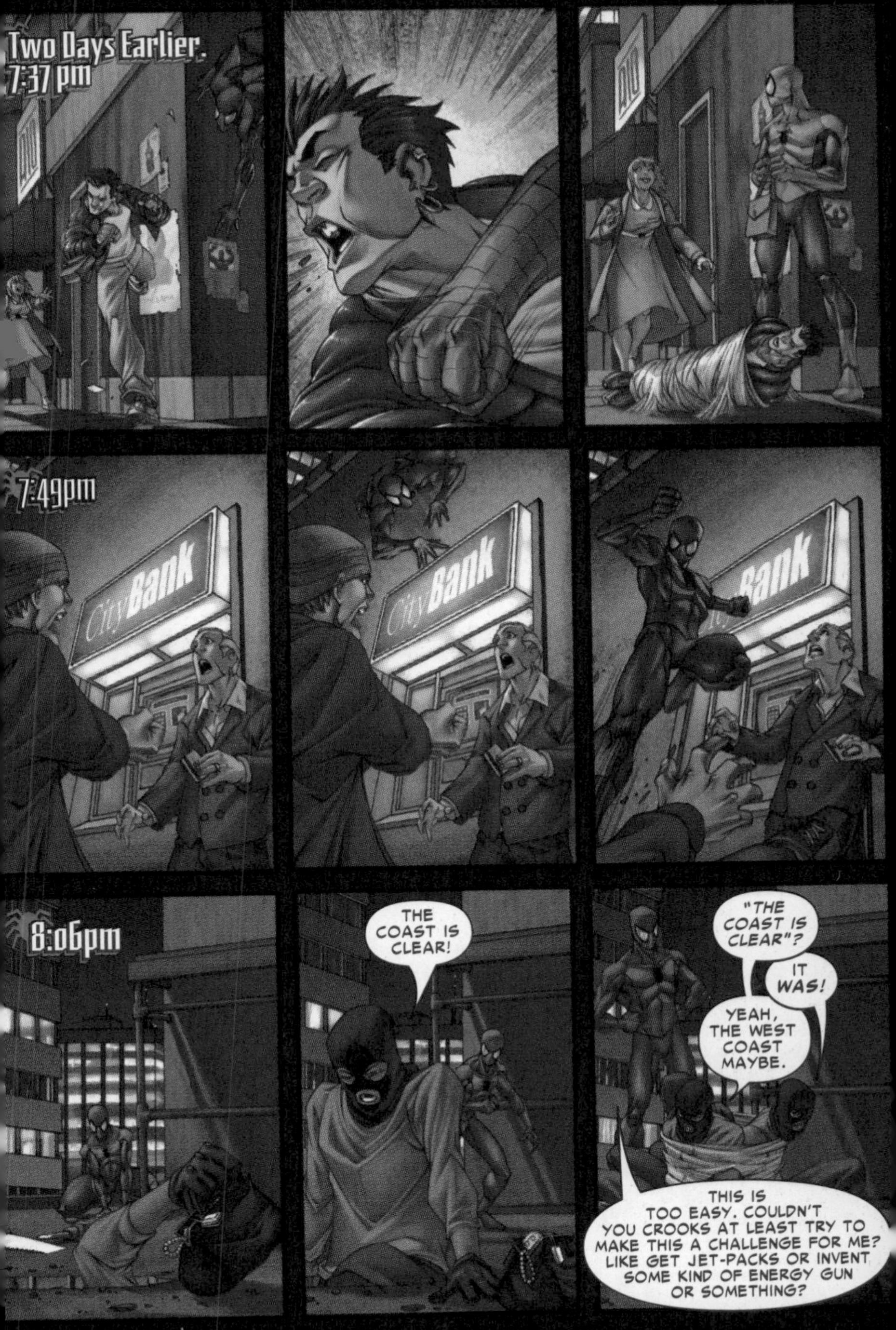
Two Days Earlier.
7:37 pm
7:49pm
City Bank
8:06pm
THE COAST IS CLEAR!
"THE COAST IS CLEAR"?
IT WAS!
YEAH, THE WEST COAST MAYBE.
THIS IS TOO EASY. COULDN'T YOU CROOKS AT LEAST TRY TO MAKE THIS A CHALLENGE FOR ME? LIKE GET JET-PACKS OR INVENT SOME KIND OF ENERGY GUN OR SOMETHING?

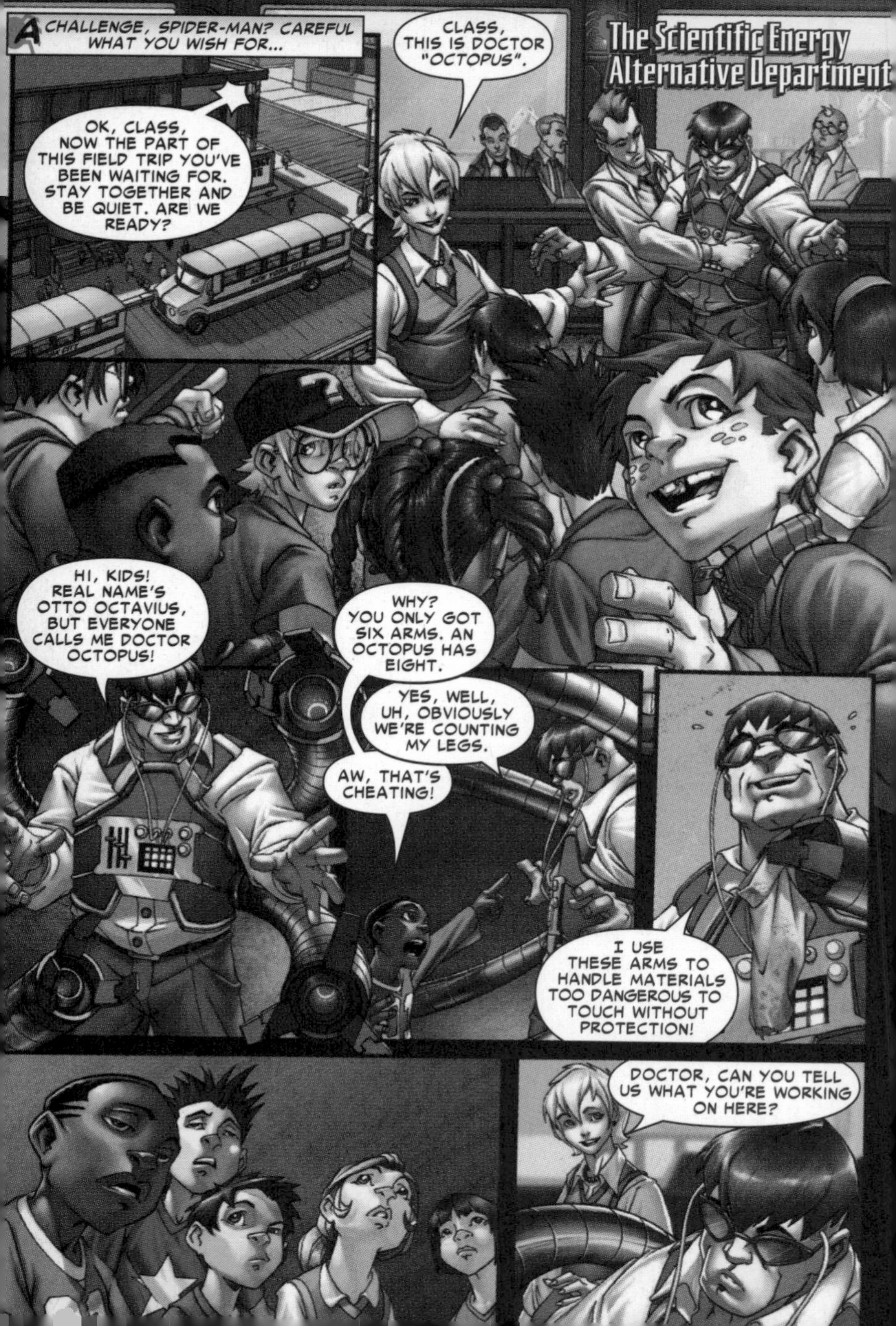
A CHALLENGE, SPIDER-MAN? CAREFUL WHAT YOU WISH FOR...
OK, CLASS, NOW THE PART OF THIS FIELD TRIP YOU'VE BEEN WAITING FOR. STAY TOGETHER AND BE QUIET. ARE WE READY?
CLASS, THIS IS DOCTOR "OCTOPUS".
The Scientific Energy Alternative Department
HI, KIDS! REAL NAME'S OTTO OCTAVIUS, BUT EVERYONE CALLS ME DOCTOR OCTOPUS!
WHY? YOU ONLY GOT SIX ARMS. AN OCTOPUS HAS EIGHT.
YES, WELL, UH, OBVIOUSLY WE'RE COUNTING MY LEGS.
AW, THAT'S CHEATING!
I USE THESE ARMS TO HANDLE MATERIALS TOO DANGEROUS TO TOUCH WITHOUT PROTECTION!
DOCTOR, CAN YOU TELL US WHAT YOU'RE WORKING ON HERE?

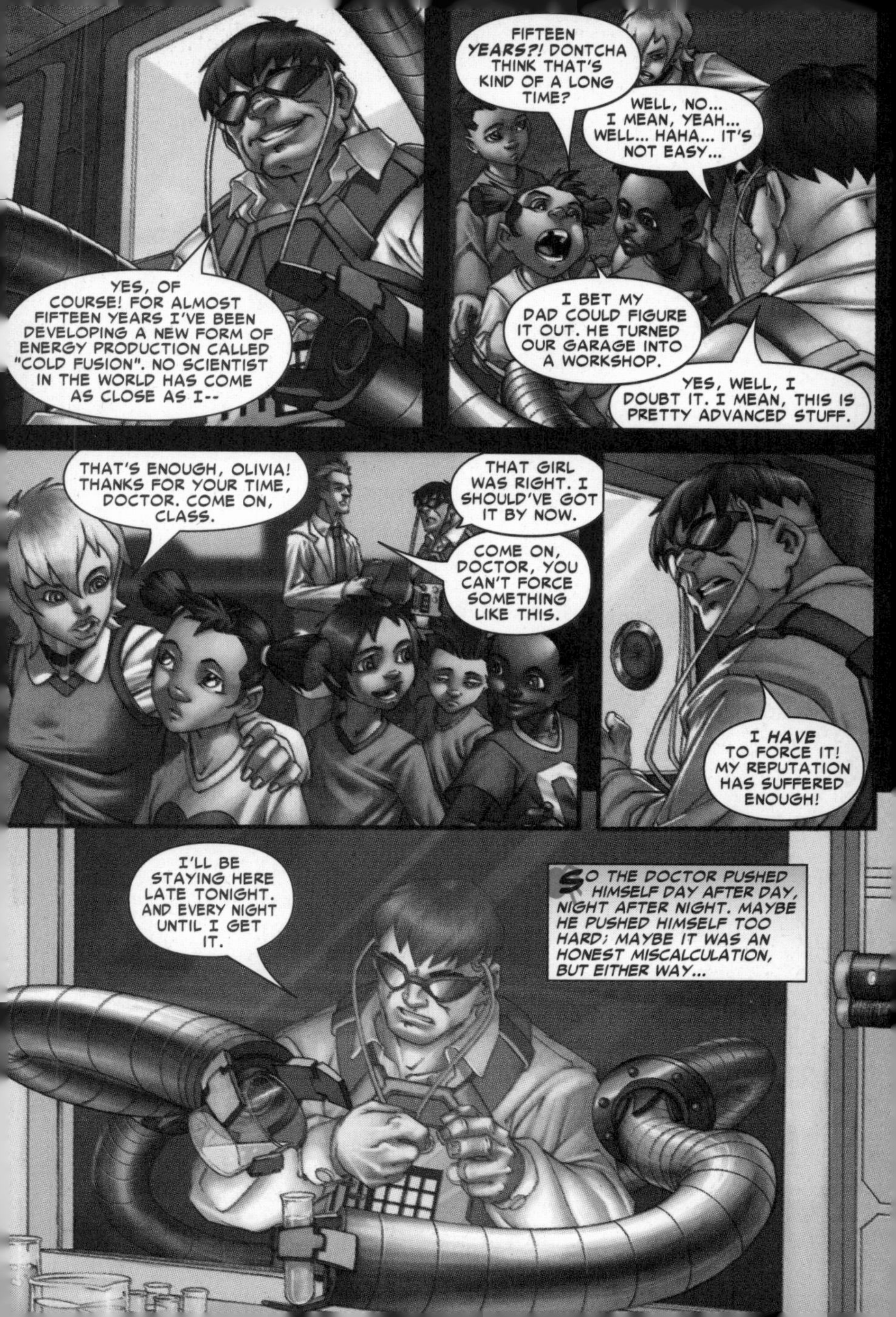

YES, OF COURSE! FOR ALMOST FIFTEEN YEARS I'VE BEEN DEVELOPING A NEW FORM OF ENERGY PRODUCTION CALLED "COLD FUSION". NO SCIENTIST IN THE WORLD HAS COME AS CLOSE AS I--
FIFTEEN *YEARS?!* DONTCHA THINK THAT'S KIND OF A LONG TIME?
WELL, NO... I MEAN, YEAH... WELL... HAHA... IT'S NOT EASY...
I BET MY DAD COULD FIGURE IT OUT. HE TURNED OUR GARAGE INTO A WORKSHOP.
YES, WELL, I DOUBT IT. I MEAN, THIS IS PRETTY ADVANCED STUFF.
THAT'S ENOUGH, OLIVIA! THANKS FOR YOUR TIME, DOCTOR. COME ON, CLASS.
THAT GIRL WAS RIGHT. I SHOULD'VE GOT IT BY NOW.
COME ON, DOCTOR, YOU CAN'T FORCE SOMETHING LIKE THIS.
I *HAVE* TO FORCE IT! MY REPUTATION HAS SUFFERED ENOUGH!
I'LL BE STAYING HERE LATE TONIGHT. AND EVERY NIGHT UNTIL I GET IT.
SO THE DOCTOR PUSHED HIMSELF DAY AFTER DAY, NIGHT AFTER NIGHT. MAYBE HE PUSHED HIMSELF TOO HARD; MAYBE IT WAS AN HONEST MISCALCULATION, BUT EITHER WAY...

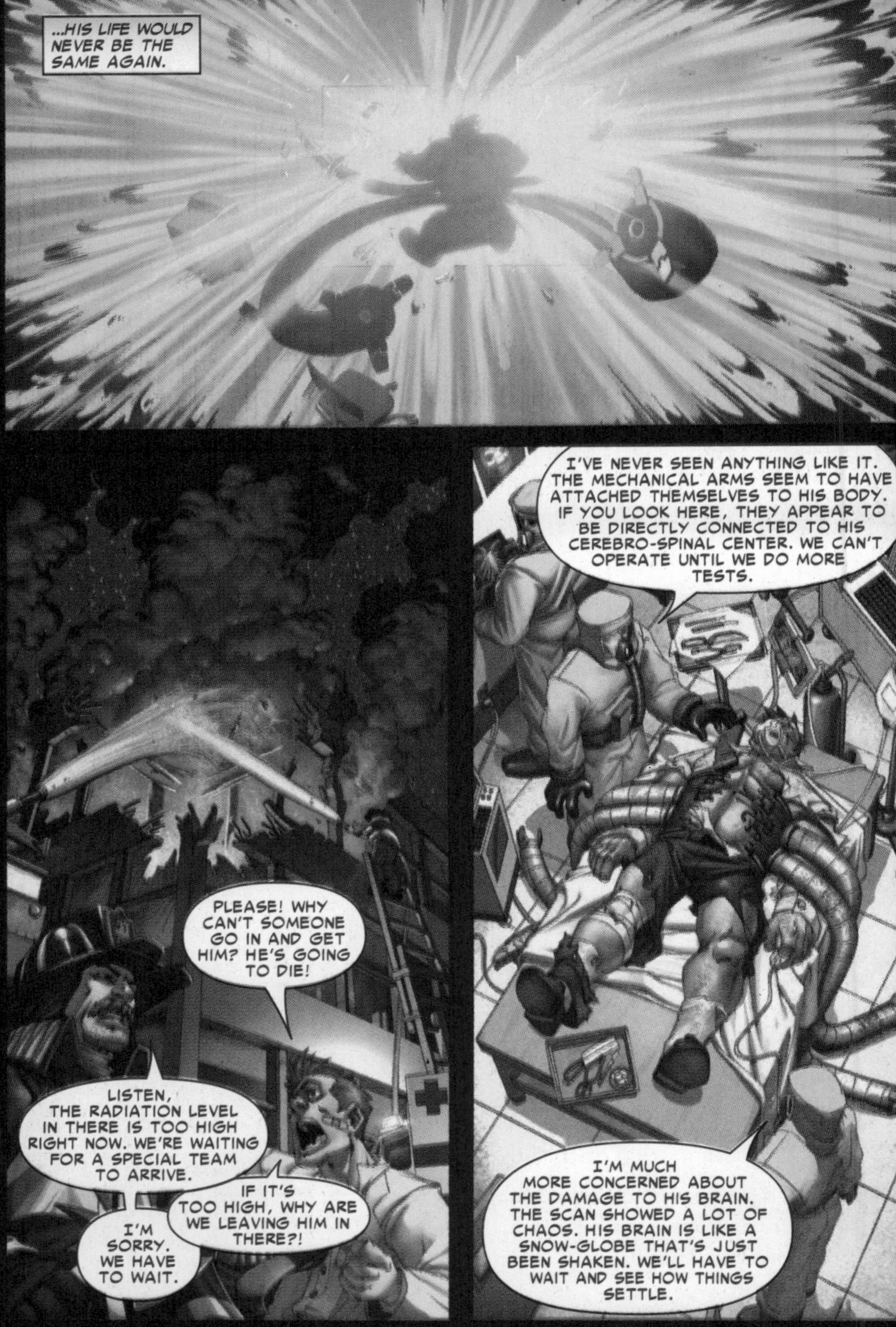
...HIS LIFE WOULD NEVER BE THE SAME AGAIN.
PLEASE! WHY CAN'T SOMEONE GO IN AND GET HIM? HE'S GOING TO DIE!
LISTEN, THE RADIATION LEVEL IN THERE IS TOO HIGH RIGHT NOW. WE'RE WAITING FOR A SPECIAL TEAM TO ARRIVE.
IF IT'S TOO HIGH, WHY ARE WE LEAVING HIM IN THERE?!
I'M SORRY. WE HAVE TO WAIT.
I'VE NEVER SEEN ANYTHING LIKE IT. THE MECHANICAL ARMS SEEM TO HAVE ATTACHED THEMSELVES TO HIS BODY. IF YOU LOOK HERE, THEY APPEAR TO BE DIRECTLY CONNECTED TO HIS CEREBRO-SPINAL CENTER. WE CAN'T OPERATE UNTIL WE DO MORE TESTS.
I'M MUCH MORE CONCERNED ABOUT THE DAMAGE TO HIS BRAIN. THE SCAN SHOWED A LOT OF CHAOS. HIS BRAIN IS LIKE A SNOW-GLOBE THAT'S JUST BEEN SHAKEN. WE'LL HAVE TO WAIT AND SEE HOW THINGS SETTLE.

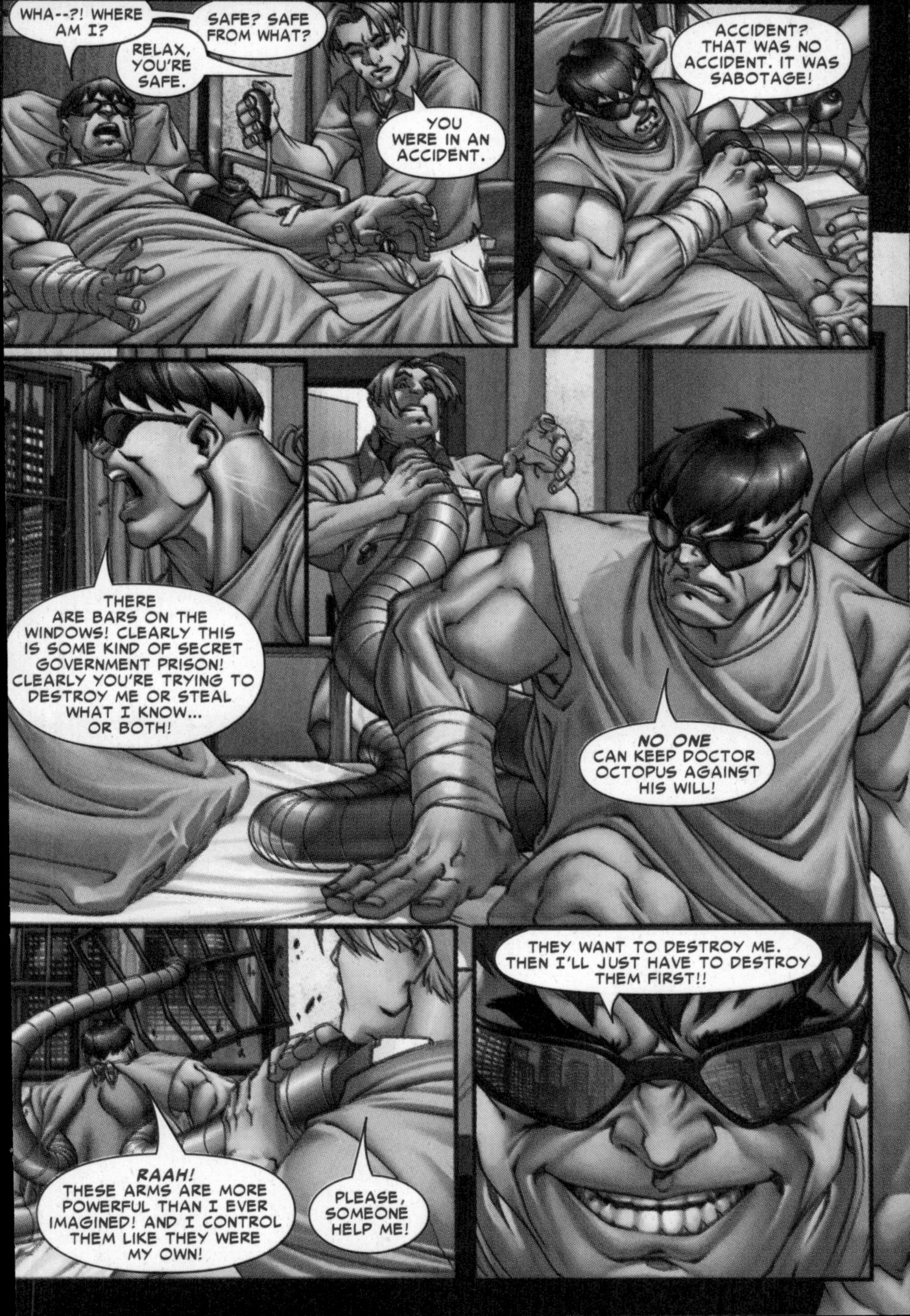
WHA--?! WHERE AM I?
RELAX, YOU'RE SAFE.
SAFE? SAFE FROM WHAT?
YOU WERE IN AN ACCIDENT.
ACCIDENT? THAT WAS NO ACCIDENT. IT WAS SABOTAGE!
THERE ARE BARS ON THE WINDOWS! CLEARLY THIS IS SOME KIND OF SECRET GOVERNMENT PRISON! CLEARLY YOU'RE TRYING TO DESTROY ME OR STEAL WHAT I KNOW... OR BOTH!
NO ONE CAN KEEP DOCTOR OCTOPUS AGAINST HIS WILL!
RAAH! THESE ARMS ARE MORE POWERFUL THAN I EVER IMAGINED! AND I CONTROL THEM LIKE THEY WERE MY OWN!
PLEASE, SOMEONE HELP ME!
THEY WANT TO DESTROY ME. THEN I'LL JUST HAVE TO DESTROY THEM FIRST!!

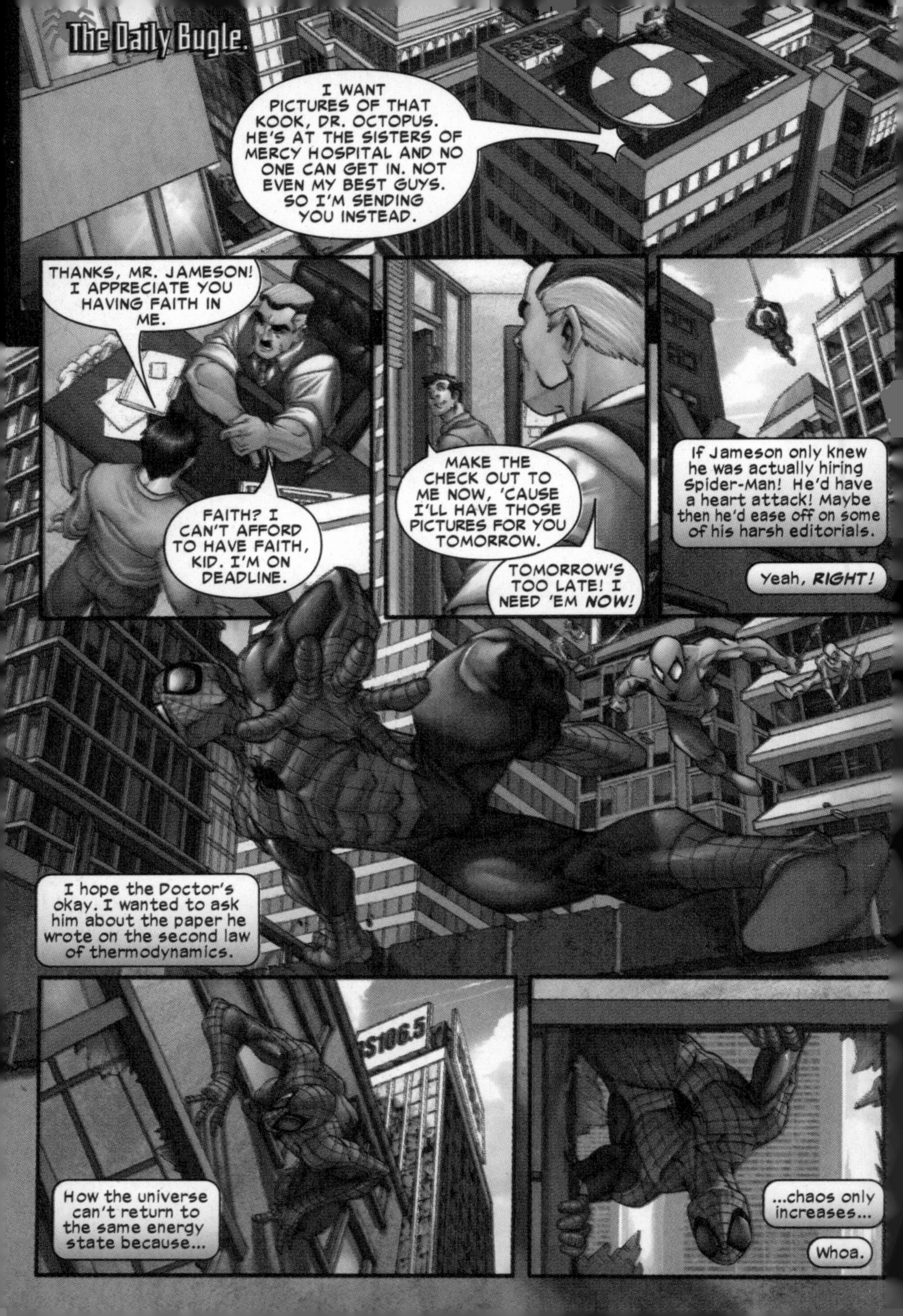
The Daily Bugle.
I WANT PICTURES OF THAT KOOK, DR. OCTOPUS. HE'S AT THE SISTERS OF MERCY HOSPITAL AND NO ONE CAN GET IN. NOT EVEN MY BEST GUYS. SO I'M SENDING YOU INSTEAD.
THANKS, MR. JAMESON! I APPRECIATE YOU HAVING FAITH IN ME.
FAITH? I CAN'T AFFORD TO HAVE FAITH, KID. I'M ON DEADLINE.
MAKE THE CHECK OUT TO ME NOW, 'CAUSE I'LL HAVE THOSE PICTURES FOR YOU TOMORROW.
TOMORROW'S TOO LATE! I NEED 'EM *NOW!*
If Jameson only knew he was actually hiring Spider-Man! He'd have a heart attack! Maybe then he'd ease off on some of his harsh editorials.
Yeah, ***RIGHT!***
I hope the Doctor's okay. I wanted to ask him about the paper he wrote on the second law of thermodynamics.
How the universe can't return to the same energy state because...
...chaos only increases...
Whoa.

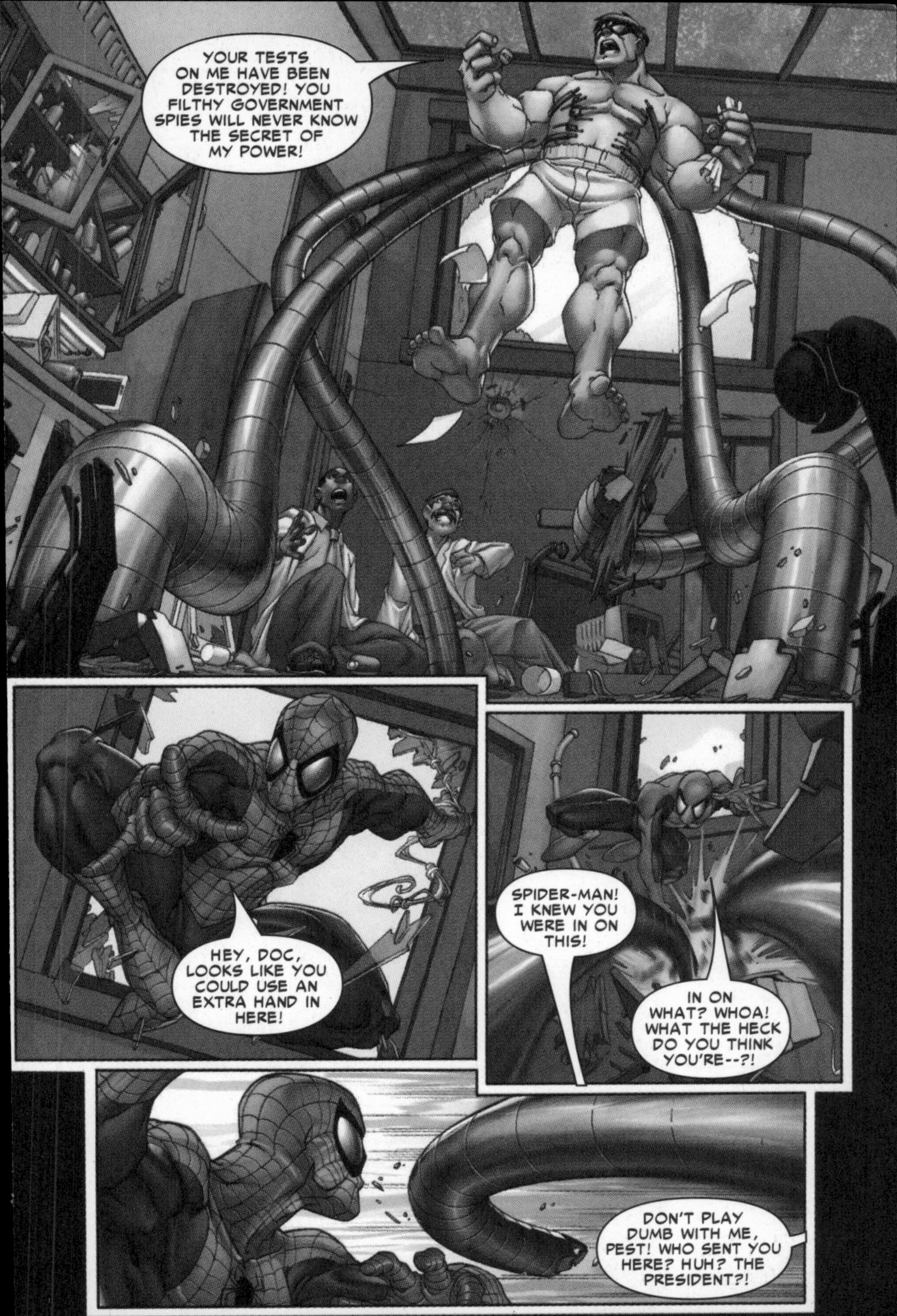
YOUR TESTS ON ME HAVE BEEN DESTROYED! YOU FILTHY GOVERNMENT SPIES WILL NEVER KNOW THE SECRET OF MY POWER!
HEY, DOC, LOOKS LIKE YOU COULD USE AN EXTRA HAND IN HERE!
SPIDER-MAN! I KNEW YOU WERE IN ON THIS!
IN ON WHAT? WHOA! WHAT THE HECK DO YOU THINK YOU'RE--?!
DON'T PLAY DUMB WITH ME, PEST! WHO SENT YOU HERE? HUH? THE PRESIDENT?!

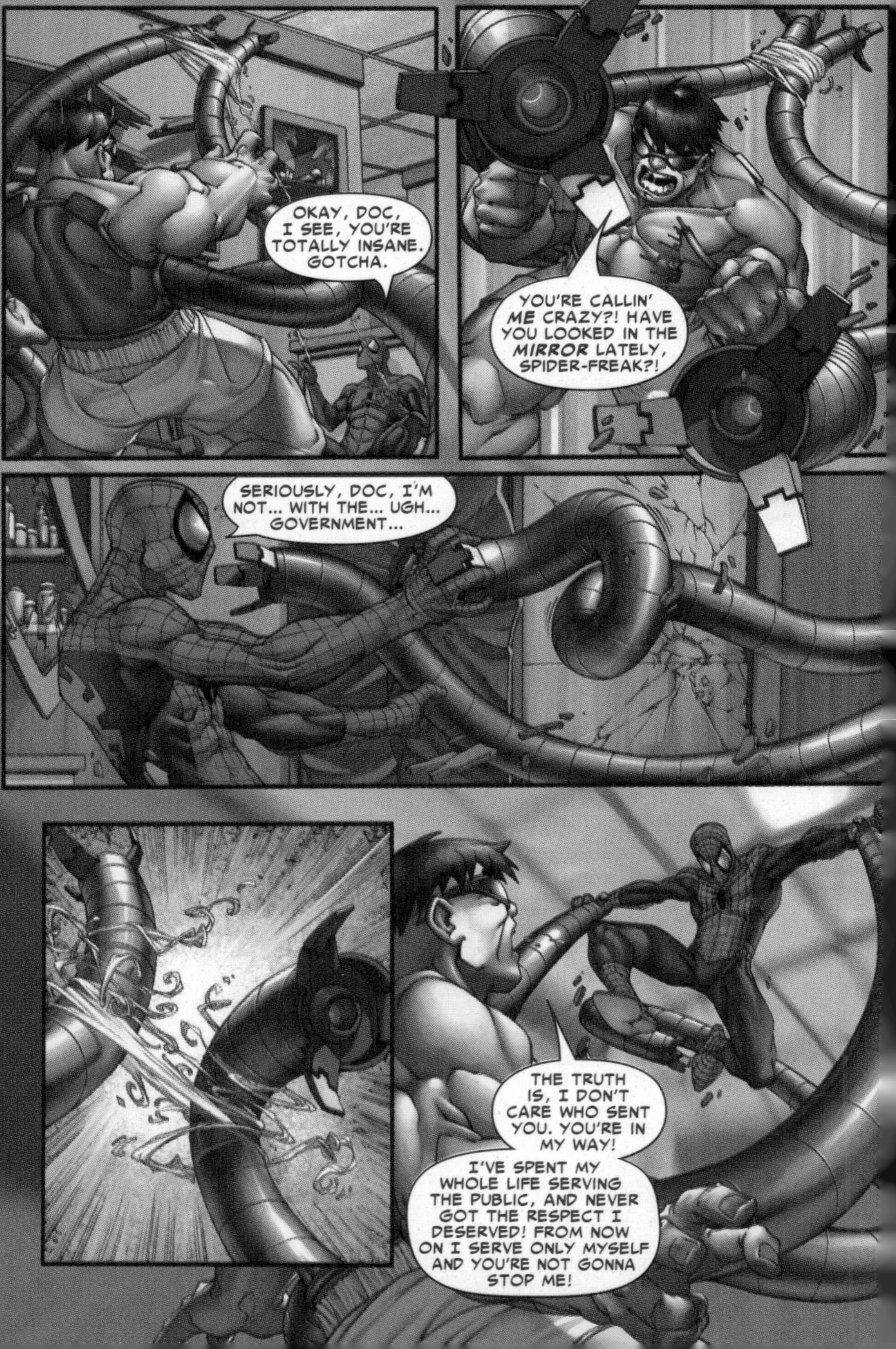

OKAY, DOC, I SEE, YOU'RE TOTALLY INSANE. GOTCHA.
YOU'RE CALLIN' *ME* CRAZY?! HAVE YOU LOOKED IN THE *MIRROR* LATELY, SPIDER-FREAK?!
SERIOUSLY, DOC, I'M NOT... WITH THE... UGH... GOVERNMENT...
THE TRUTH IS, I DON'T CARE WHO SENT YOU. YOU'RE IN MY WAY!
I'VE SPENT MY WHOLE LIFE SERVING THE PUBLIC, AND NEVER GOT THE RESPECT I DESERVED! FROM NOW ON I SERVE ONLY MYSELF AND YOU'RE NOT GONNA STOP ME!

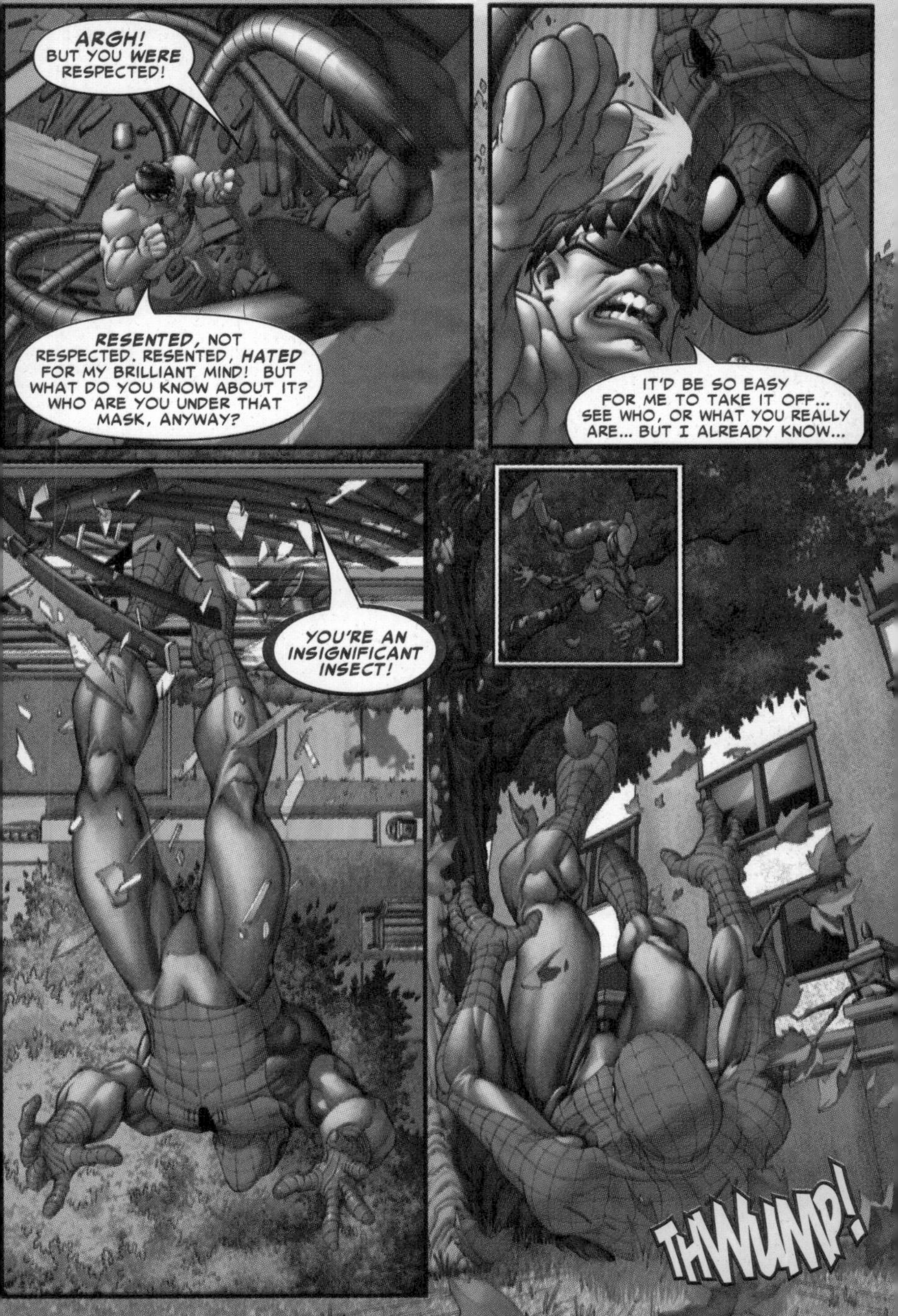
ARGH! BUT YOU WERE RESPECTED!
RESENTED, NOT RESPECTED. RESENTED, HATED FOR MY BRILLIANT MIND! BUT WHAT DO YOU KNOW ABOUT IT? WHO ARE YOU UNDER THAT MASK, ANYWAY?
IT'D BE SO EASY FOR ME TO TAKE IT OFF... SEE WHO, OR WHAT YOU REALLY ARE... BUT I ALREADY KNOW...
YOU'RE AN INSIGNIFICANT INSECT!
THWUMP!

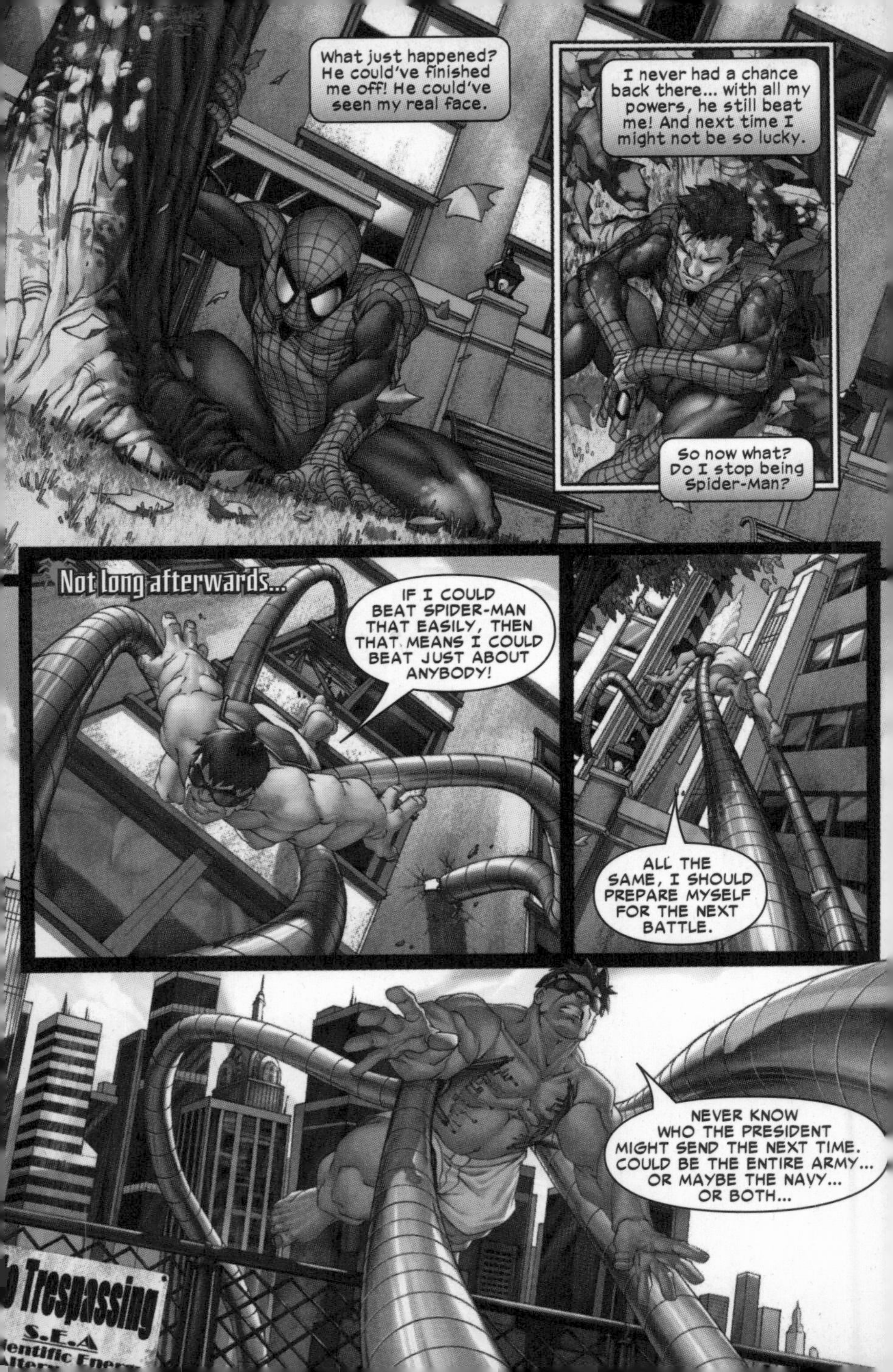
What just happened? He could've finished me off! He could've seen my real face.
I never had a chance back there... with all my powers, he still beat me! And next time I might not be so lucky.
So now what? Do I stop being Spider-Man?
Not long afterwards...
IF I COULD BEAT SPIDER-MAN THAT EASILY, THEN THAT MEANS I COULD BEAT JUST ABOUT ANYBODY!
ALL THE SAME, I SHOULD PREPARE MYSELF FOR THE NEXT BATTLE.
NEVER KNOW WHO THE PRESIDENT MIGHT SEND THE NEXT TIME. COULD BE THE ENTIRE ARMY... OR MAYBE THE NAVY... OR BOTH...
S.E.A

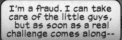

I'm a fraud. I can take care of the little guys, but as soon as a real challenge comes along--

OH, HELLO, BETTY? PETER PARKER. IS JAMESON THERE? OH, WELL, OK, COULD YOU JUST TELL HIM I'M NOT GONNA HAVE THE PICTURES OF DR. OCTOPUS FOR HIM?

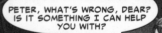

I KNOW HE WILL, BUT THERE'S NOTHING I CAN DO. IN FACT, I'M NOT SURE I'LL BE ABLE TO GET ANY MORE PICTURES AT ALL... NO, IT'S OK. SO LONG, BETTY.

PETER, WHAT'S WRONG, DEAR? IS IT SOMETHING I CAN HELP YOU WITH?

NO, AUNT MAY. THIS IS JUST... SOMETHING I HAVE TO DEAL WITH MYSELF. I'LL GET THROUGH IT. ANYWAY, I'VE GOT HOMEWORK I SHOULD DO.

WELL, IN CASE YOU WANT TO TALK... I'M HERE.

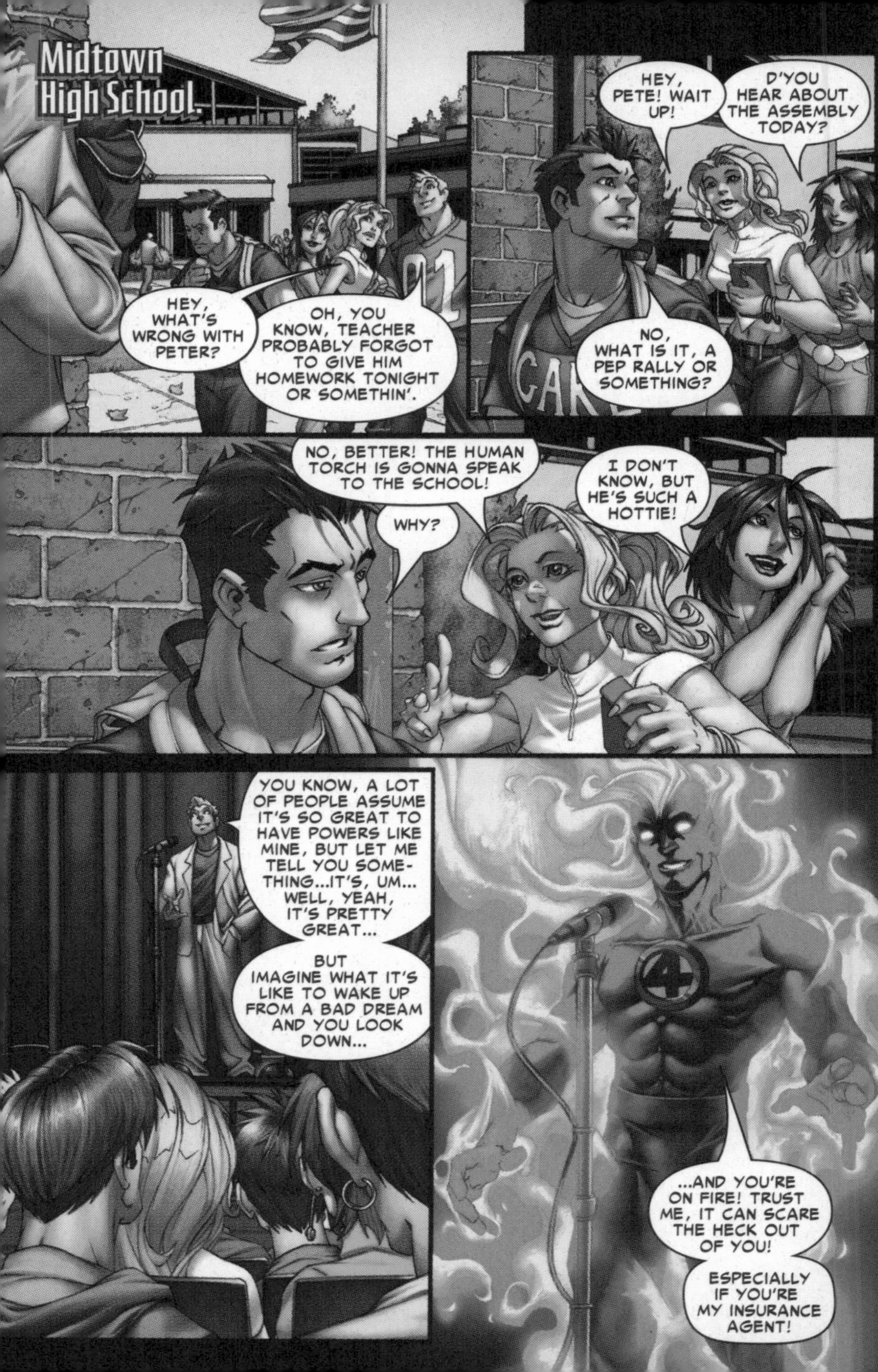
Midtown High School.
HEY, WHAT'S WRONG WITH PETER?
OH, YOU KNOW, TEACHER PROBABLY FORGOT TO GIVE HIM HOMEWORK TONIGHT OR SOMETHIN'.
HEY, PETE! WAIT UP!
D'YOU HEAR ABOUT THE ASSEMBLY TODAY?
NO, WHAT IS IT, A PEP RALLY OR SOMETHING?
NO, BETTER! THE HUMAN TORCH IS GONNA SPEAK TO THE SCHOOL!
WHY?
I DON'T KNOW, BUT HE'S SUCH A HOTTIE!
YOU KNOW, A LOT OF PEOPLE ASSUME IT'S SO GREAT TO HAVE POWERS LIKE MINE, BUT LET ME TELL YOU SOME-THING...IT'S, UM... WELL, YEAH, IT'S PRETTY GREAT...
BUT IMAGINE WHAT IT'S LIKE TO WAKE UP FROM A BAD DREAM AND YOU LOOK DOWN...
...AND YOU'RE ON FIRE! TRUST ME, IT CAN SCARE THE HECK OUT OF YOU!
ESPECIALLY IF YOU'RE MY INSURANCE AGENT!

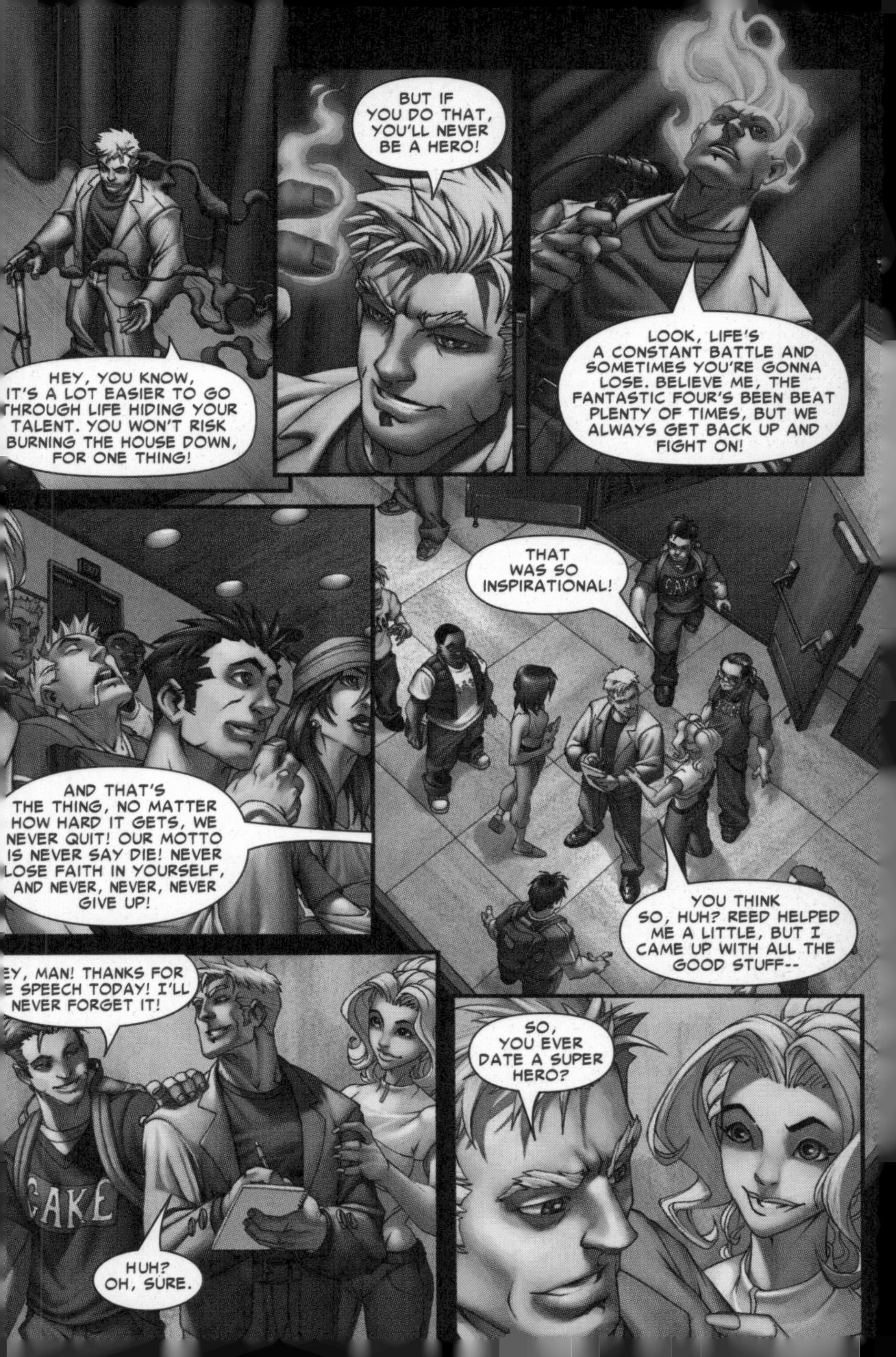
HEY, YOU KNOW, IT'S A LOT EASIER TO GO THROUGH LIFE HIDING YOUR TALENT. YOU WON'T RISK BURNING THE HOUSE DOWN, FOR ONE THING!
BUT IF YOU DO THAT, YOU'LL NEVER BE A HERO!
LOOK, LIFE'S A CONSTANT BATTLE AND SOMETIMES YOU'RE GONNA LOSE. BELIEVE ME, THE FANTASTIC FOUR'S BEEN BEAT PLENTY OF TIMES, BUT WE ALWAYS GET BACK UP AND FIGHT ON!
AND THAT'S THE THING, NO MATTER HOW HARD IT GETS, WE NEVER QUIT! OUR MOTTO IS NEVER SAY DIE! NEVER LOSE FAITH IN YOURSELF, AND NEVER, NEVER, NEVER GIVE UP!
THAT WAS SO INSPIRATIONAL!
YOU THINK SO, HUH? REED HELPED ME A LITTLE, BUT I CAME UP WITH ALL THE GOOD STUFF--
EY, MAN! THANKS FOR E SPEECH TODAY! I'LL NEVER FORGET IT!
HUH? OH, SURE.
SO, YOU EVER DATE A SUPER HERO?

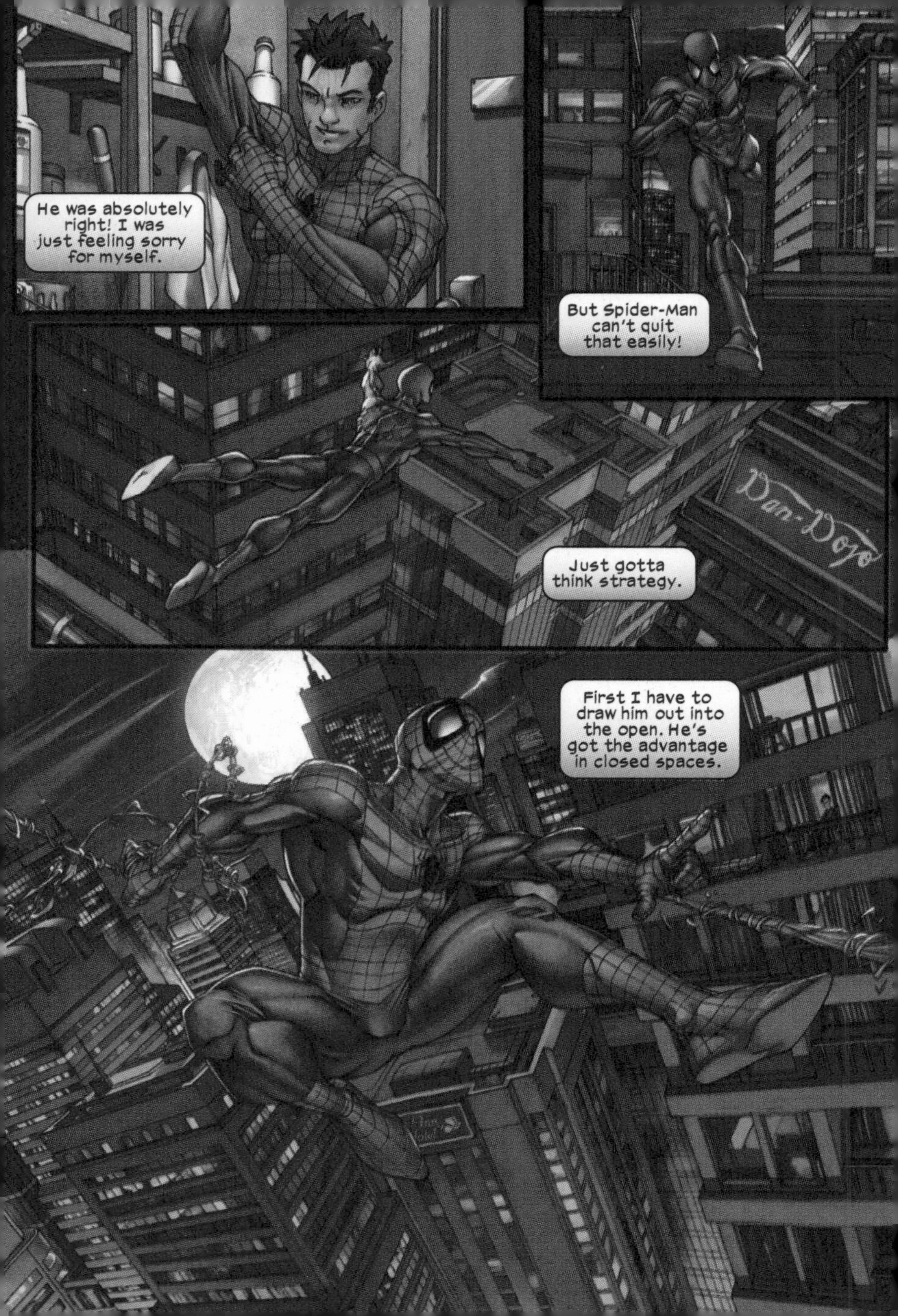
He was absolutely right! I was just feeling sorry for myself.
But Spider-Man can't quit that easily!
Dan-Dojo
Just gotta think strategy.
First I have to draw him out into the open. He's got the advantage in closed spaces.

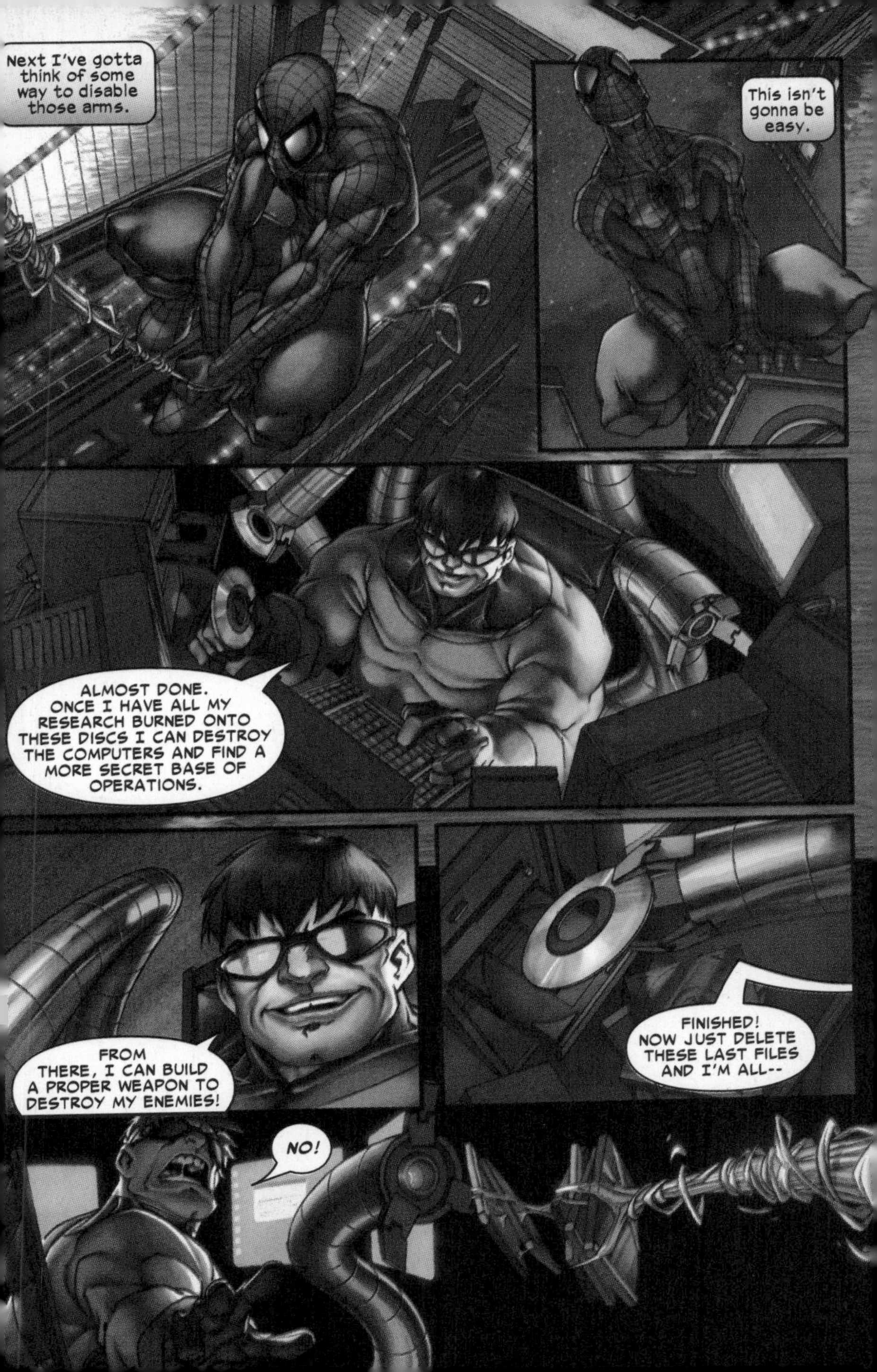
Next I've gotta think of some way to disable those arms.
This isn't gonna be easy.
ALMOST DONE. ONCE I HAVE ALL MY RESEARCH BURNED ONTO THESE DISCS I CAN DESTROY THE COMPUTERS AND FIND A MORE SECRET BASE OF OPERATIONS.
FROM THERE, I CAN BUILD A PROPER WEAPON TO DESTROY MY ENEMIES!
FINISHED! NOW JUST DELETE THESE LAST FILES AND I'M ALL--
NO!

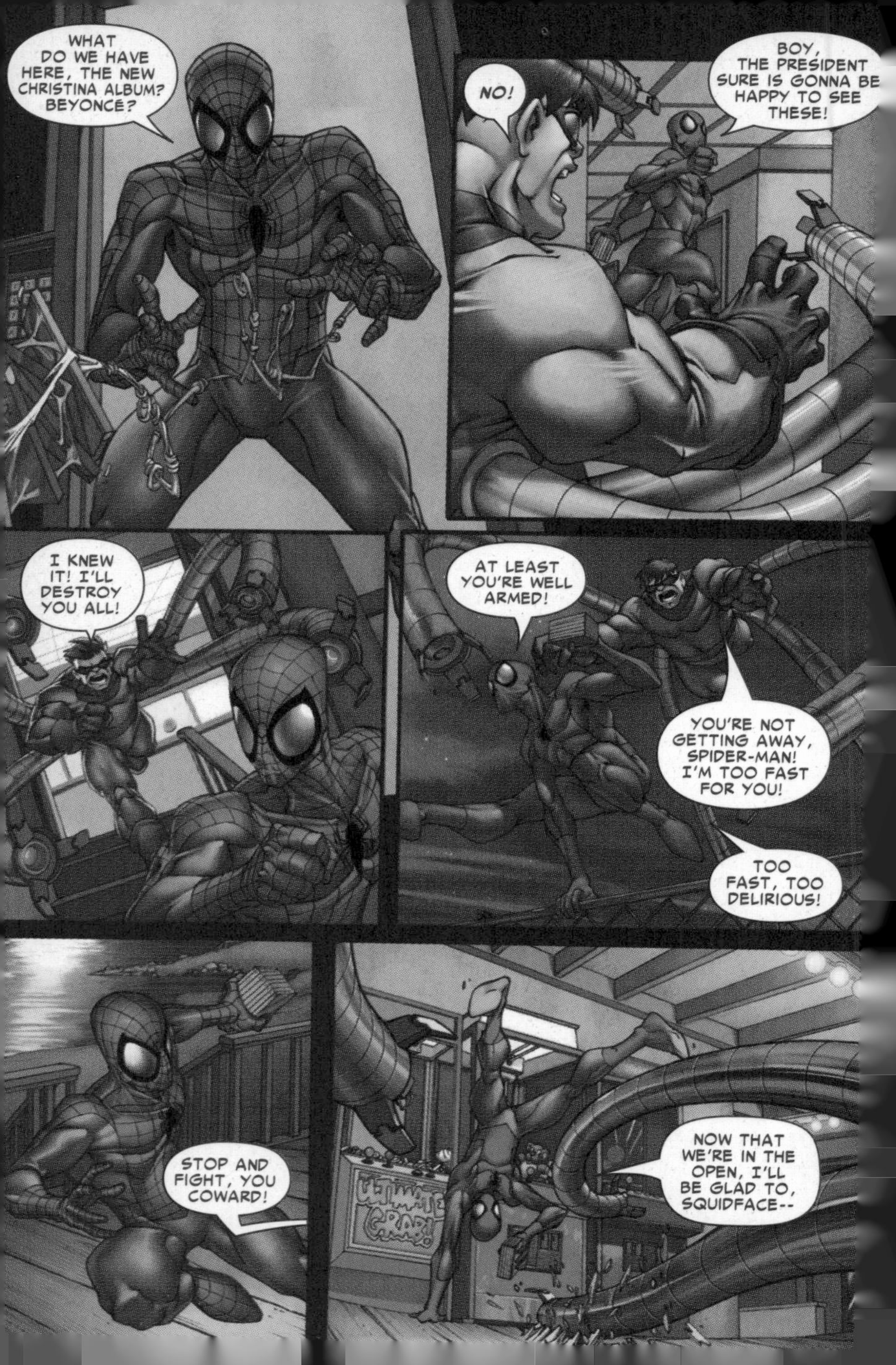
WHAT DO WE HAVE HERE, THE NEW CHRISTINA ALBUM? BEYONCÉ?
NO!
BOY, THE PRESIDENT SURE IS GONNA BE HAPPY TO SEE THESE!
I KNEW IT! I'LL DESTROY YOU ALL!
AT LEAST YOU'RE WELL ARMED!
YOU'RE NOT GETTING AWAY, SPIDER-MAN! I'M TOO FAST FOR YOU!
TOO FAST, TOO DELIRIOUS!
STOP AND FIGHT, YOU COWARD!
NOW THAT WE'RE IN THE OPEN, I'LL BE GLAD TO, SQUIDFACE--

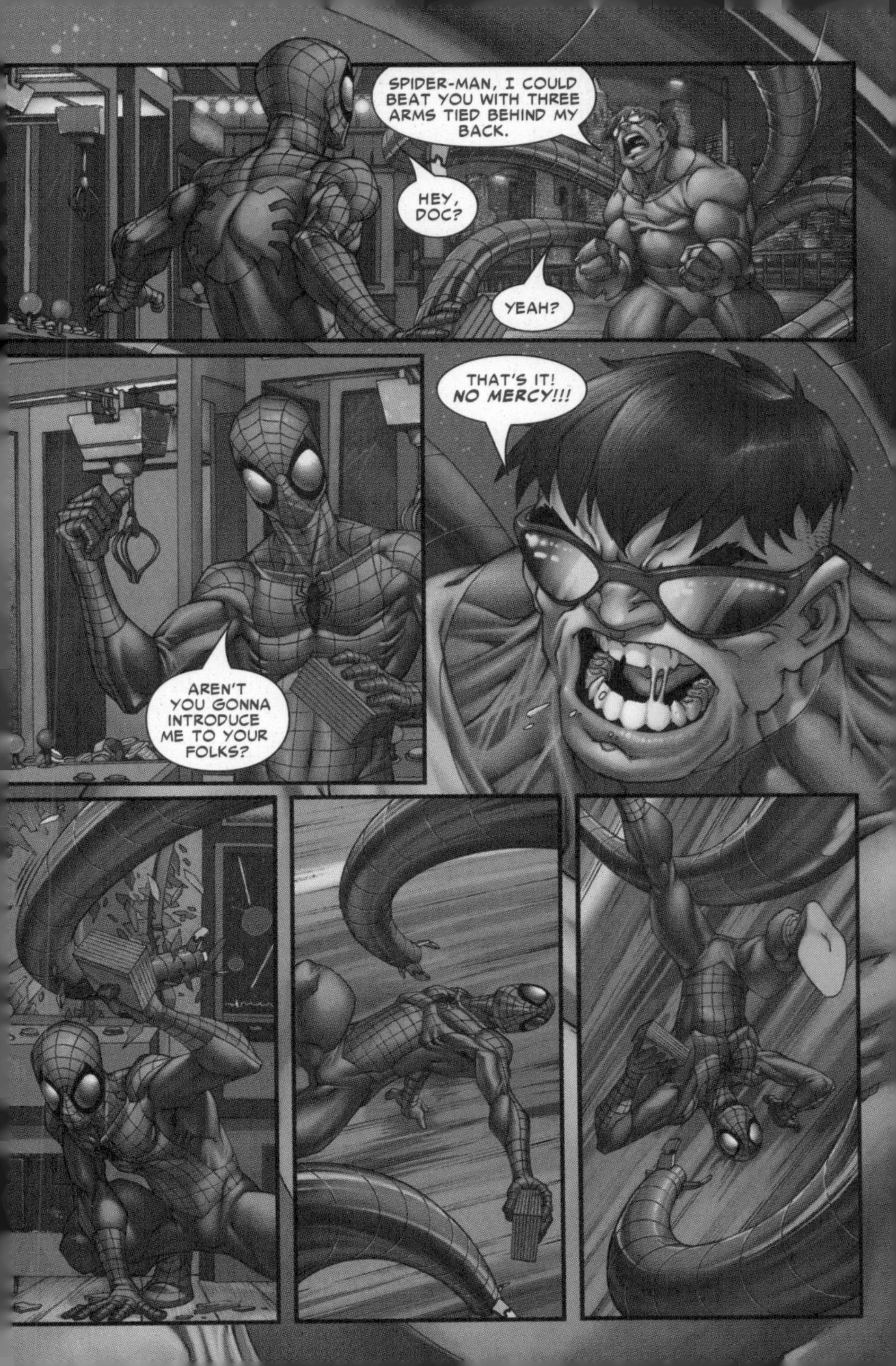
SPIDER-MAN, I COULD BEAT YOU WITH THREE ARMS TIED BEHIND MY BACK.
HEY, DOC?
YEAH?
THAT'S IT! NO MERCY!!!
AREN'T YOU GONNA INTRODUCE ME TO YOUR FOLKS?

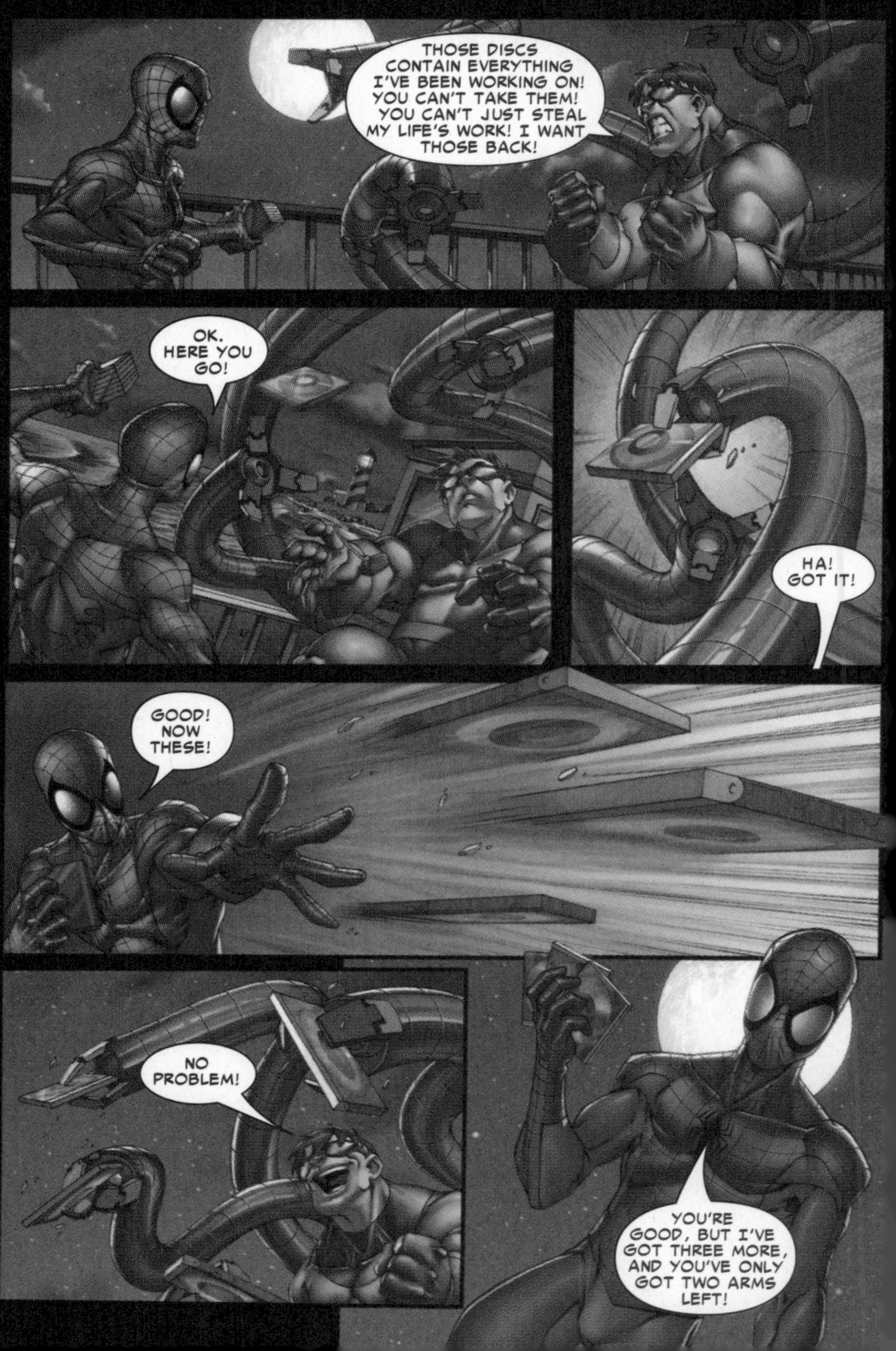
THOSE DISCS CONTAIN EVERYTHING I'VE BEEN WORKING ON! YOU CAN'T TAKE THEM! YOU CAN'T JUST STEAL MY LIFE'S WORK! I WANT THOSE BACK!
OK. HERE YOU GO!
HA! GOT IT!
GOOD! NOW THESE!
NO PROBLEM!
YOU'RE GOOD, BUT I'VE GOT THREE MORE, AND YOU'VE ONLY GOT TWO ARMS LEFT!

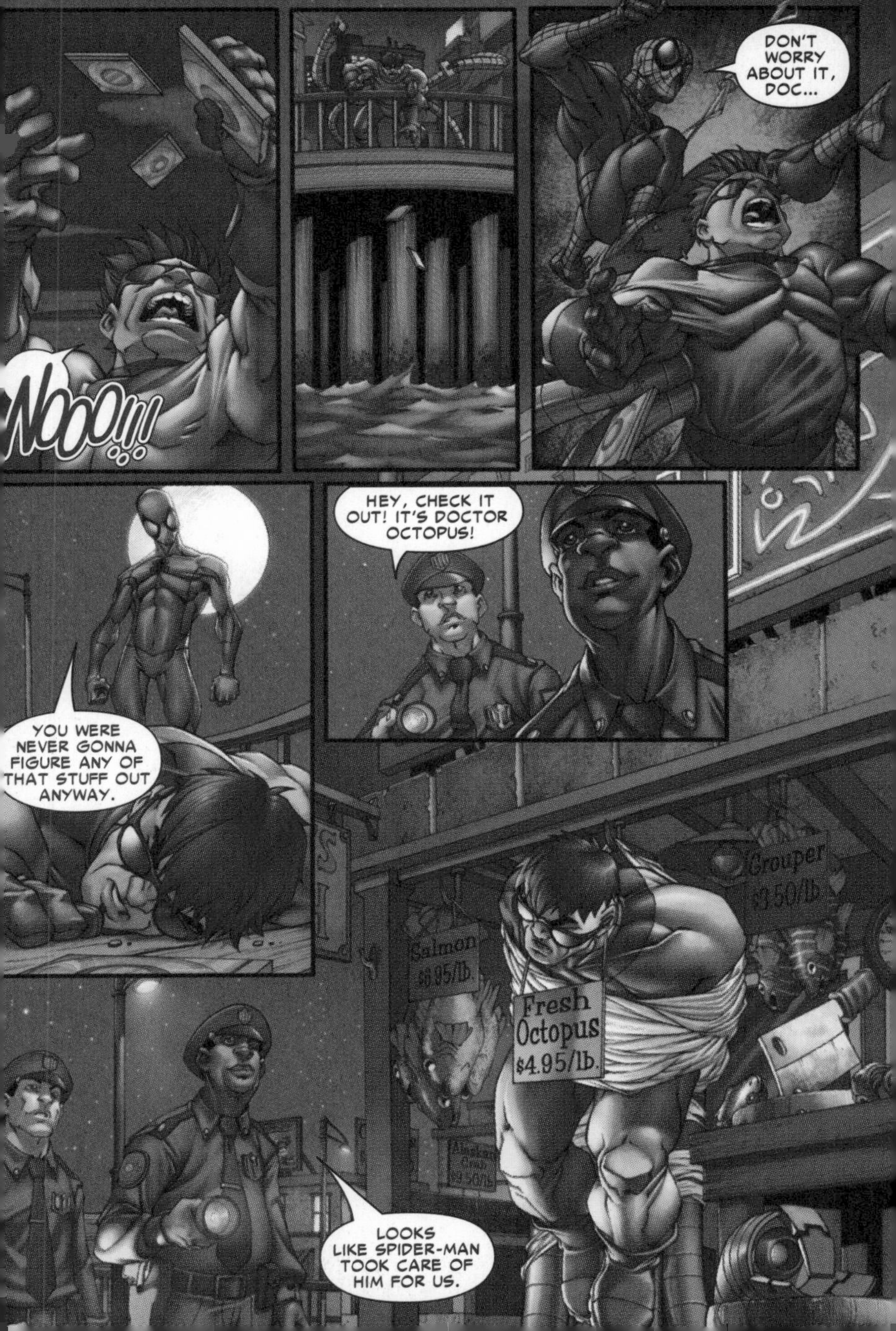
NOOO!!!
DON'T WORRY ABOUT IT, DOC...
YOU WERE NEVER GONNA FIGURE ANY OF THAT STUFF OUT ANYWAY.
HEY, CHECK IT OUT! IT'S DOCTOR OCTOPUS!
Grouper $3.50/lb.
Salmon $6.95/lb.
Fresh Octopus $4.95/lb.
LOOKS LIKE SPIDER-MAN TOOK CARE OF HIM FOR US.

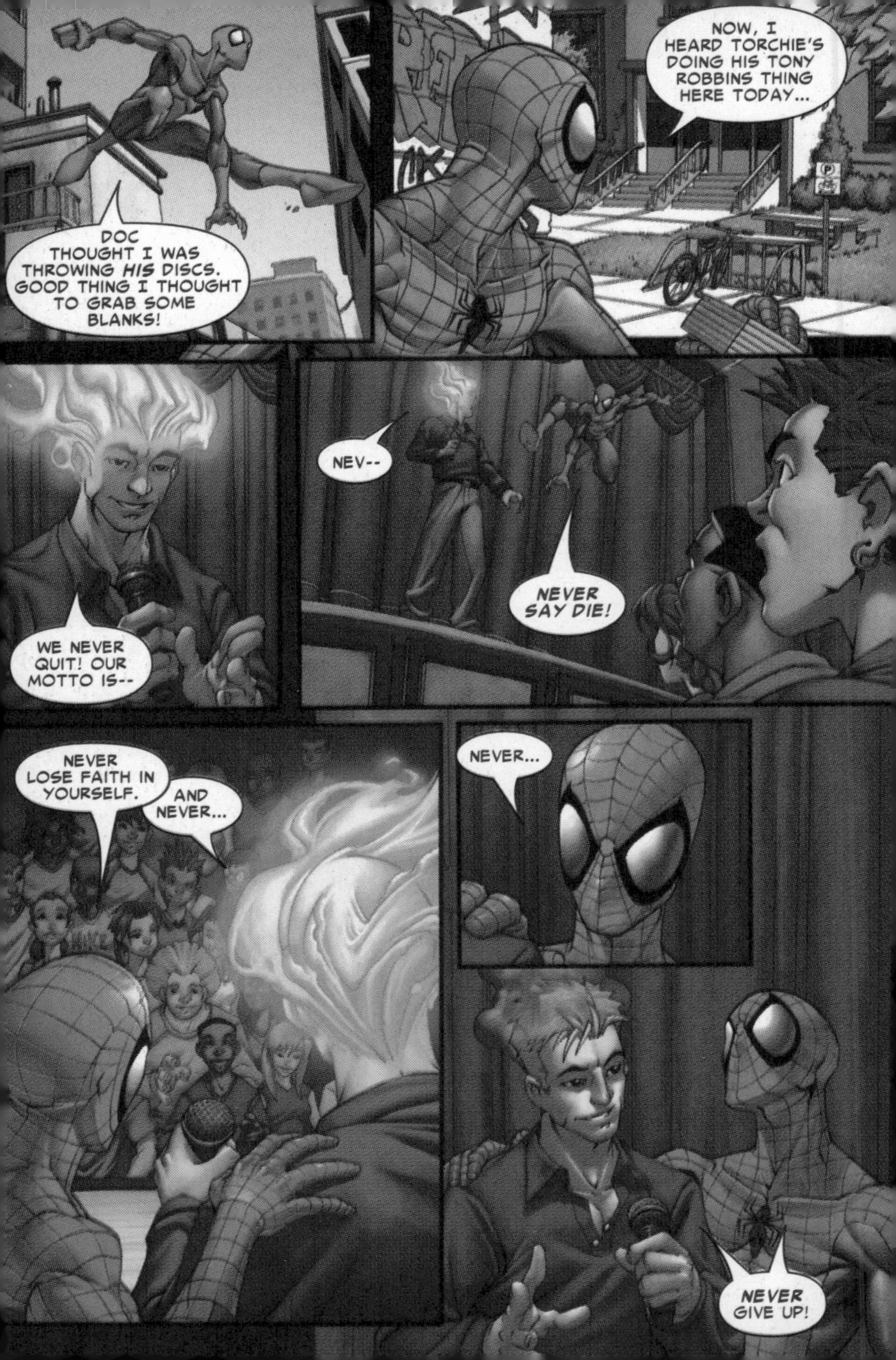
DOC THOUGHT I WAS THROWING *HIS* DISCS. GOOD THING I THOUGHT TO GRAB SOME BLANKS!
NOW, I HEARD TORCHIE'S DOING HIS TONY ROBBINS THING HERE TODAY...
WE NEVER QUIT! OUR MOTTO IS--
NEV--
NEVER SAY DIE!
NEVER LOSE FAITH IN YOURSELF.
AND NEVER...
NEVER...
NEVER GIVE UP!

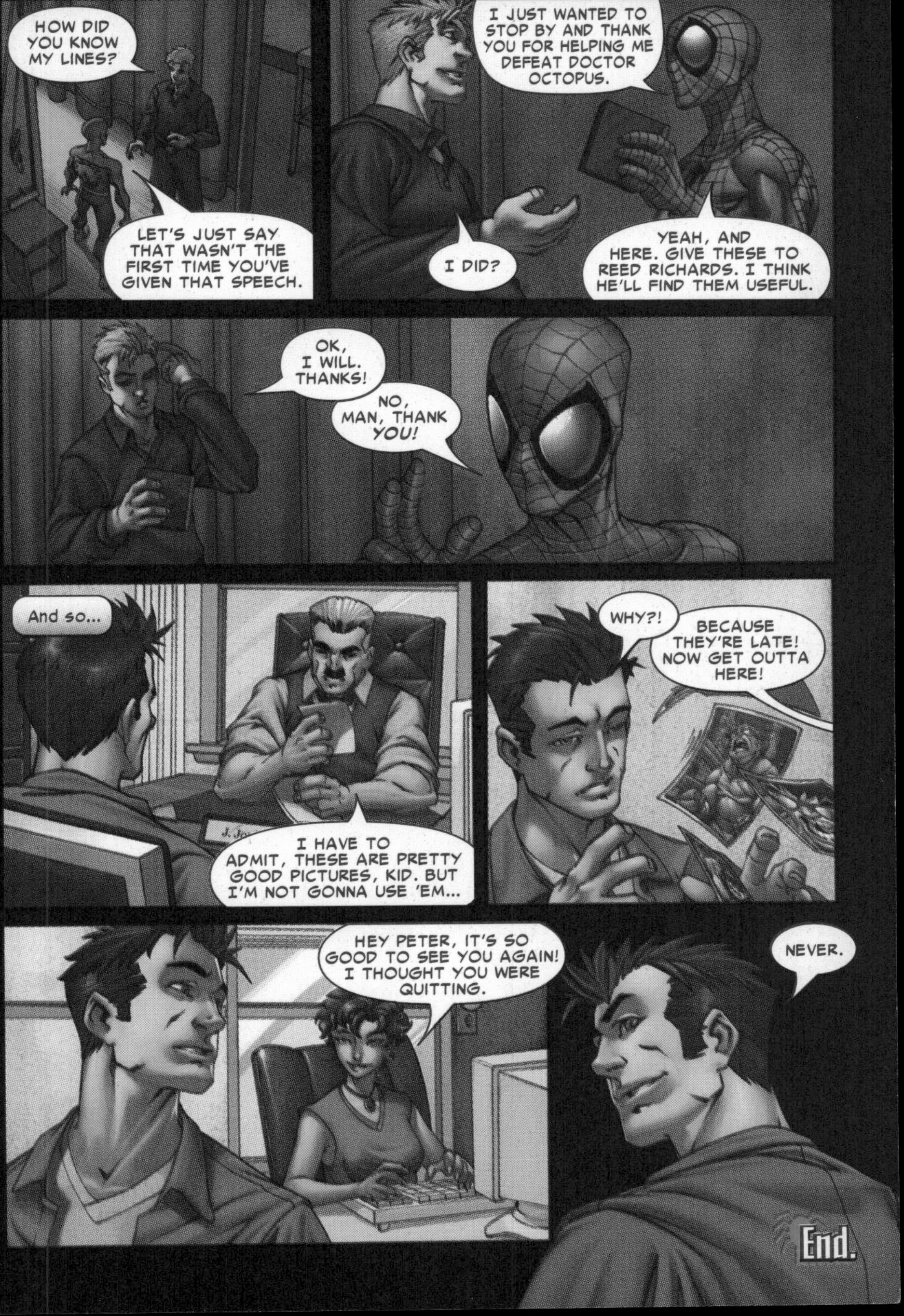
HOW DID YOU KNOW MY LINES?
LET'S JUST SAY THAT WASN'T THE FIRST TIME YOU'VE GIVEN THAT SPEECH.
I JUST WANTED TO STOP BY AND THANK YOU FOR HELPING ME DEFEAT DOCTOR OCTOPUS.
I DID?
YEAH, AND HERE. GIVE THESE TO REED RICHARDS. I THINK HE'LL FIND THEM USEFUL.
OK, I WILL. THANKS!
NO, MAN, THANK YOU!
And so...
I HAVE TO ADMIT, THESE ARE PRETTY GOOD PICTURES, KID. BUT I'M NOT GONNA USE 'EM...
WHY?!
BECAUSE THEY'RE LATE! NOW GET OUTTA HERE!
HEY PETER, IT'S SO GOOD TO SEE YOU AGAIN! I THOUGHT YOU WERE QUITTING.
NEVER.
End.

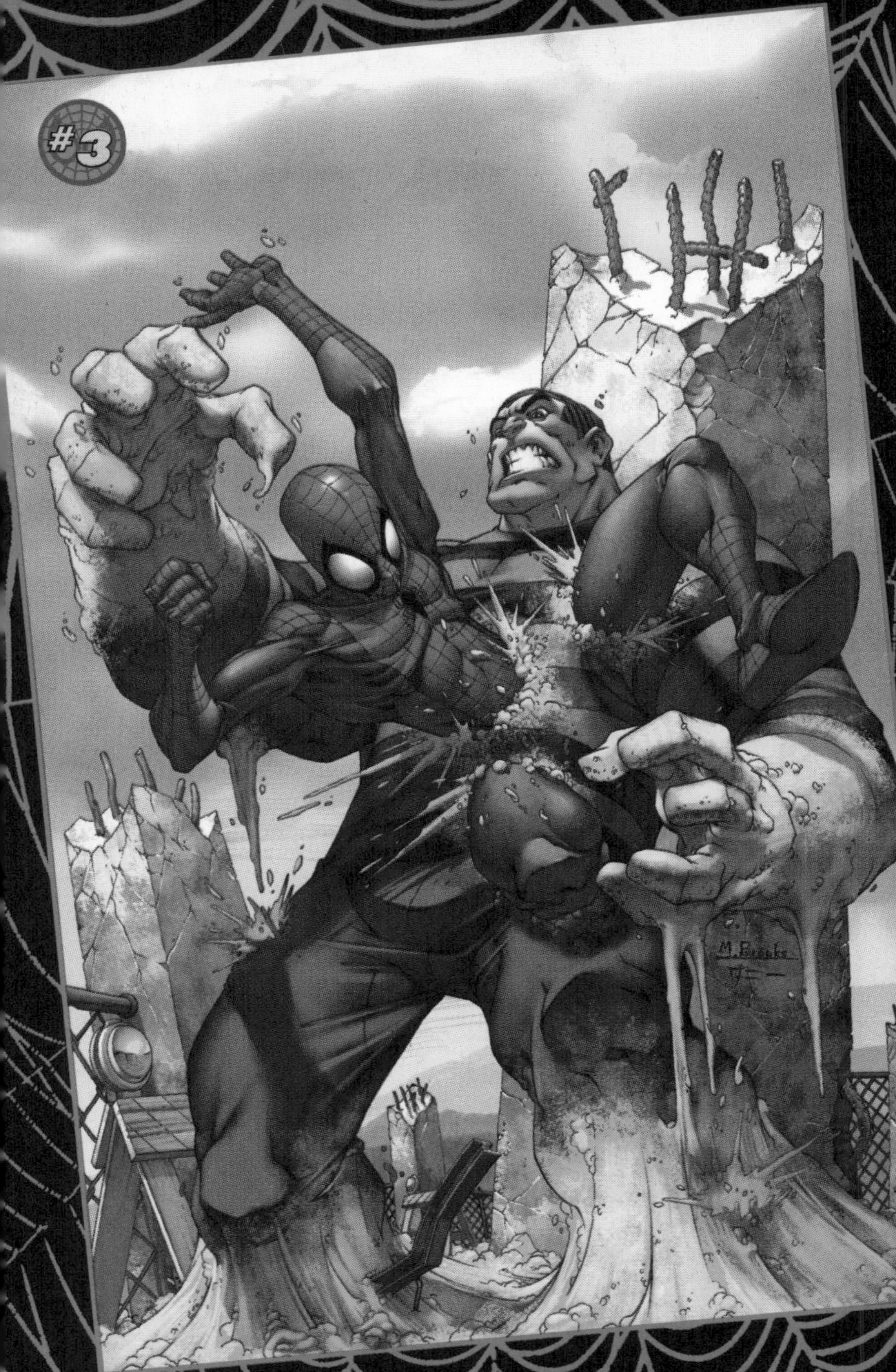
#3
M. Brooks

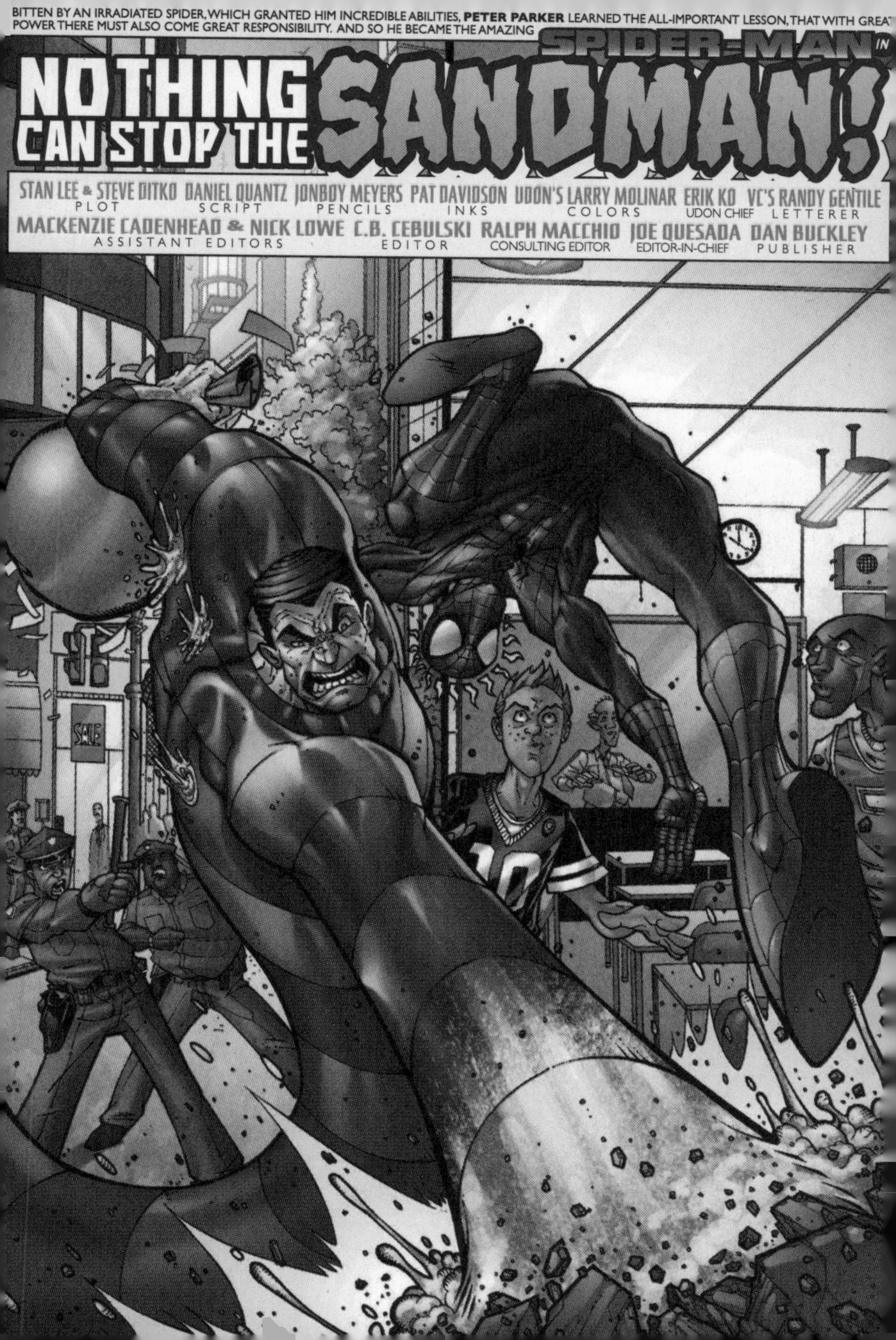
BITTEN BY AN IRRADIATED SPIDER, WHICH GRANTED HIM INCREDIBLE ABILITIES, PETER PARKER LEARNED THE ALL-IMPORTANT LESSON, THAT WITH GREAT POWER THERE MUST ALSO COME GREAT RESPONSIBILITY. AND SO HE BECAME THE AMAZING SPIDER-MAN IN
NOTHING CAN STOP THE SANDMAN!
STAN LEE & STEVE DITKO PLOT
DANIEL QUANTZ SCRIPT
JONBOY MEYERS PENCILS
PAT DAVIDSON INKS
UDON'S LARRY MOLINAR COLORS
ERIK KO UDON CHIEF
VC'S RANDY GENTILE LETTERER
MACKENZIE CADENHEAD & NICK LOWE ASSISTANT EDITORS
C.B. CEBULSKI EDITOR
RALPH MACCHIO CONSULTING EDITOR
JOE QUESADA EDITOR-IN-CHIEF
DAN BUCKLEY PUBLISHER
SALE

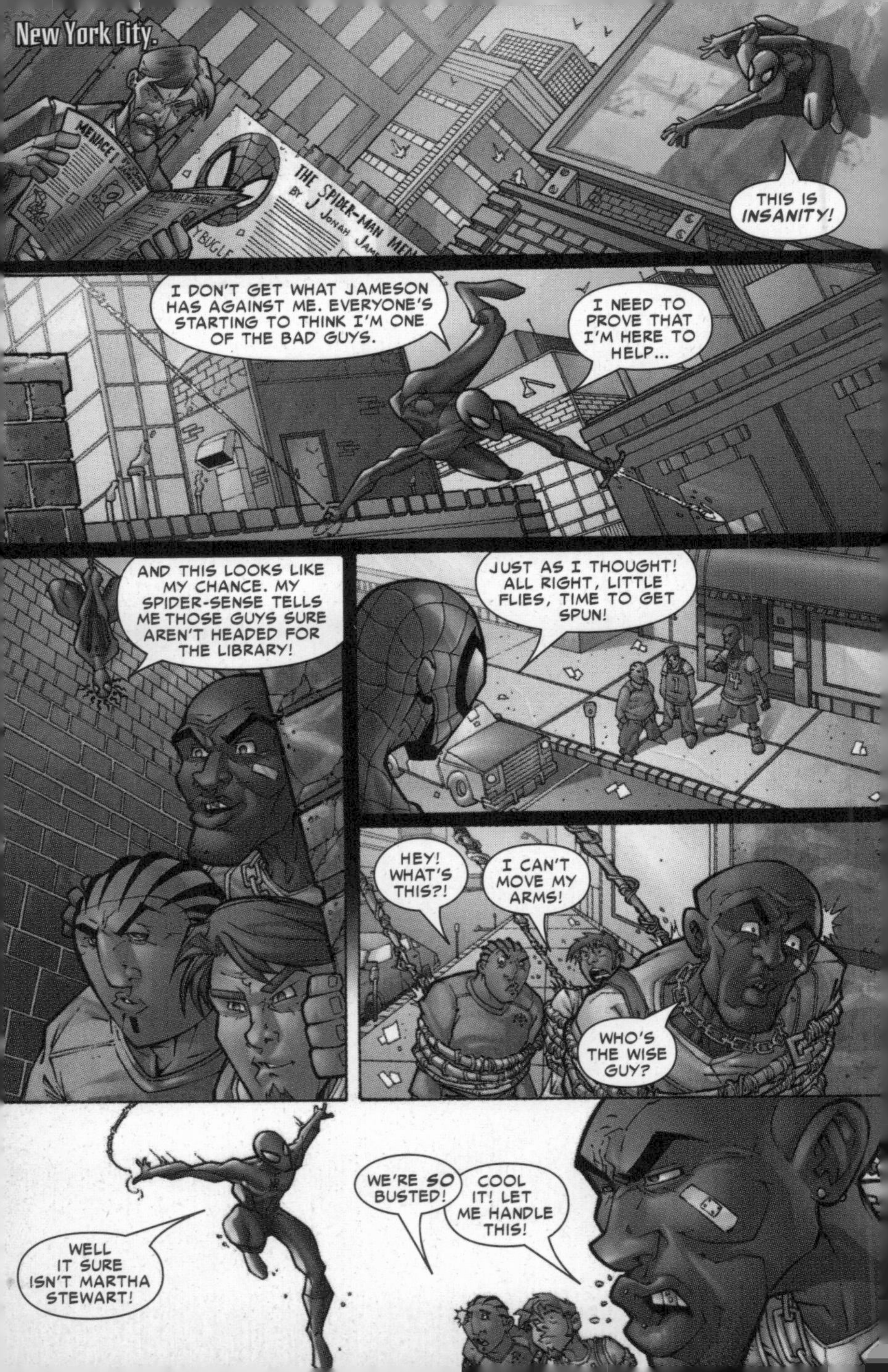
New York City.
MENACE!
THE SPIDER-MAN MENACE BY J JONAH JAMESON
THIS IS INSANITY!
I DON'T GET WHAT JAMESON HAS AGAINST ME. EVERYONE'S STARTING TO THINK I'M ONE OF THE BAD GUYS.
I NEED TO PROVE THAT I'M HERE TO HELP...
AND THIS LOOKS LIKE MY CHANCE. MY SPIDER-SENSE TELLS ME THOSE GUYS SURE AREN'T HEADED FOR THE LIBRARY!
JUST AS I THOUGHT! ALL RIGHT, LITTLE FLIES, TIME TO GET SPUN!
HEY! WHAT'S THIS?!
I CAN'T MOVE MY ARMS!
WHO'S THE WISE GUY?
WELL IT SURE ISN'T MARTHA STEWART!
WE'RE *SO* BUSTED!
COOL IT! LET ME HANDLE THIS!

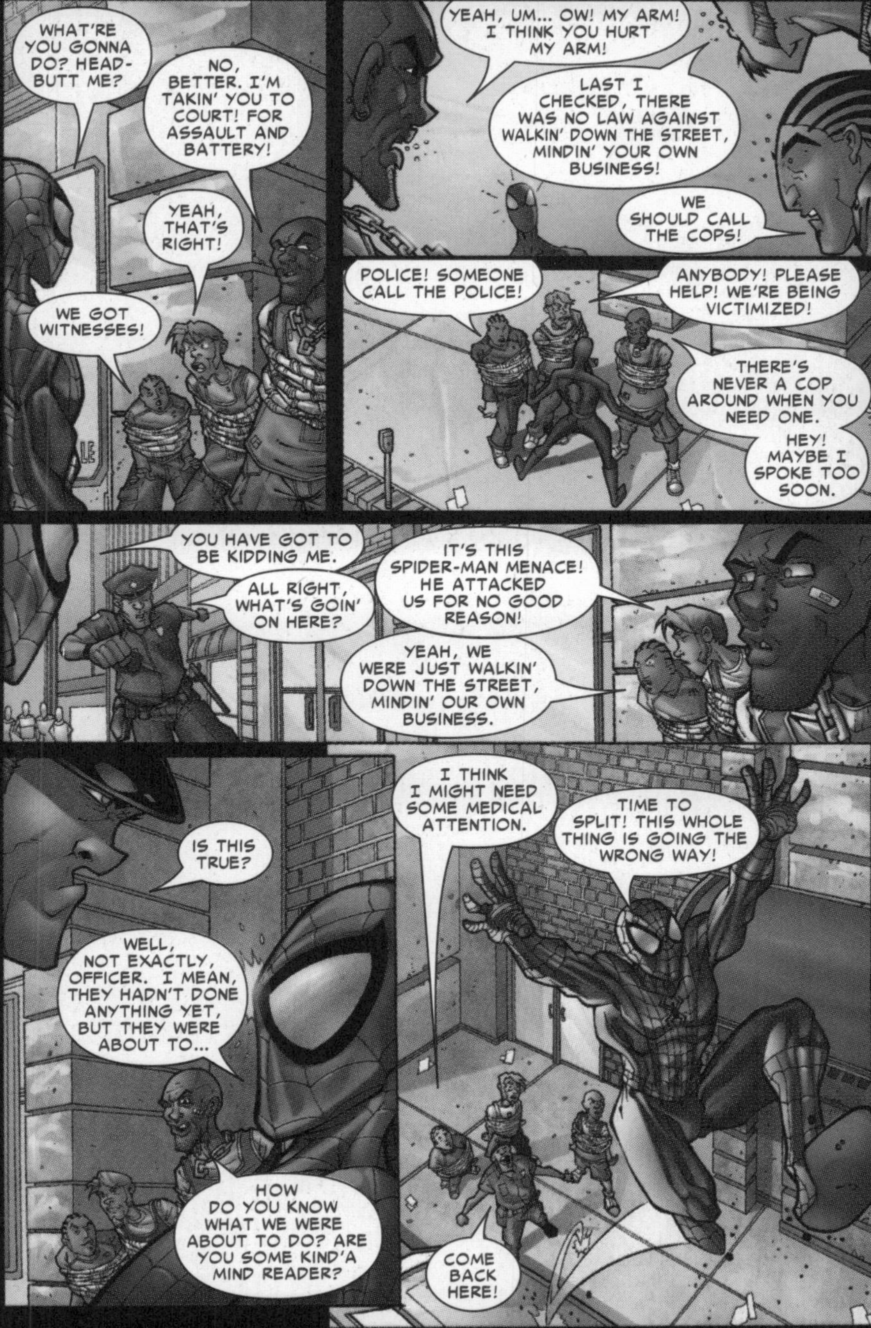
WHAT'RE YOU GONNA DO? HEAD-BUTT ME?
NO, BETTER. I'M TAKIN' YOU TO COURT! FOR ASSAULT AND BATTERY!
YEAH, THAT'S RIGHT!
WE GOT WITNESSES!
YEAH, UM... OW! MY ARM! I THINK YOU HURT MY ARM!
LAST I CHECKED, THERE WAS NO LAW AGAINST WALKIN' DOWN THE STREET, MINDIN' YOUR OWN BUSINESS!
WE SHOULD CALL THE COPS!
POLICE! SOMEONE CALL THE POLICE!
ANYBODY! PLEASE HELP! WE'RE BEING VICTIMIZED!
THERE'S NEVER A COP AROUND WHEN YOU NEED ONE.
HEY! MAYBE I SPOKE TOO SOON.
YOU HAVE GOT TO BE KIDDING ME.
ALL RIGHT, WHAT'S GOIN' ON HERE?
IT'S THIS SPIDER-MAN MENACE! HE ATTACKED US FOR NO GOOD REASON!
YEAH, WE WERE JUST WALKIN' DOWN THE STREET, MINDIN' OUR OWN BUSINESS.
IS THIS TRUE?
WELL, NOT EXACTLY, OFFICER. I MEAN, THEY HADN'T DONE ANYTHING YET, BUT THEY WERE ABOUT TO...
HOW DO YOU KNOW WHAT WE WERE ABOUT TO DO? ARE YOU SOME KIND'A MIND READER?
I THINK I MIGHT NEED SOME MEDICAL ATTENTION.
TIME TO SPLIT! THIS WHOLE THING IS GOING THE WRONG WAY!
COME BACK HERE!

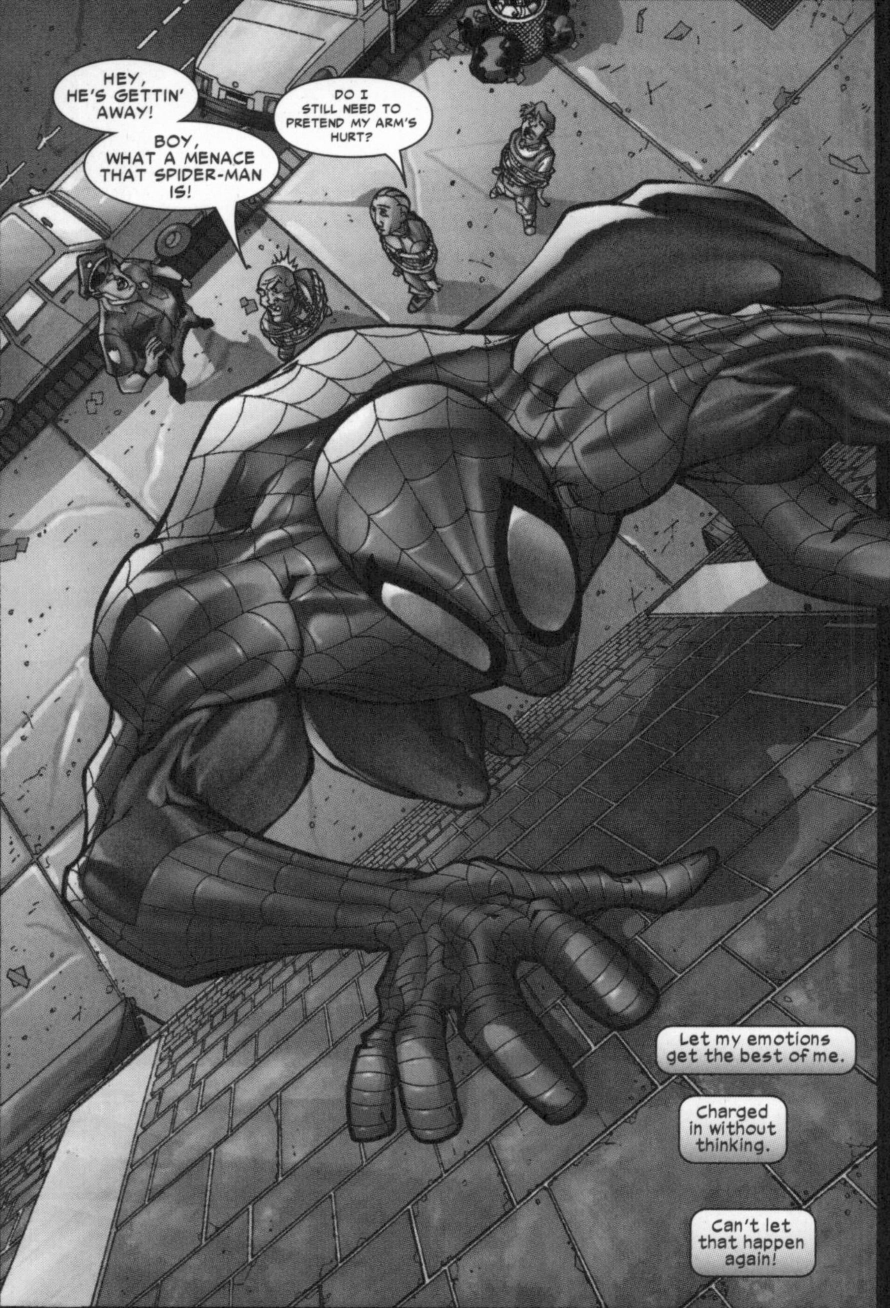
HEY, HE'S GETTIN' AWAY!
BOY, WHAT A MENACE THAT SPIDER-MAN IS!
DO I STILL NEED TO PRETEND MY ARM'S HURT?
Let my emotions get the best of me.
Charged in without thinking.
Can't let that happen again!

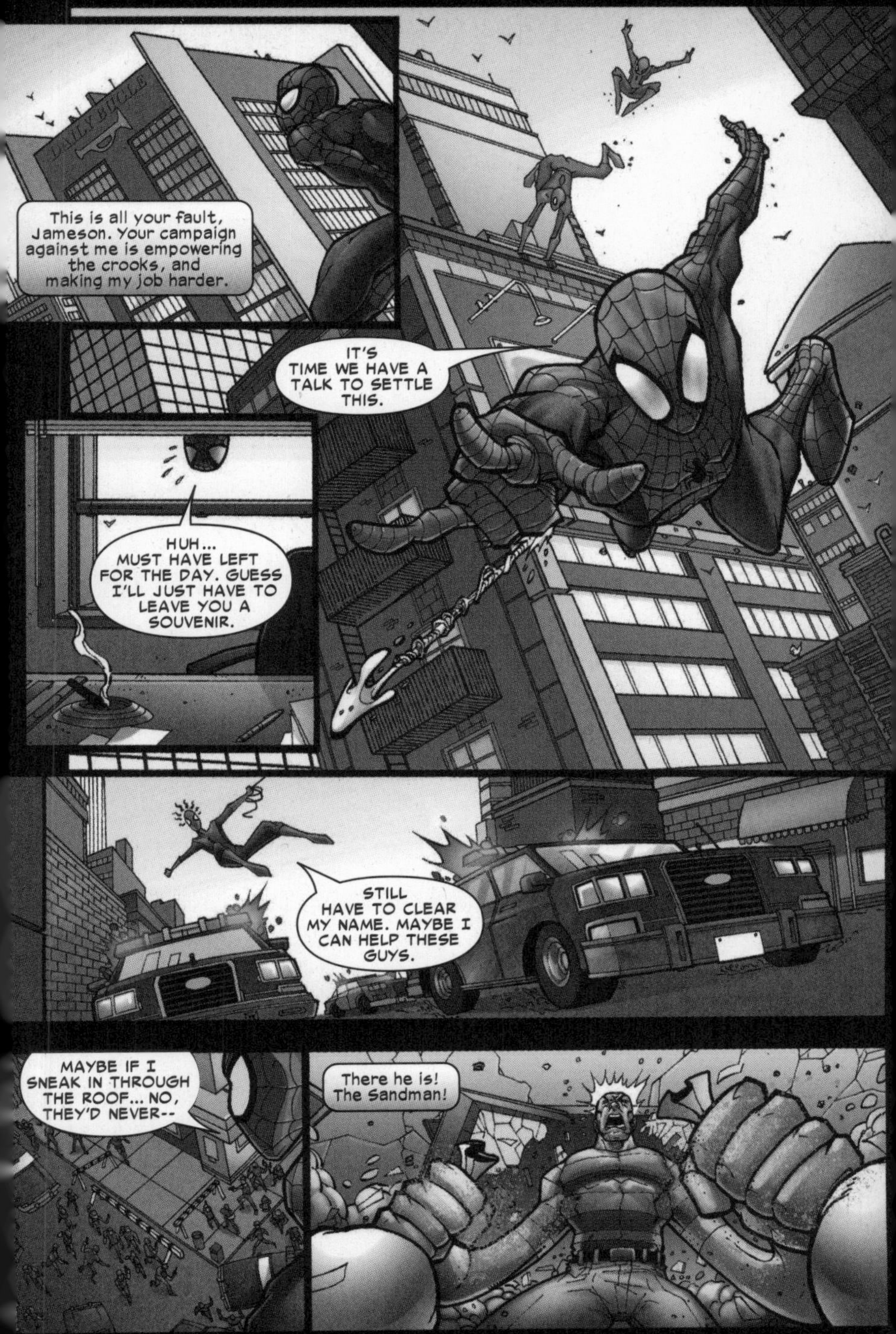

This is all your fault, Jameson. Your campaign against me is empowering the crooks, and making my job harder.
IT'S TIME WE HAVE A TALK TO SETTLE THIS.
HUH... MUST HAVE LEFT FOR THE DAY. GUESS I'LL JUST HAVE TO LEAVE YOU A SOUVENIR.
STILL HAVE TO CLEAR MY NAME. MAYBE I CAN HELP THESE GUYS.
MAYBE IF I SNEAK IN THROUGH THE ROOF... NO, THEY'D NEVER--
There he is! The Sandman!

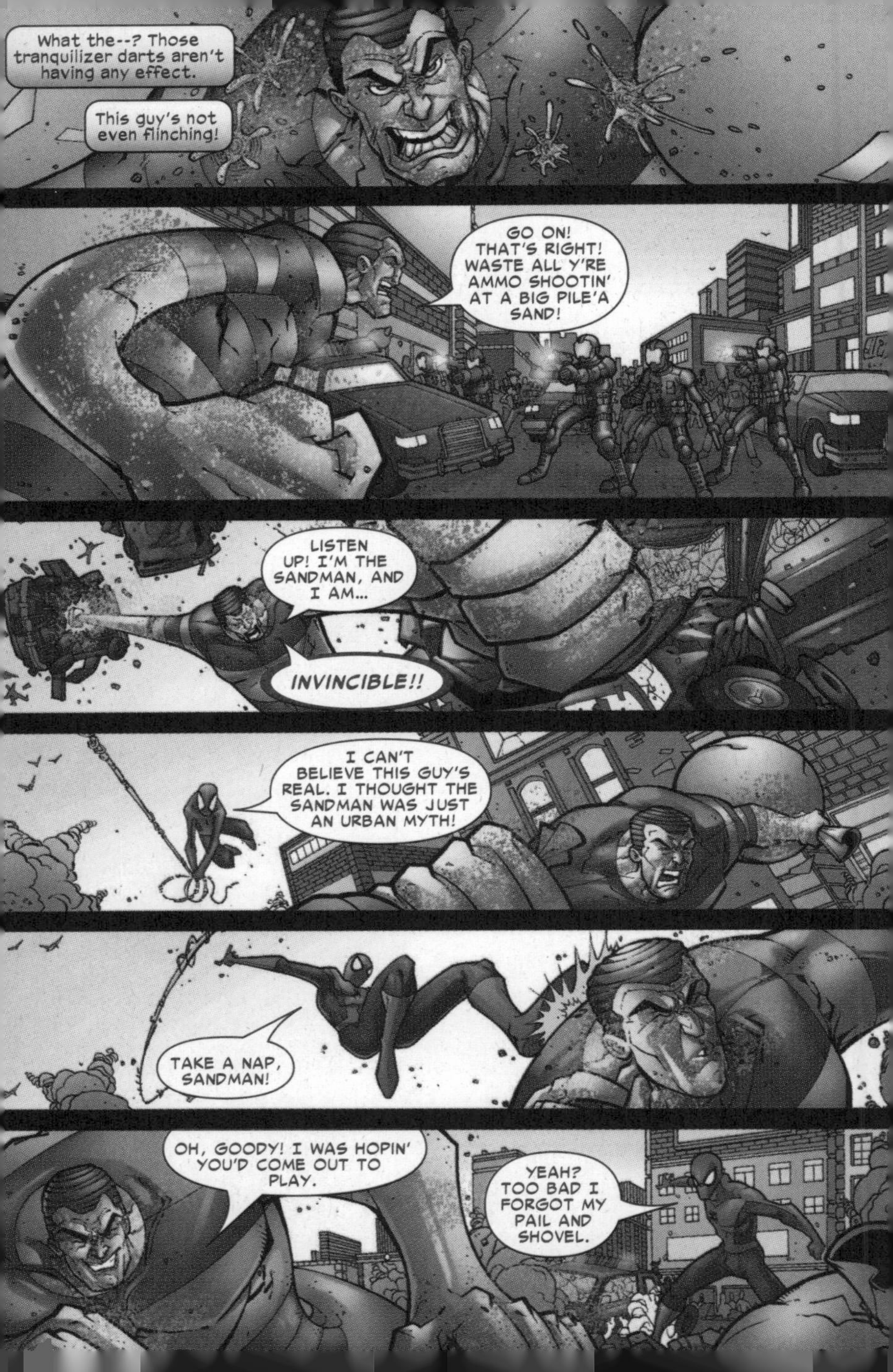
What the--? Those tranquilizer darts aren't having any effect.
This guy's not even flinching!
GO ON! THAT'S RIGHT! WASTE ALL Y'RE AMMO SHOOTIN' AT A BIG PILE'A SAND!
LISTEN UP! I'M THE SANDMAN, AND I AM...
INVINCIBLE!!
I CAN'T BELIEVE THIS GUY'S REAL. I THOUGHT THE SANDMAN WAS JUST AN URBAN MYTH!
TAKE A NAP, SANDMAN!
OH, GOODY! I WAS HOPIN' YOU'D COME OUT TO PLAY.
YEAH? TOO BAD I FORGOT MY PAIL AND SHOVEL.

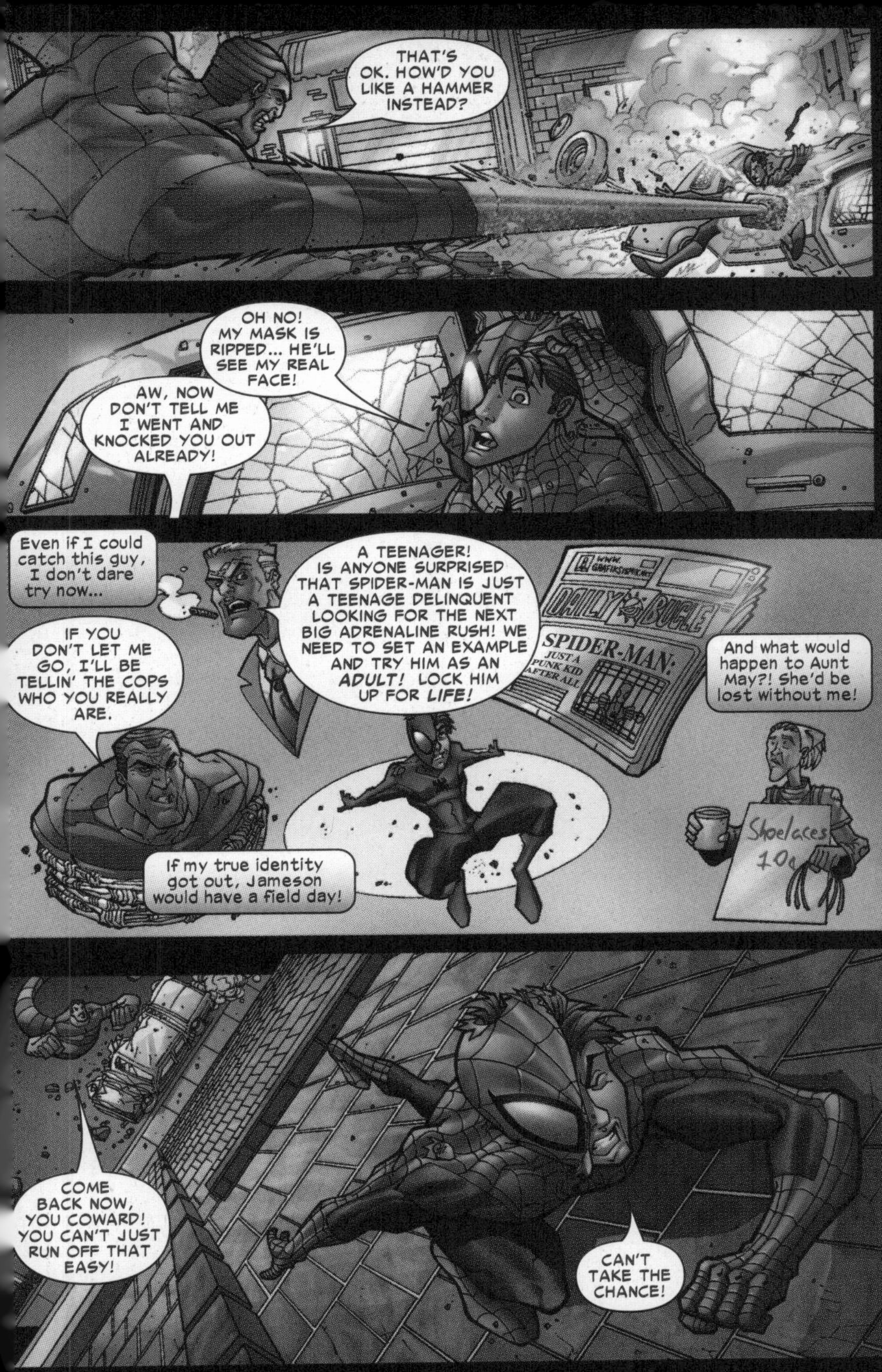

THAT'S OK. HOW'D YOU LIKE A HAMMER INSTEAD?
OH NO! MY MASK IS RIPPED... HE'LL SEE MY REAL FACE!
AW, NOW DON'T TELL ME I WENT AND KNOCKED YOU OUT ALREADY!
Even if I could catch this guy, I don't dare try now...
A TEENAGER! IS ANYONE SURPRISED THAT SPIDER-MAN IS JUST A TEENAGE DELINQUENT LOOKING FOR THE NEXT BIG ADRENALINE RUSH! WE NEED TO SET AN EXAMPLE AND TRY HIM AS AN ADULT! LOCK HIM UP FOR LIFE!
DAILY BUGLE
SPIDER-MAN: JUST A PUNK KID AFTER ALL
IF YOU DON'T LET ME GO, I'LL BE TELLIN' THE COPS WHO YOU REALLY ARE.
And what would happen to Aunt May?! She'd be lost without me!
Shoelaces 10¢
If my true identity got out, Jameson would have a field day!
COME BACK NOW, YOU COWARD! YOU CAN'T JUST RUN OFF THAT EASY!
CAN'T TAKE THE CHANCE!

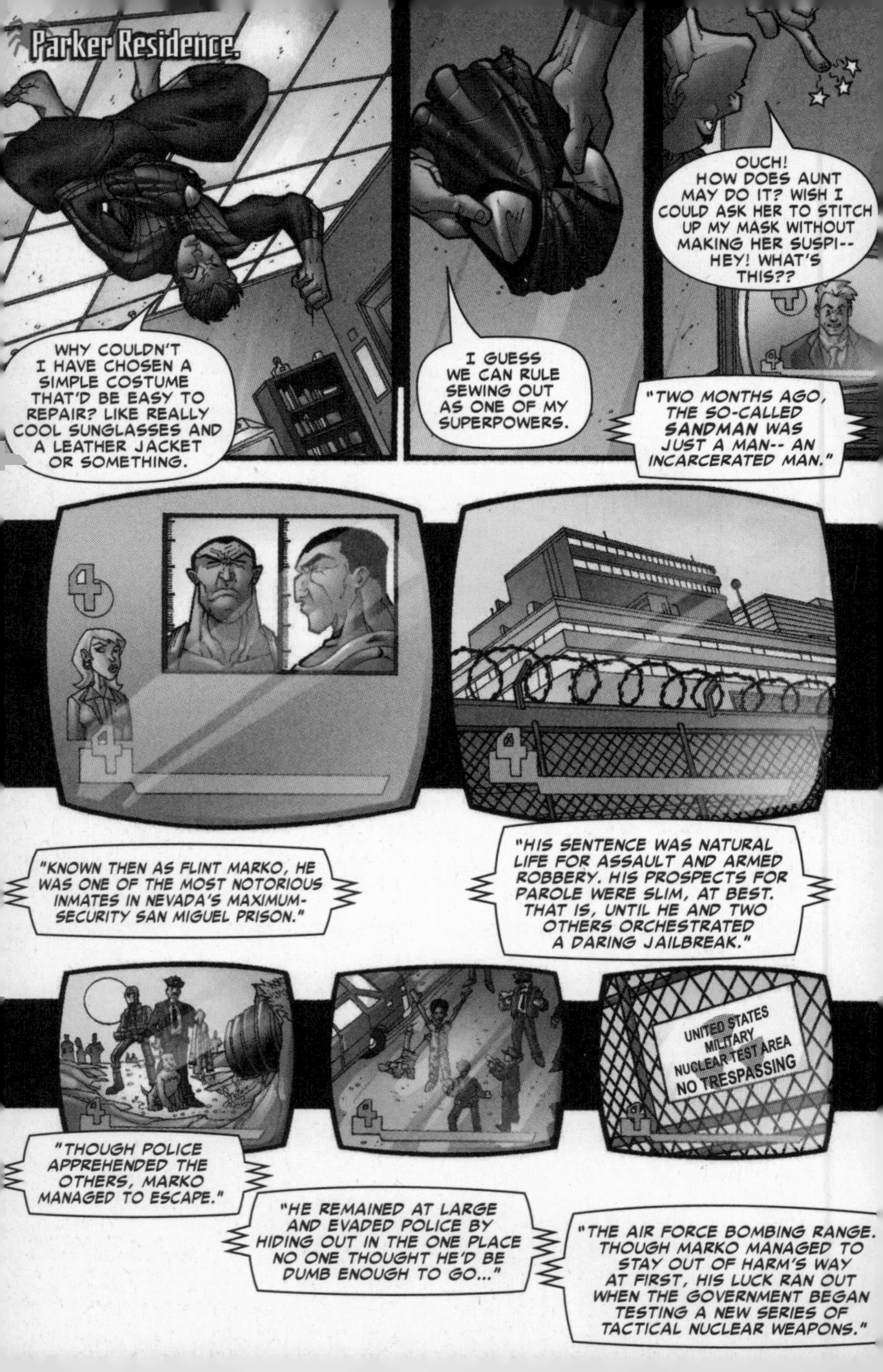
Parker Residence.
WHY COULDN'T I HAVE CHOSEN A SIMPLE COSTUME THAT'D BE EASY TO REPAIR? LIKE REALLY COOL SUNGLASSES AND A LEATHER JACKET OR SOMETHING.
I GUESS WE CAN RULE SEWING OUT AS ONE OF MY SUPERPOWERS.
OUCH! HOW DOES AUNT MAY DO IT? WISH I COULD ASK HER TO STITCH UP MY MASK WITHOUT MAKING HER SUSPI-- HEY! WHAT'S THIS??
"TWO MONTHS AGO, THE SO-CALLED SANDMAN WAS JUST A MAN-- AN INCARCERATED MAN."
"KNOWN THEN AS FLINT MARKO, HE WAS ONE OF THE MOST NOTORIOUS INMATES IN NEVADA'S MAXIMUM-SECURITY SAN MIGUEL PRISON."
"HIS SENTENCE WAS NATURAL LIFE FOR ASSAULT AND ARMED ROBBERY. HIS PROSPECTS FOR PAROLE WERE SLIM, AT BEST. THAT IS, UNTIL HE AND TWO OTHERS ORCHESTRATED A DARING JAILBREAK."
UNITED STATES MILITARY NUCLEAR TEST AREA NO TRESPASSING
"THOUGH POLICE APPREHENDED THE OTHERS, MARKO MANAGED TO ESCAPE."
"HE REMAINED AT LARGE AND EVADED POLICE BY HIDING OUT IN THE ONE PLACE NO ONE THOUGHT HE'D BE DUMB ENOUGH TO GO..."
"THE AIR FORCE BOMBING RANGE. THOUGH MARKO MANAGED TO STAY OUT OF HARM'S WAY AT FIRST, HIS LUCK RAN OUT WHEN THE GOVERNMENT BEGAN TESTING A NEW SERIES OF TACTICAL NUCLEAR WEAPONS."

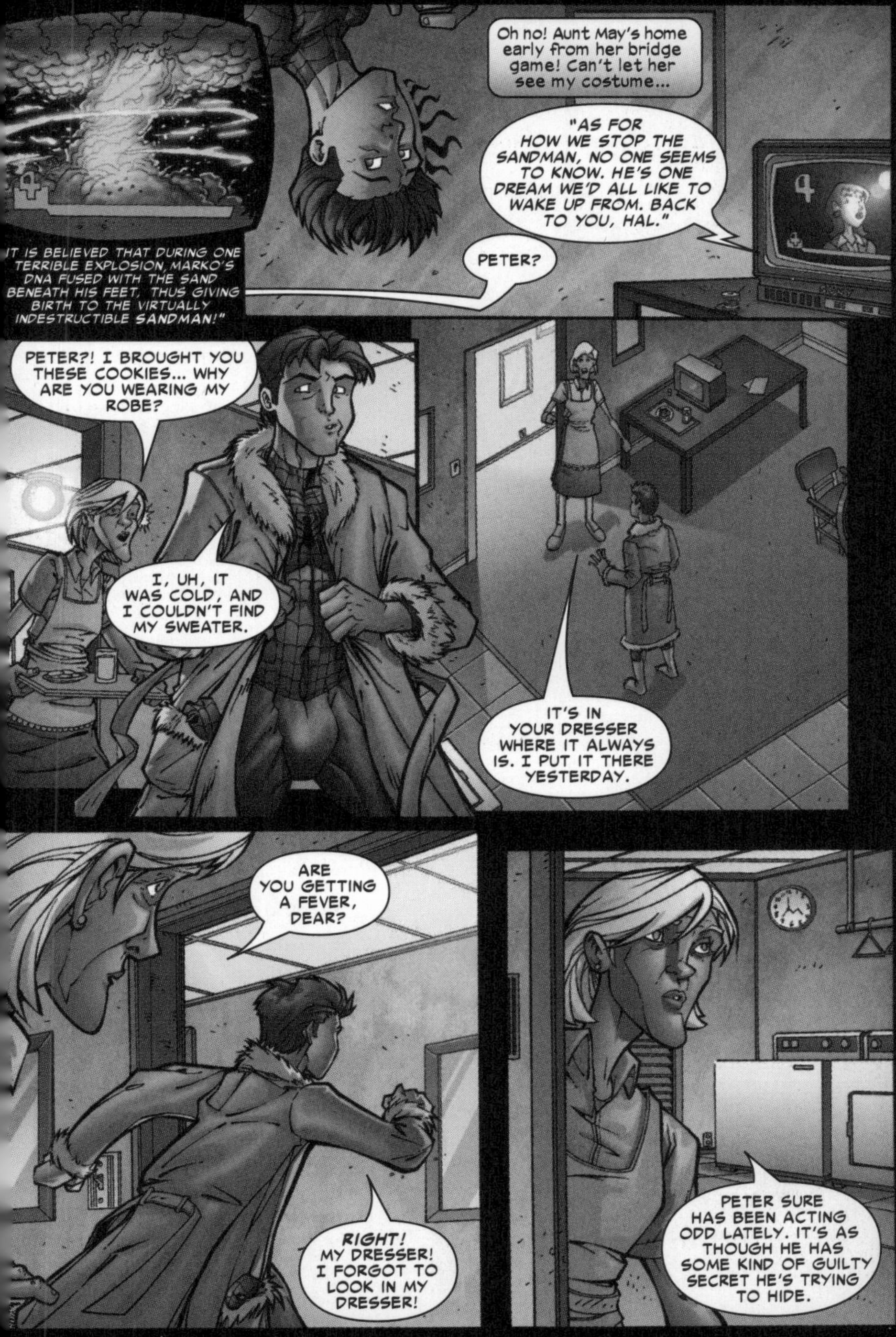
IT IS BELIEVED THAT DURING ONE TERRIBLE EXPLOSION, MARKO'S DNA FUSED WITH THE SAND BENEATH HIS FEET, THUS GIVING BIRTH TO THE VIRTUALLY INDESTRUCTIBLE SANDMAN!"
Oh no! Aunt May's home early from her bridge game! Can't let her see my costume...
"AS FOR HOW WE STOP THE SANDMAN, NO ONE SEEMS TO KNOW. HE'S ONE DREAM WE'D ALL LIKE TO WAKE UP FROM. BACK TO YOU, HAL."
PETER?
PETER?! I BROUGHT YOU THESE COOKIES... WHY ARE YOU WEARING MY ROBE?
I, UH, IT WAS COLD, AND I COULDN'T FIND MY SWEATER.
IT'S IN YOUR DRESSER WHERE IT ALWAYS IS. I PUT IT THERE YESTERDAY.
ARE YOU GETTING A FEVER, DEAR?
RIGHT! MY DRESSER! I FORGOT TO LOOK IN MY DRESSER!
PETER SURE HAS BEEN ACTING ODD LATELY. IT'S AS THOUGH HE HAS SOME KIND OF GUILTY SECRET HE'S TRYING TO HIDE.

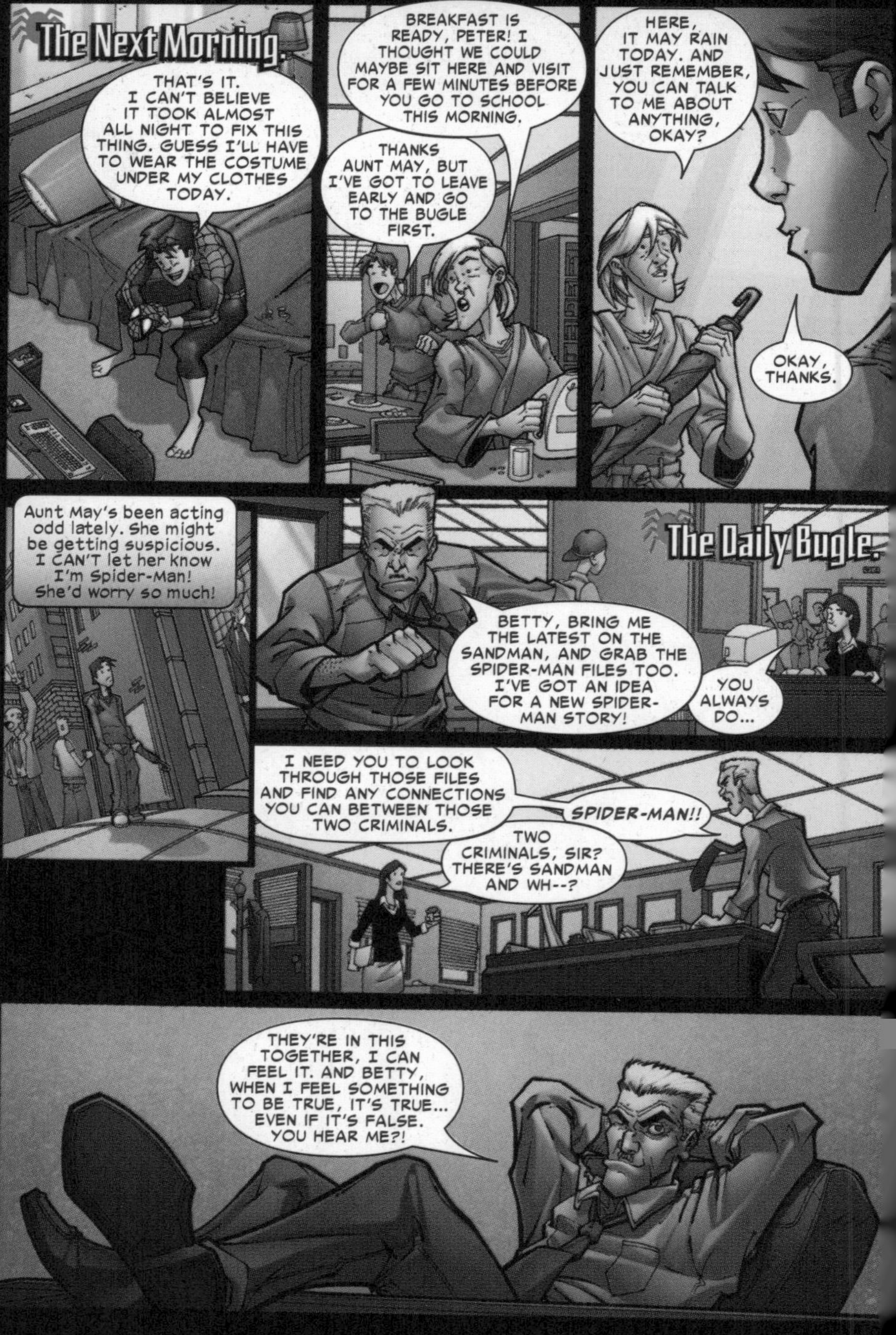
The Next Morning.
THAT'S IT. I CAN'T BELIEVE IT TOOK ALMOST ALL NIGHT TO FIX THIS THING. GUESS I'LL HAVE TO WEAR THE COSTUME UNDER MY CLOTHES TODAY.
BREAKFAST IS READY, PETER! I THOUGHT WE COULD MAYBE SIT HERE AND VISIT FOR A FEW MINUTES BEFORE YOU GO TO SCHOOL THIS MORNING.
THANKS AUNT MAY, BUT I'VE GOT TO LEAVE EARLY AND GO TO THE BUGLE FIRST.
HERE, IT MAY RAIN TODAY. AND JUST REMEMBER, YOU CAN TALK TO ME ABOUT ANYTHING, OKAY?
OKAY, THANKS.
Aunt May's been acting odd lately. She might be getting suspicious. I CAN'T let her know I'm Spider-Man! She'd worry so much!
The Daily Bugle.
BETTY, BRING ME THE LATEST ON THE SANDMAN, AND GRAB THE SPIDER-MAN FILES TOO. I'VE GOT AN IDEA FOR A NEW SPIDER-MAN STORY!
YOU ALWAYS DO...
I NEED YOU TO LOOK THROUGH THOSE FILES AND FIND ANY CONNECTIONS YOU CAN BETWEEN THOSE TWO CRIMINALS.
TWO CRIMINALS, SIR? THERE'S SANDMAN AND WH--?
SPIDER-MAN!!
THEY'RE IN THIS TOGETHER, I CAN FEEL IT. AND BETTY, WHEN I FEEL SOMETHING TO BE TRUE, IT'S TRUE... EVEN IF IT'S FALSE. YOU HEAR ME?!

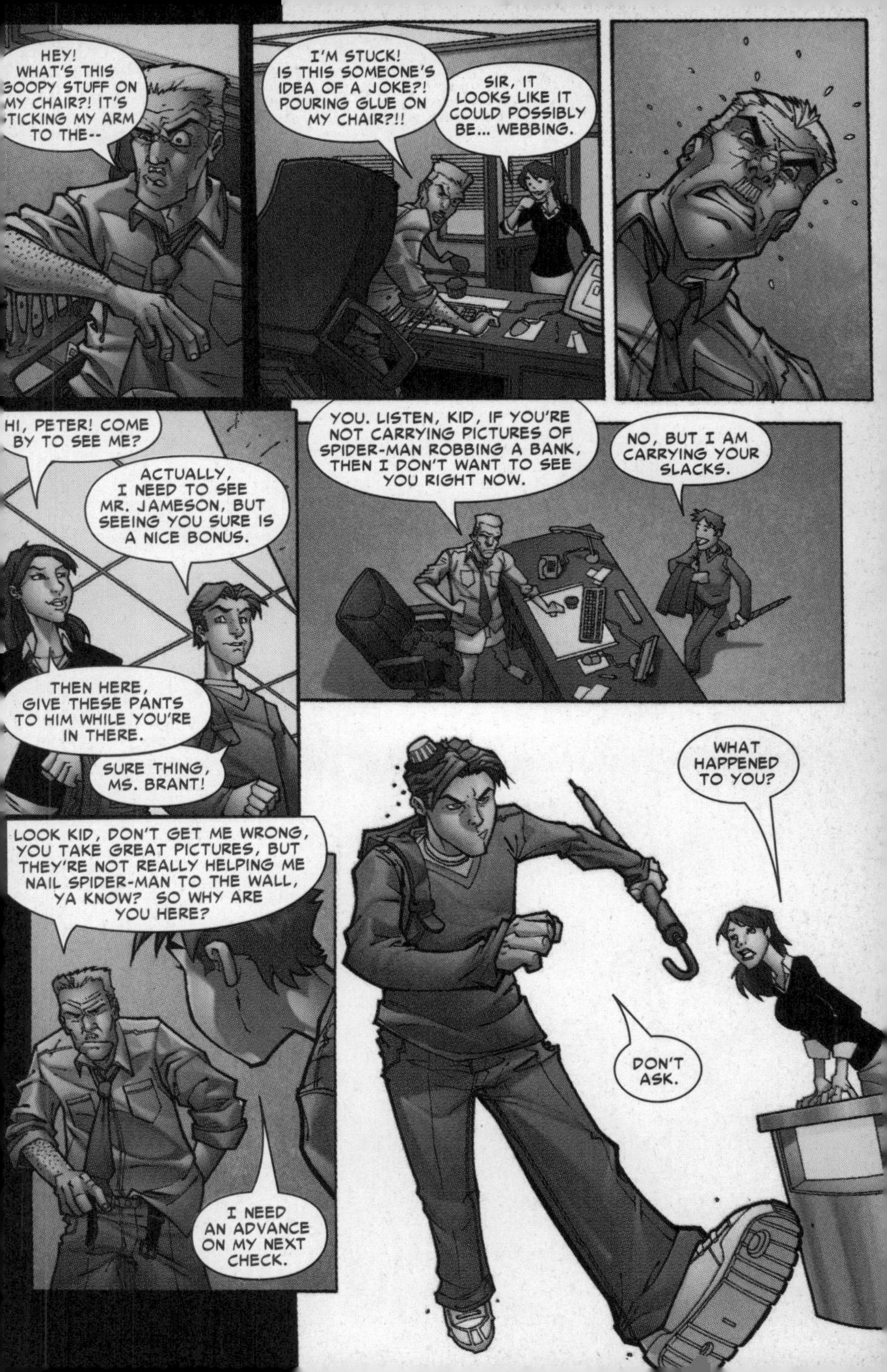
HEY! WHAT'S THIS GOOPY STUFF ON MY CHAIR?! IT'S STICKING MY ARM TO THE--
I'M STUCK! IS THIS SOMEONE'S IDEA OF A JOKE?! POURING GLUE ON MY CHAIR?!!
SIR, IT LOOKS LIKE IT COULD POSSIBLY BE... WEBBING.
HI, PETER! COME BY TO SEE ME?
ACTUALLY, I NEED TO SEE MR. JAMESON, BUT SEEING YOU SURE IS A NICE BONUS.
THEN HERE, GIVE THESE PANTS TO HIM WHILE YOU'RE IN THERE.
SURE THING, MS. BRANT!
YOU. LISTEN, KID, IF YOU'RE NOT CARRYING PICTURES OF SPIDER-MAN ROBBING A BANK, THEN I DON'T WANT TO SEE YOU RIGHT NOW.
NO, BUT I AM CARRYING YOUR SLACKS.
LOOK KID, DON'T GET ME WRONG, YOU TAKE GREAT PICTURES, BUT THEY'RE NOT REALLY HELPING ME NAIL SPIDER-MAN TO THE WALL, YA KNOW? SO WHY ARE YOU HERE?
I NEED AN ADVANCE ON MY NEXT CHECK.
WHAT HAPPENED TO YOU?
DON'T ASK.

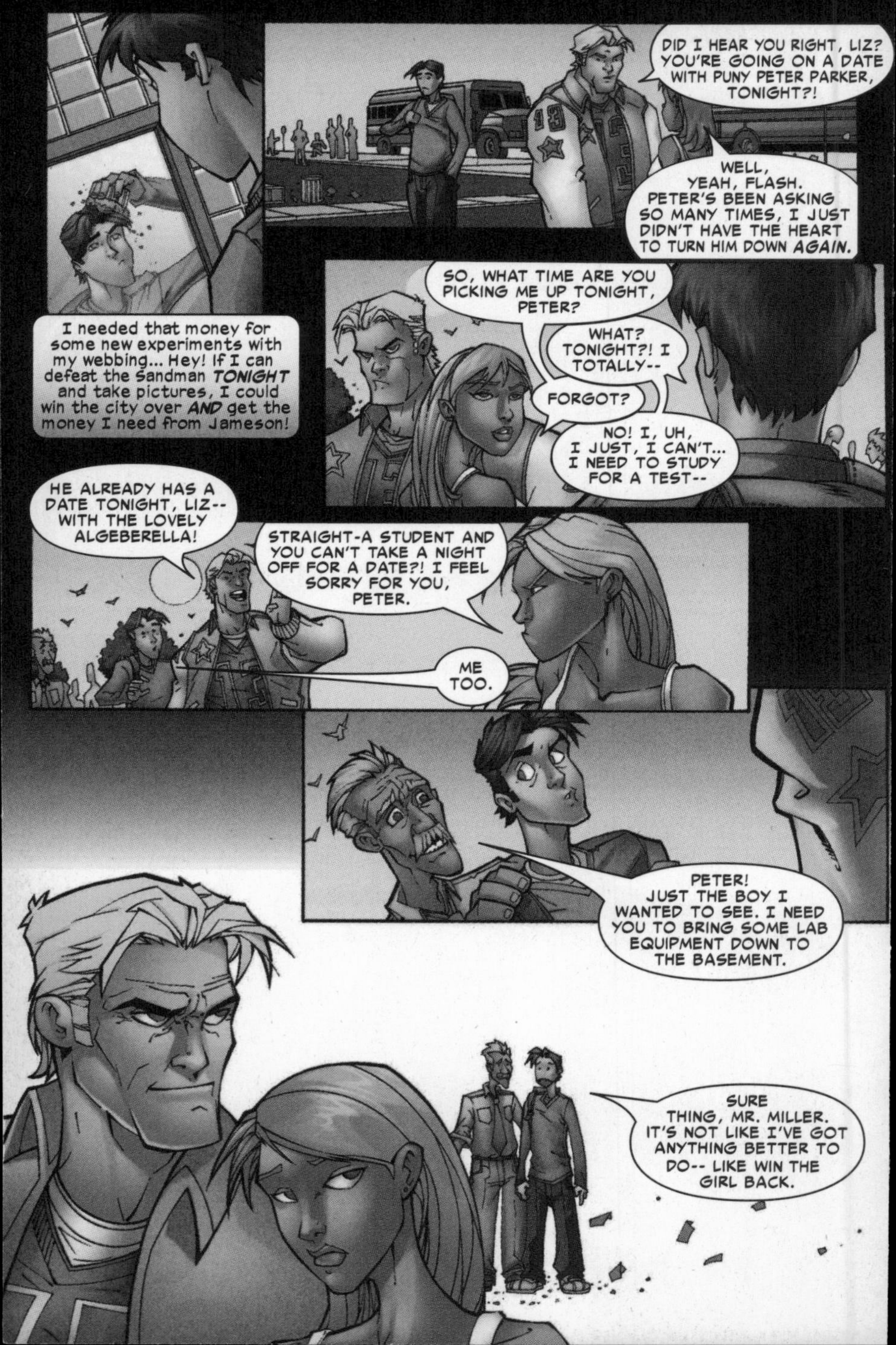

DID I HEAR YOU RIGHT, LIZ? YOU'RE GOING ON A DATE WITH PUNY PETER PARKER, TONIGHT?!
WELL, YEAH, FLASH. PETER'S BEEN ASKING SO MANY TIMES, I JUST DIDN'T HAVE THE HEART TO TURN HIM DOWN AGAIN.
I needed that money for some new experiments with my webbing... Hey! If I can defeat the Sandman TONIGHT and take pictures, I could win the city over AND get the money I need from Jameson!
SO, WHAT TIME ARE YOU PICKING ME UP TONIGHT, PETER?
WHAT? TONIGHT?! I TOTALLY--
FORGOT?
NO! I, UH, I JUST, I CAN'T... I NEED TO STUDY FOR A TEST--
HE ALREADY HAS A DATE TONIGHT, LIZ-- WITH THE LOVELY ALGEBERELLA!
STRAIGHT-A STUDENT AND YOU CAN'T TAKE A NIGHT OFF FOR A DATE?! I FEEL SORRY FOR YOU, PETER.
ME TOO.
PETER! JUST THE BOY I WANTED TO SEE. I NEED YOU TO BRING SOME LAB EQUIPMENT DOWN TO THE BASEMENT.
SURE THING, MR. MILLER. IT'S NOT LIKE I'VE GOT ANYTHING BETTER TO DO-- LIKE WIN THE GIRL BACK.

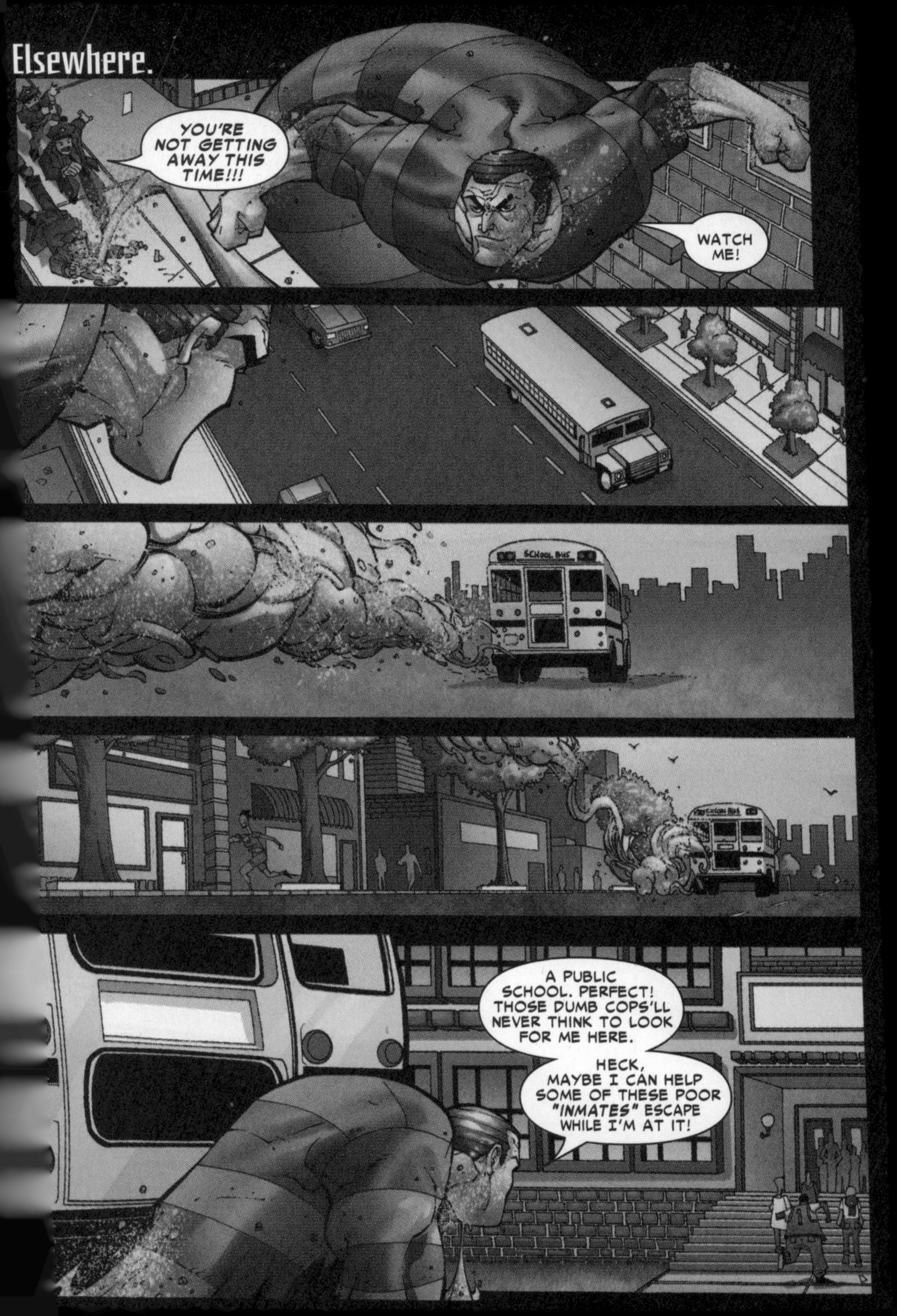
Elsewhere.
YOU'RE NOT GETTING AWAY THIS TIME!!!
WATCH ME!
SCHOOL BUS
A PUBLIC SCHOOL. PERFECT! THOSE DUMB COPS'LL NEVER THINK TO LOOK FOR ME HERE.
HECK, MAYBE I CAN HELP SOME OF THESE POOR "INMATES" ESCAPE WHILE I'M AT IT!

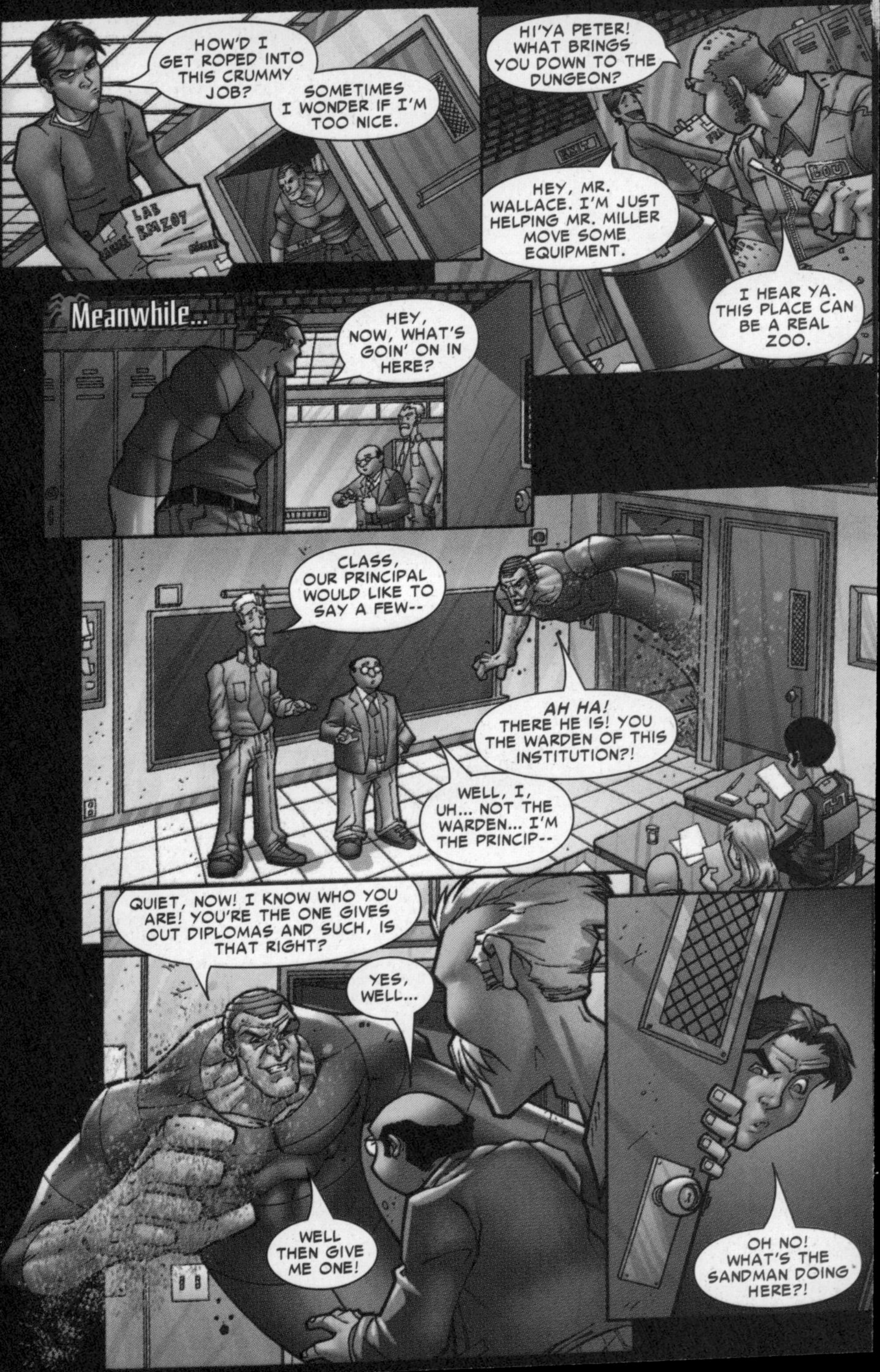
HOW'D I GET ROPED INTO THIS CRUMMY JOB?
SOMETIMES I WONDER IF I'M TOO NICE.
HI'YA PETER! WHAT BRINGS YOU DOWN TO THE DUNGEON?
HEY, MR. WALLACE. I'M JUST HELPING MR. MILLER MOVE SOME EQUIPMENT.
I HEAR YA. THIS PLACE CAN BE A REAL ZOO.
Meanwhile...
HEY, NOW, WHAT'S GOIN' ON IN HERE?
CLASS, OUR PRINCIPAL WOULD LIKE TO SAY A FEW--
AH HA! THERE HE IS! YOU THE WARDEN OF THIS INSTITUTION?!
WELL, I, UH... NOT THE WARDEN... I'M THE PRINCIP--
QUIET, NOW! I KNOW WHO YOU ARE! YOU'RE THE ONE GIVES OUT DIPLOMAS AND SUCH, IS THAT RIGHT?
YES, WELL...
WELL THEN GIVE ME ONE!
OH NO! WHAT'S THE SANDMAN DOING HERE?!

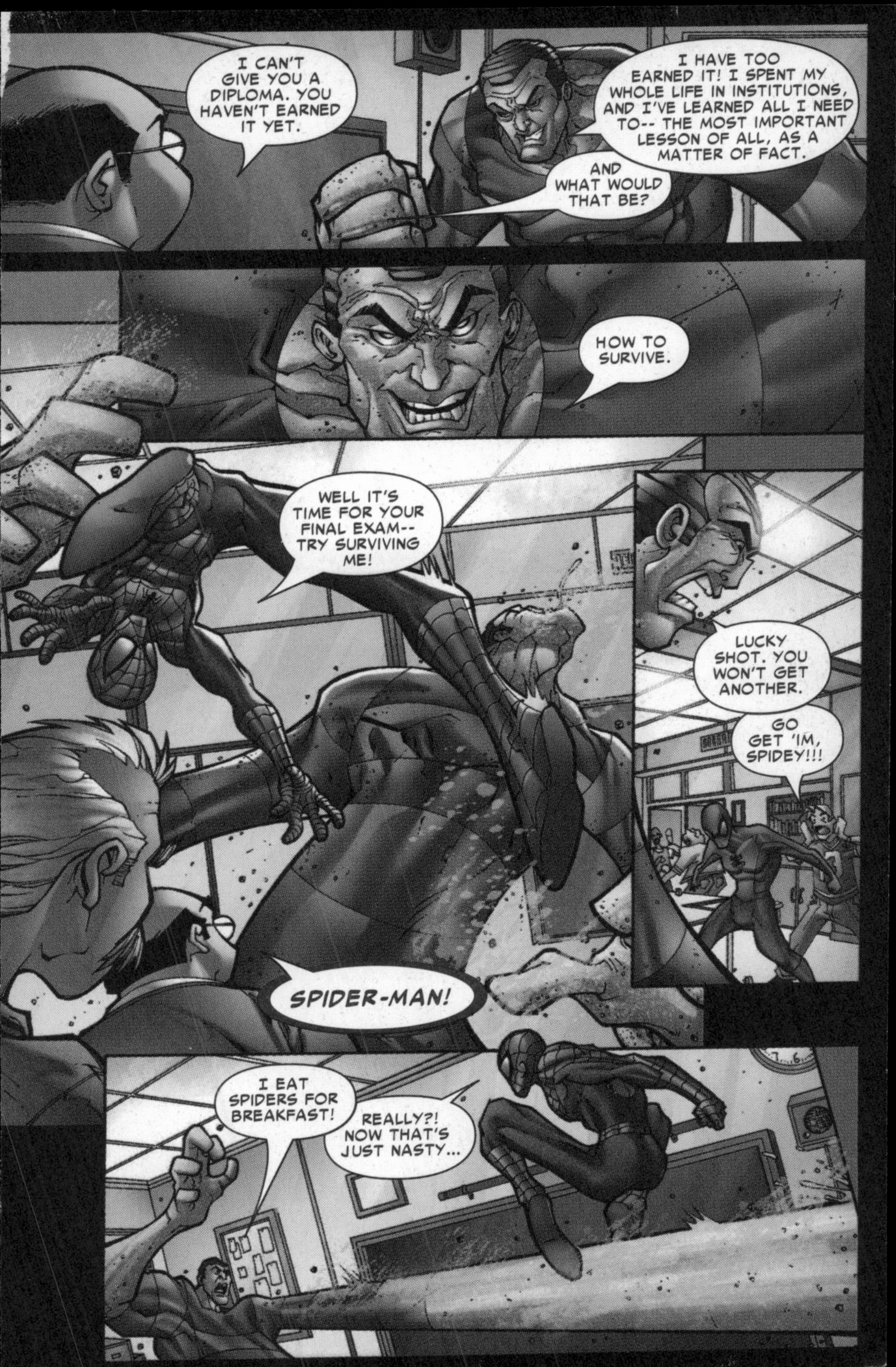
I CAN'T GIVE YOU A DIPLOMA. YOU HAVEN'T EARNED IT YET.
I HAVE TOO EARNED IT! I SPENT MY WHOLE LIFE IN INSTITUTIONS, AND I'VE LEARNED ALL I NEED TO-- THE MOST IMPORTANT LESSON OF ALL, AS A MATTER OF FACT.
AND WHAT WOULD THAT BE?
HOW TO SURVIVE.
WELL IT'S TIME FOR YOUR FINAL EXAM-- TRY SURVIVING ME!
SPIDER-MAN!
LUCKY SHOT. YOU WON'T GET ANOTHER.
GO GET 'IM, SPIDEY!!!
I EAT SPIDERS FOR BREAKFAST!
REALLY?! NOW THAT'S JUST NASTY...

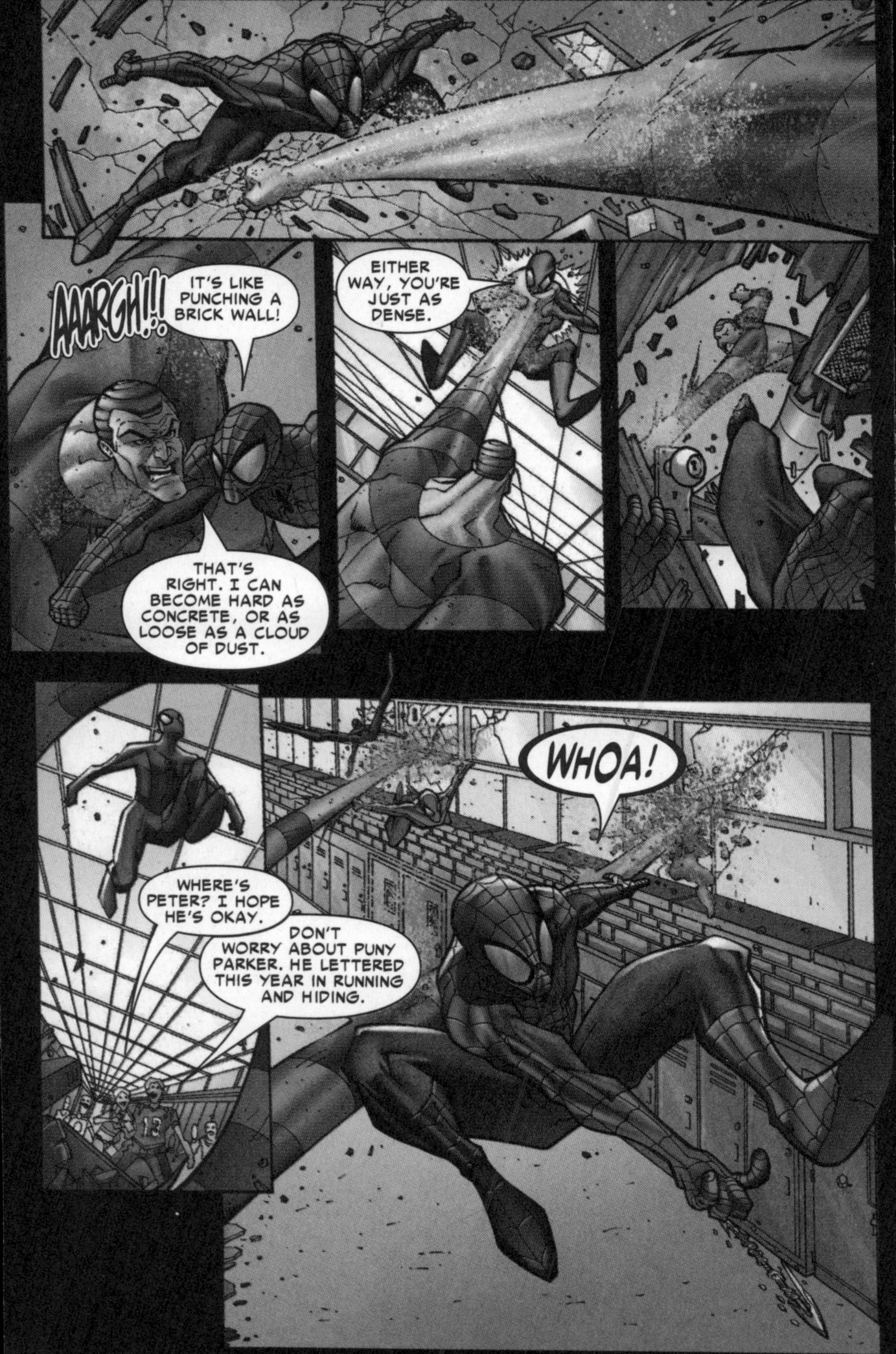
AAARGH!!!
IT'S LIKE PUNCHING A BRICK WALL!
THAT'S RIGHT. I CAN BECOME HARD AS CONCRETE, OR AS LOOSE AS A CLOUD OF DUST.
EITHER WAY, YOU'RE JUST AS DENSE.
WHOA!
WHERE'S PETER? I HOPE HE'S OKAY.
DON'T WORRY ABOUT PUNY PARKER. HE LETTERED THIS YEAR IN RUNNING AND HIDING.

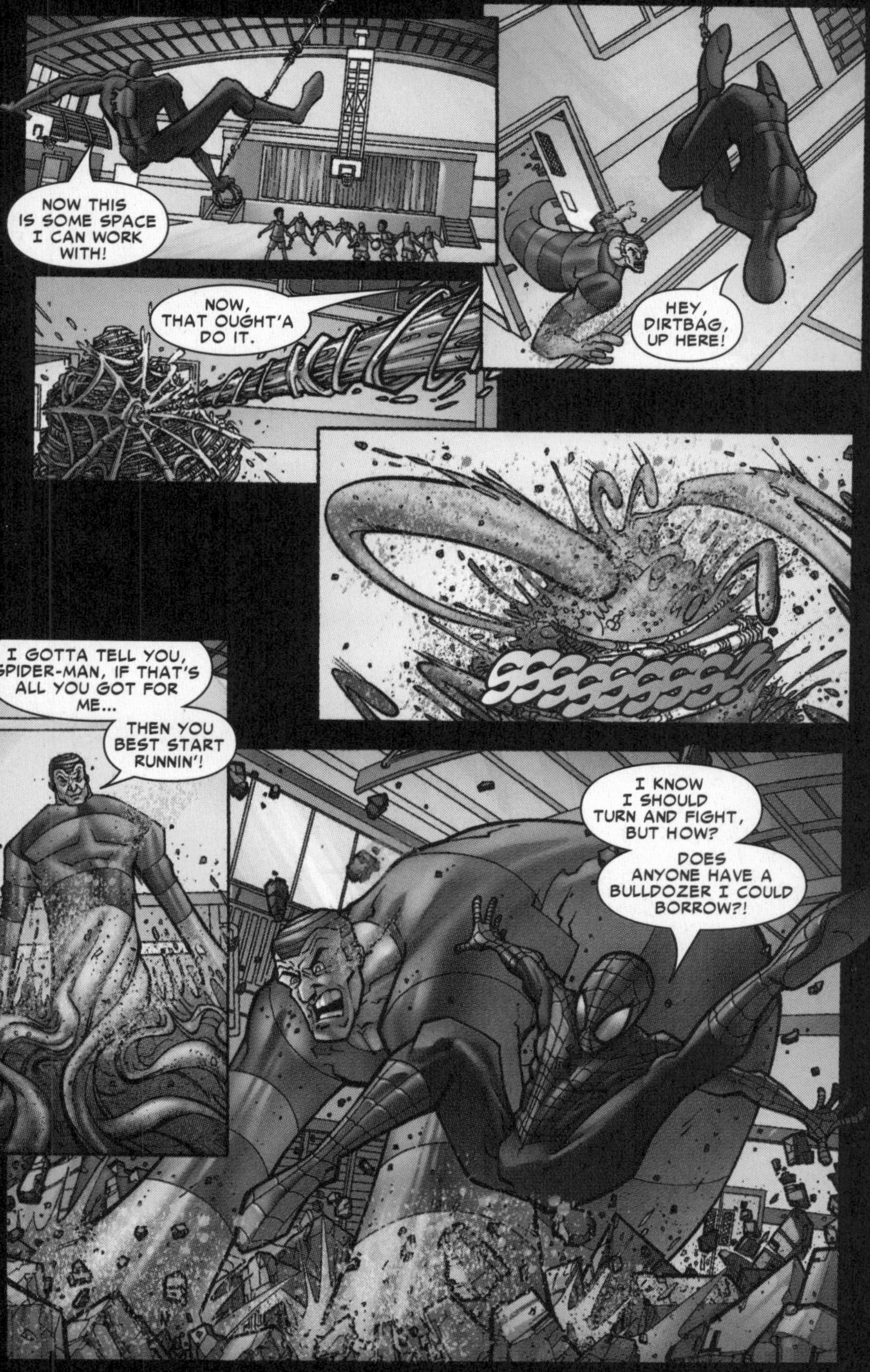
NOW THIS IS SOME SPACE I CAN WORK WITH!
HEY, DIRTBAG, UP HERE!
NOW, THAT OUGHT'A DO IT.
SSSSSSSSSS!
I GOTTA TELL YOU, SPIDER-MAN, IF THAT'S ALL YOU GOT FOR ME...
THEN YOU BEST START RUNNIN'!
I KNOW I SHOULD TURN AND FIGHT, BUT HOW?
DOES ANYONE HAVE A BULLDOZER I COULD BORROW?!

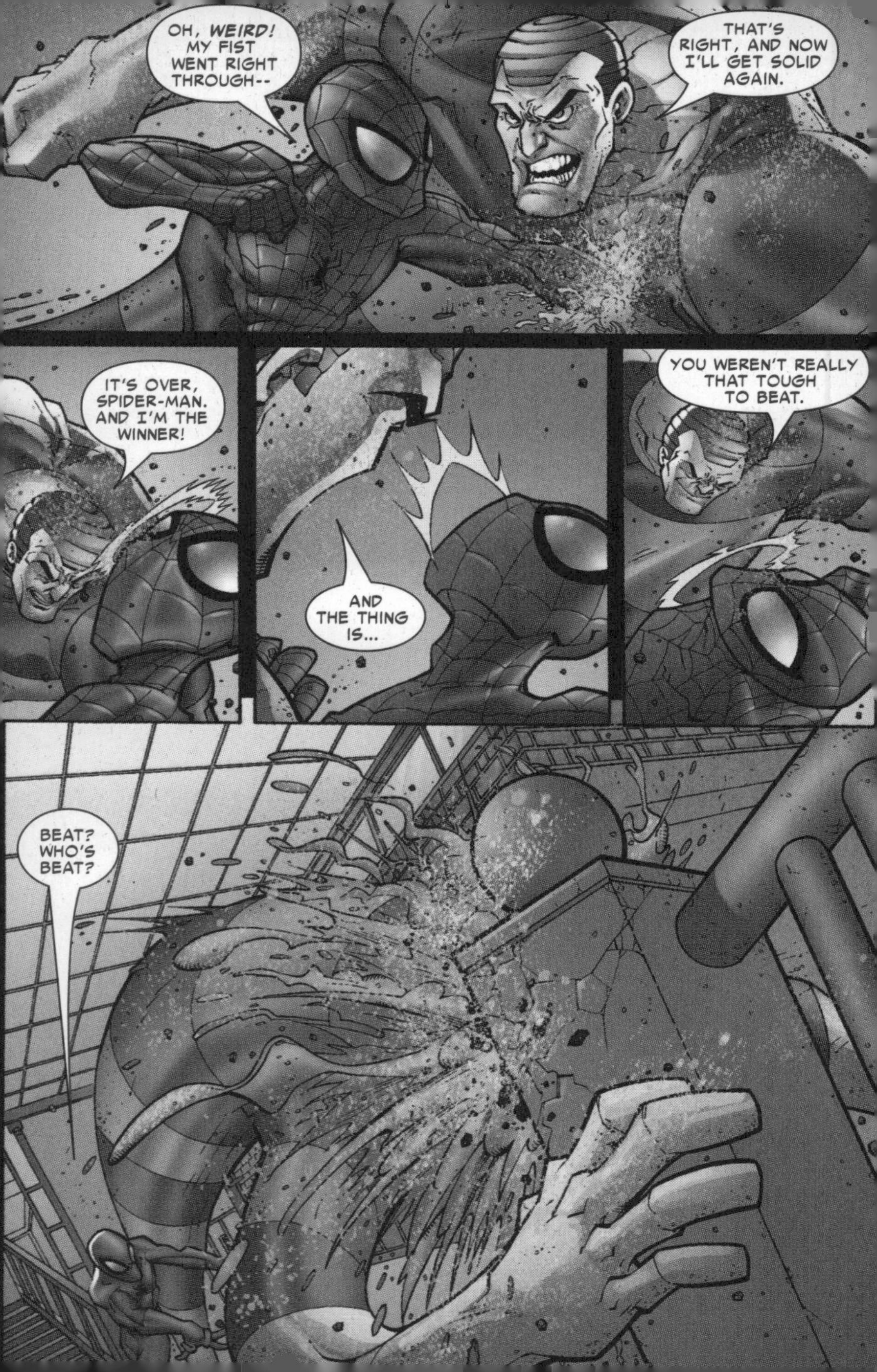
OH, WEIRD! MY FIST WENT RIGHT THROUGH--
THAT'S RIGHT, AND NOW I'LL GET SOLID AGAIN.
IT'S OVER, SPIDER-MAN. AND I'M THE WINNER!
AND THE THING IS...
YOU WEREN'T REALLY THAT TOUGH TO BEAT.
BEAT? WHO'S BEAT?

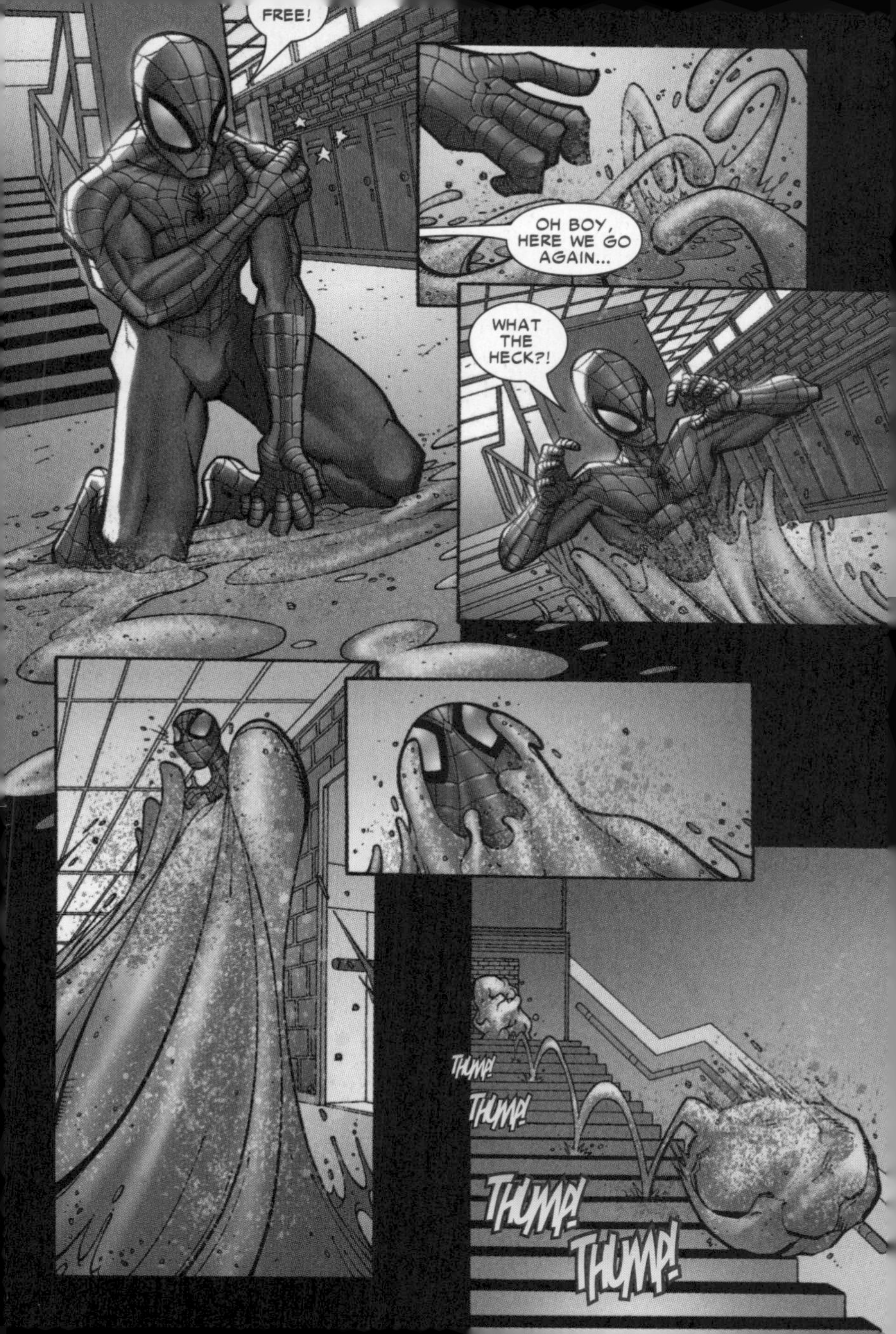
FREE!
OH BOY, HERE WE GO AGAIN...
WHAT THE HECK?!
THUMP!
THUMP!
THUMP!
THUMP!

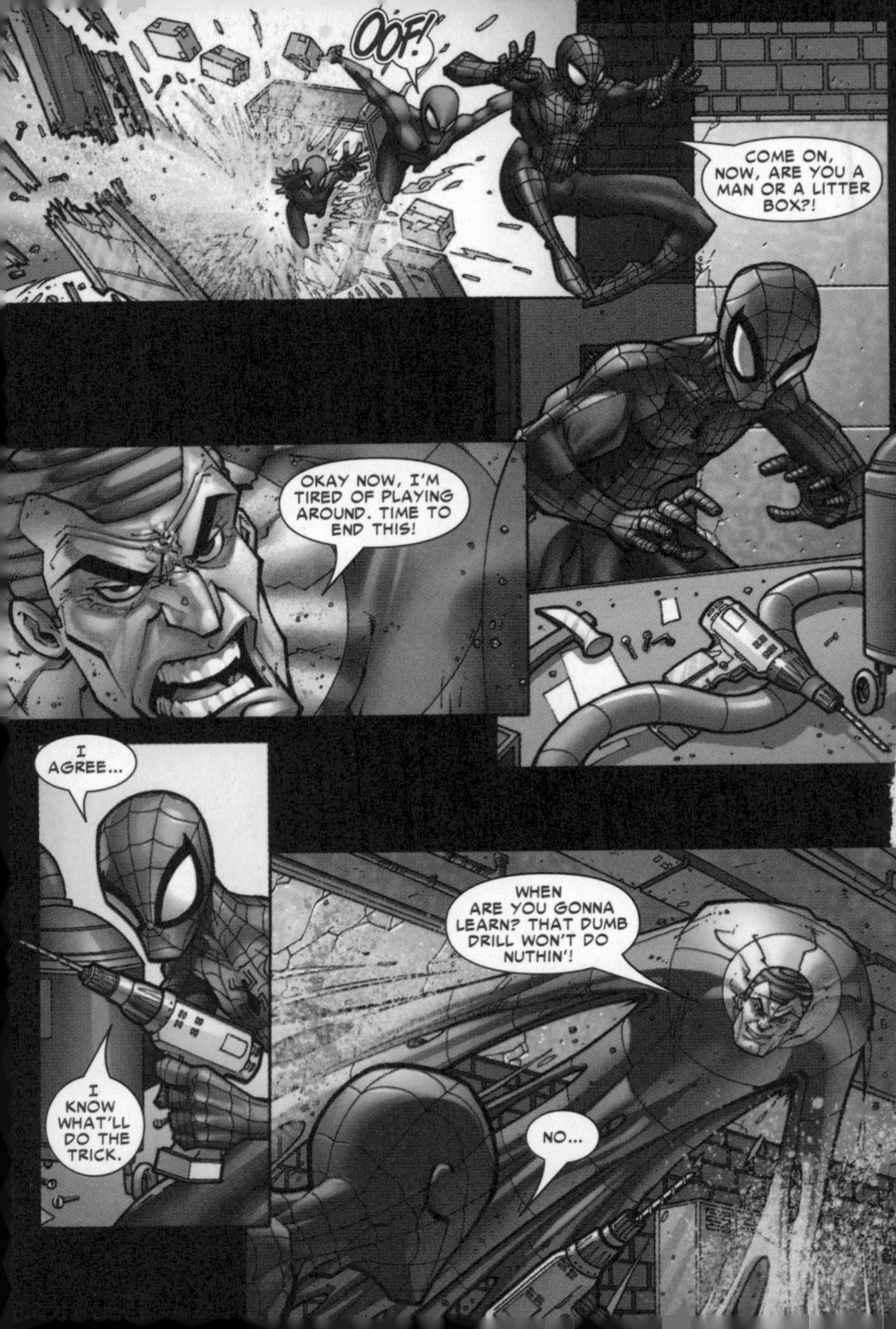
OOF!
COME ON, NOW, ARE YOU A MAN OR A LITTER BOX?!
OKAY NOW, I'M TIRED OF PLAYING AROUND. TIME TO END THIS!
I AGREE...
I KNOW WHAT'LL DO THE TRICK.
WHEN ARE YOU GONNA LEARN? THAT DUMB DRILL WON'T DO NUTHIN'!
NO...

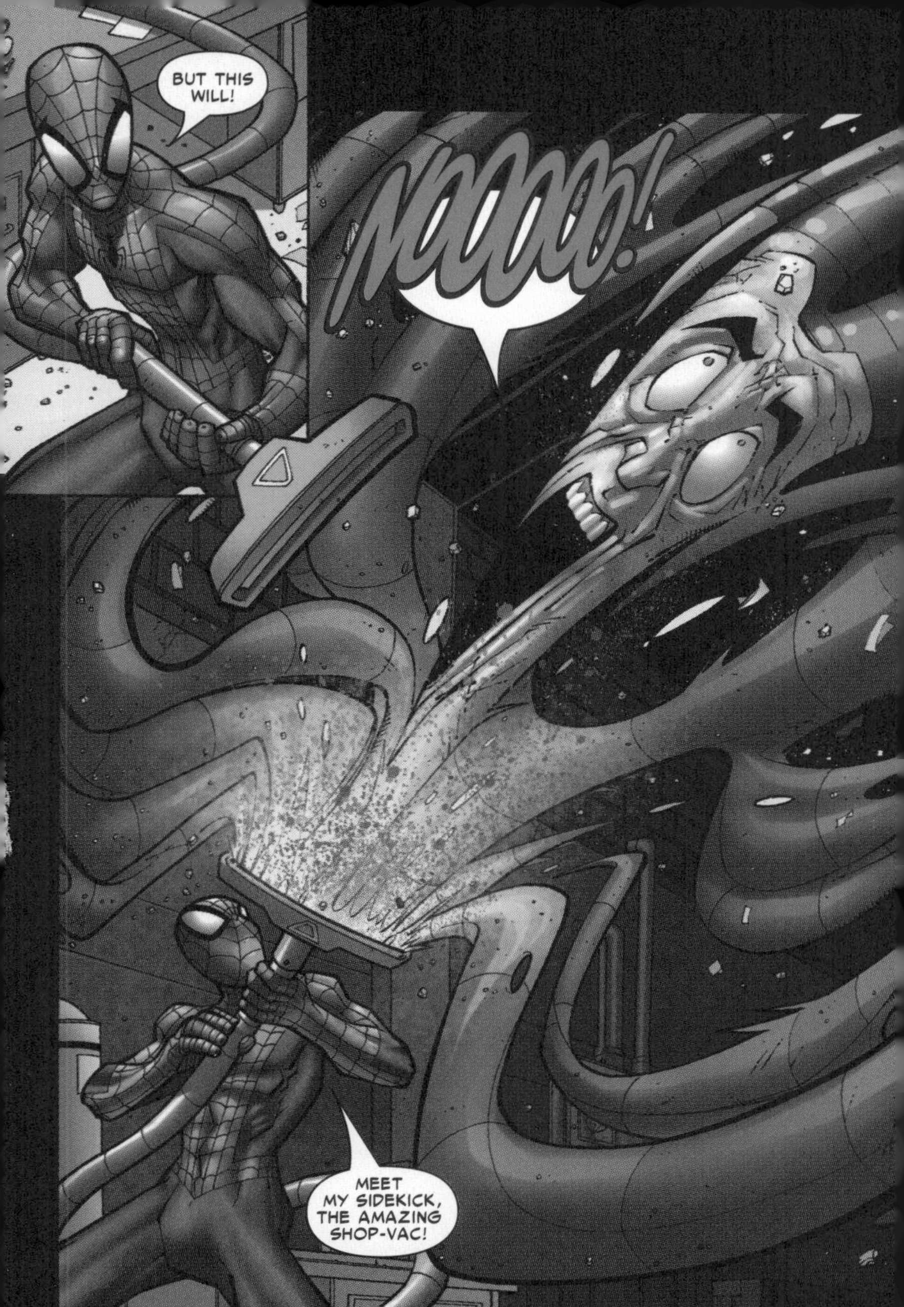
BUT THIS WILL!
NOOOOO!
MEET MY SIDEKICK, THE AMAZING SHOP-VAC!

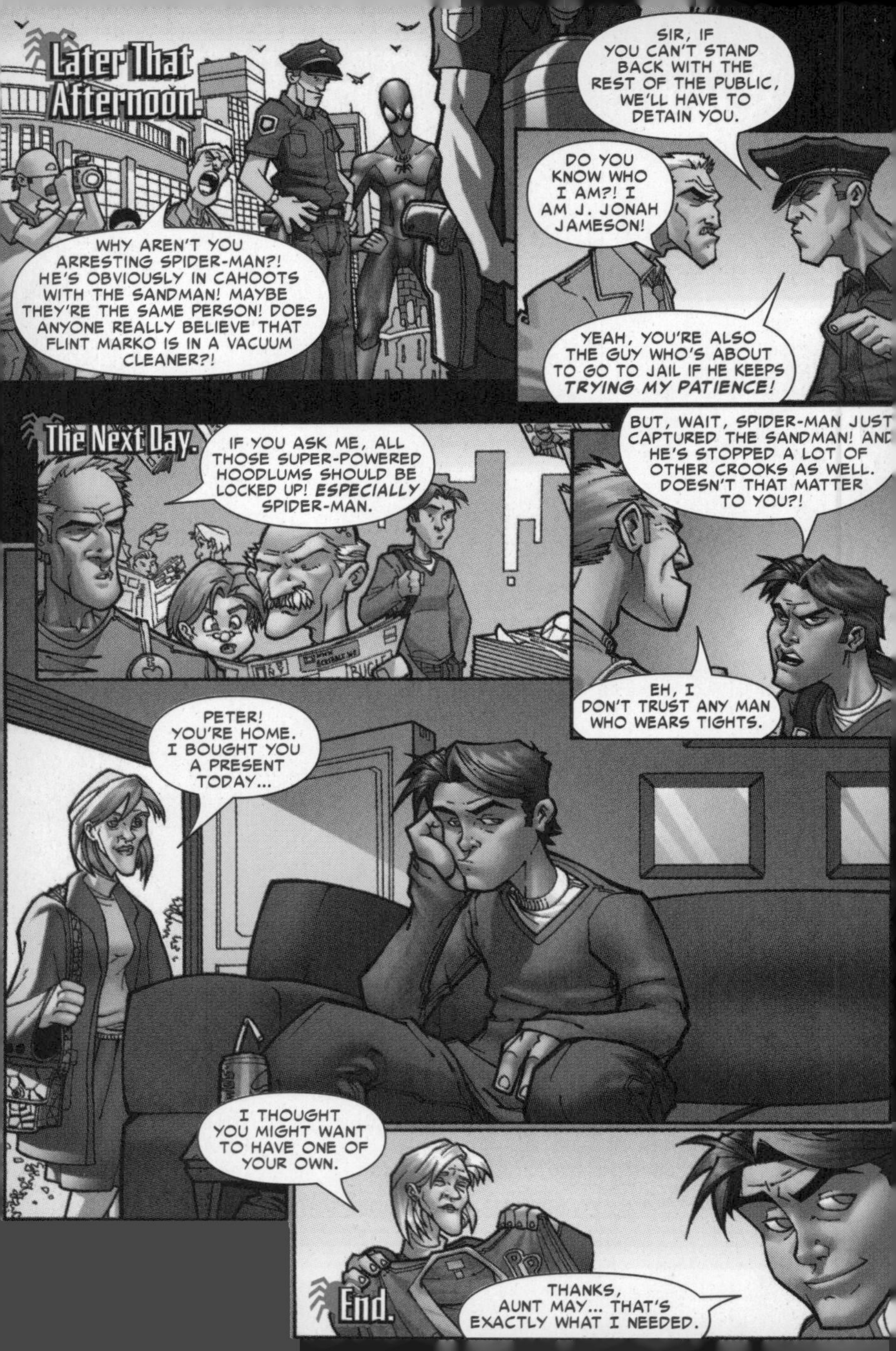
Later That Afternoon.
WHY AREN'T YOU ARRESTING SPIDER-MAN?! HE'S OBVIOUSLY IN CAHOOTS WITH THE SANDMAN! MAYBE THEY'RE THE SAME PERSON! DOES ANYONE REALLY BELIEVE THAT FLINT MARKO IS IN A VACUUM CLEANER?!
SIR, IF YOU CAN'T STAND BACK WITH THE REST OF THE PUBLIC, WE'LL HAVE TO DETAIN YOU.
DO YOU KNOW WHO I AM?! I AM J. JONAH JAMESON!
YEAH, YOU'RE ALSO THE GUY WHO'S ABOUT TO GO TO JAIL IF HE KEEPS TRYING MY PATIENCE!
The Next Day.
IF YOU ASK ME, ALL THOSE SUPER-POWERED HOODLUMS SHOULD BE LOCKED UP! ESPECIALLY SPIDER-MAN.
BUT, WAIT, SPIDER-MAN JUST CAPTURED THE SANDMAN! AND HE'S STOPPED A LOT OF OTHER CROOKS AS WELL. DOESN'T THAT MATTER TO YOU?!
EH, I DON'T TRUST ANY MAN WHO WEARS TIGHTS.
PETER! YOU'RE HOME. I BOUGHT YOU A PRESENT TODAY...
I THOUGHT YOU MIGHT WANT TO HAVE ONE OF YOUR OWN.
THANKS, AUNT MAY... THAT'S EXACTLY WHAT I NEEDED.
End.

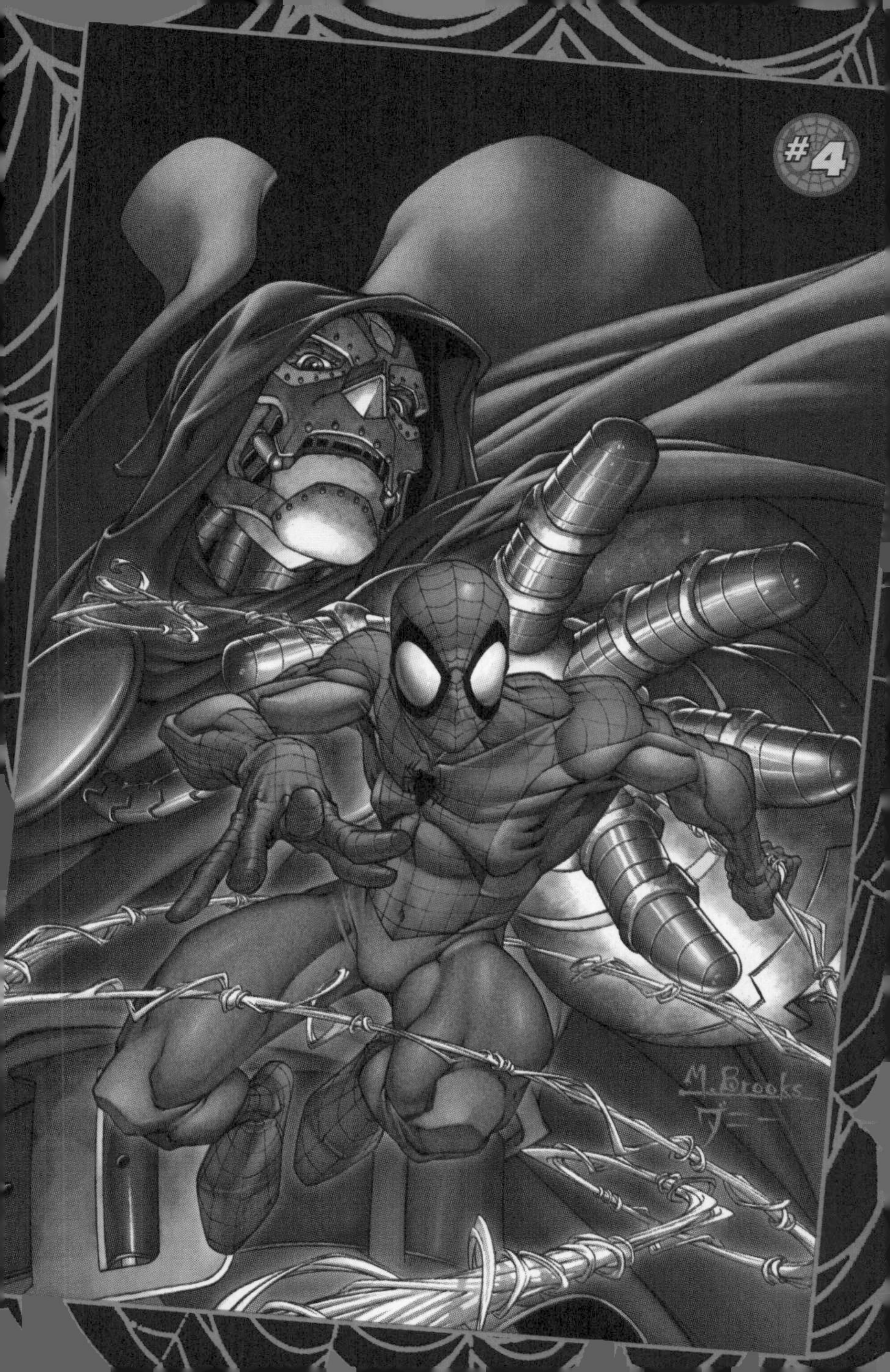
#4
M. Brooks

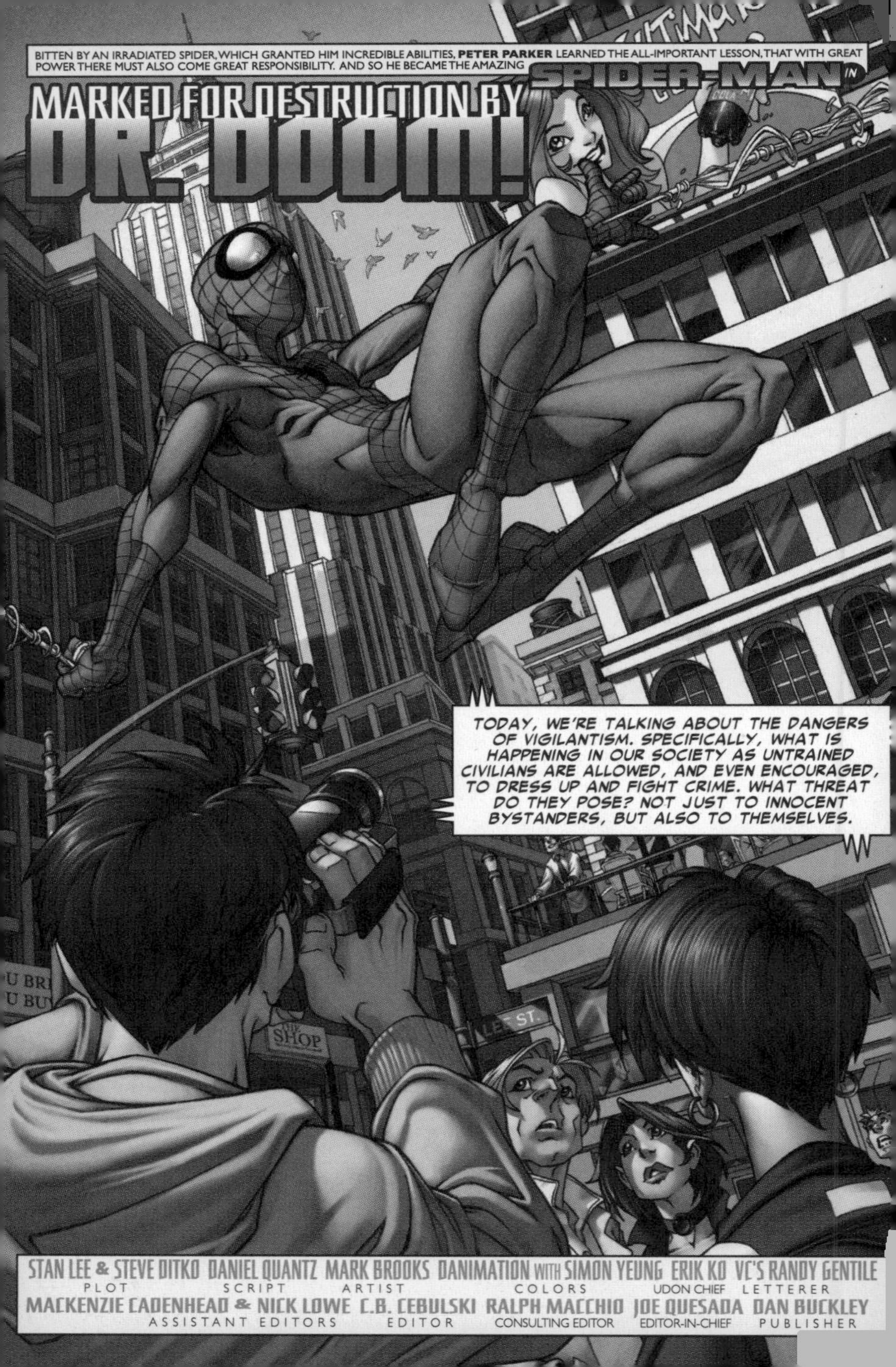
BITTEN BY AN IRRADIATED SPIDER, WHICH GRANTED HIM INCREDIBLE ABILITIES, PETER PARKER LEARNED THE ALL-IMPORTANT LESSON, THAT WITH GREAT POWER THERE MUST ALSO COME GREAT RESPONSIBILITY. AND SO HE BECAME THE AMAZING SPIDER-MAN IN
MARKED FOR DESTRUCTION BY DR. DOOM!
TODAY, WE'RE TALKING ABOUT THE DANGERS OF VIGILANTISM. SPECIFICALLY, WHAT IS HAPPENING IN OUR SOCIETY AS UNTRAINED CIVILIANS ARE ALLOWED, AND EVEN ENCOURAGED, TO DRESS UP AND FIGHT CRIME. WHAT THREAT DO THEY POSE? NOT JUST TO INNOCENT BYSTANDERS, BUT ALSO TO THEMSELVES.
THE SHOP
LEE ST.
STAN LEE & STEVE DITKO PLOT
DANIEL QUANTZ SCRIPT
MARK BROOKS ARTIST
DANIMATION WITH SIMON YEUNG COLORS
ERIK KO UDON CHIEF
VC'S RANDY GENTILE LETTERER
MACKENZIE CADENHEAD & NICK LOWE ASSISTANT EDITORS
C.B. CEBULSKI EDITOR
RALPH MACCHIO CONSULTING EDITOR
JOE QUESADA EDITOR-IN-CHIEF
DAN BUCKLEY PUBLISHER

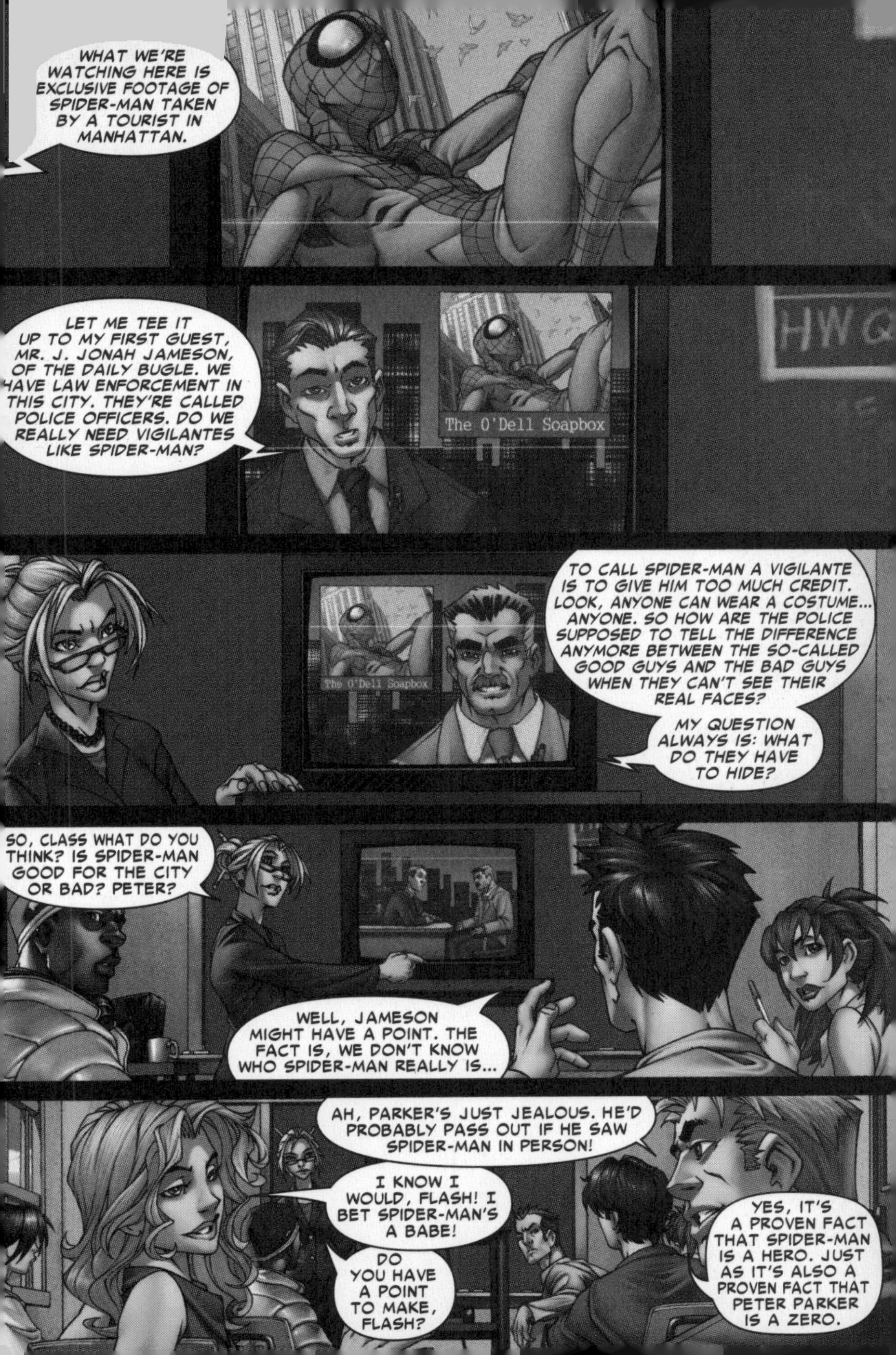
WHAT WE'RE WATCHING HERE IS EXCLUSIVE FOOTAGE OF SPIDER-MAN TAKEN BY A TOURIST IN MANHATTAN.
LET ME TEE IT UP TO MY FIRST GUEST, MR. J. JONAH JAMESON, OF THE DAILY BUGLE. WE HAVE LAW ENFORCEMENT IN THIS CITY. THEY'RE CALLED POLICE OFFICERS. DO WE REALLY NEED VIGILANTES LIKE SPIDER-MAN?
The O'Dell Soapbox
HWG
TO CALL SPIDER-MAN A VIGILANTE IS TO GIVE HIM TOO MUCH CREDIT. LOOK, ANYONE CAN WEAR A COSTUME... ANYONE. SO HOW ARE THE POLICE SUPPOSED TO TELL THE DIFFERENCE ANYMORE BETWEEN THE SO-CALLED GOOD GUYS AND THE BAD GUYS WHEN THEY CAN'T SEE THEIR REAL FACES?
MY QUESTION ALWAYS IS: WHAT DO THEY HAVE TO HIDE?
The O'Dell Soapbox
SO, CLASS WHAT DO YOU THINK? IS SPIDER-MAN GOOD FOR THE CITY OR BAD? PETER?
WELL, JAMESON MIGHT HAVE A POINT. THE FACT IS, WE DON'T KNOW WHO SPIDER-MAN REALLY IS...
AH, PARKER'S JUST JEALOUS. HE'D PROBABLY PASS OUT IF HE SAW SPIDER-MAN IN PERSON!
I KNOW I WOULD, FLASH! I BET SPIDER-MAN'S A BABE!
DO YOU HAVE A POINT TO MAKE, FLASH?
YES, IT'S A PROVEN FACT THAT SPIDER-MAN IS A HERO. JUST AS IT'S ALSO A PROVEN FACT THAT PETER PARKER IS A ZERO.

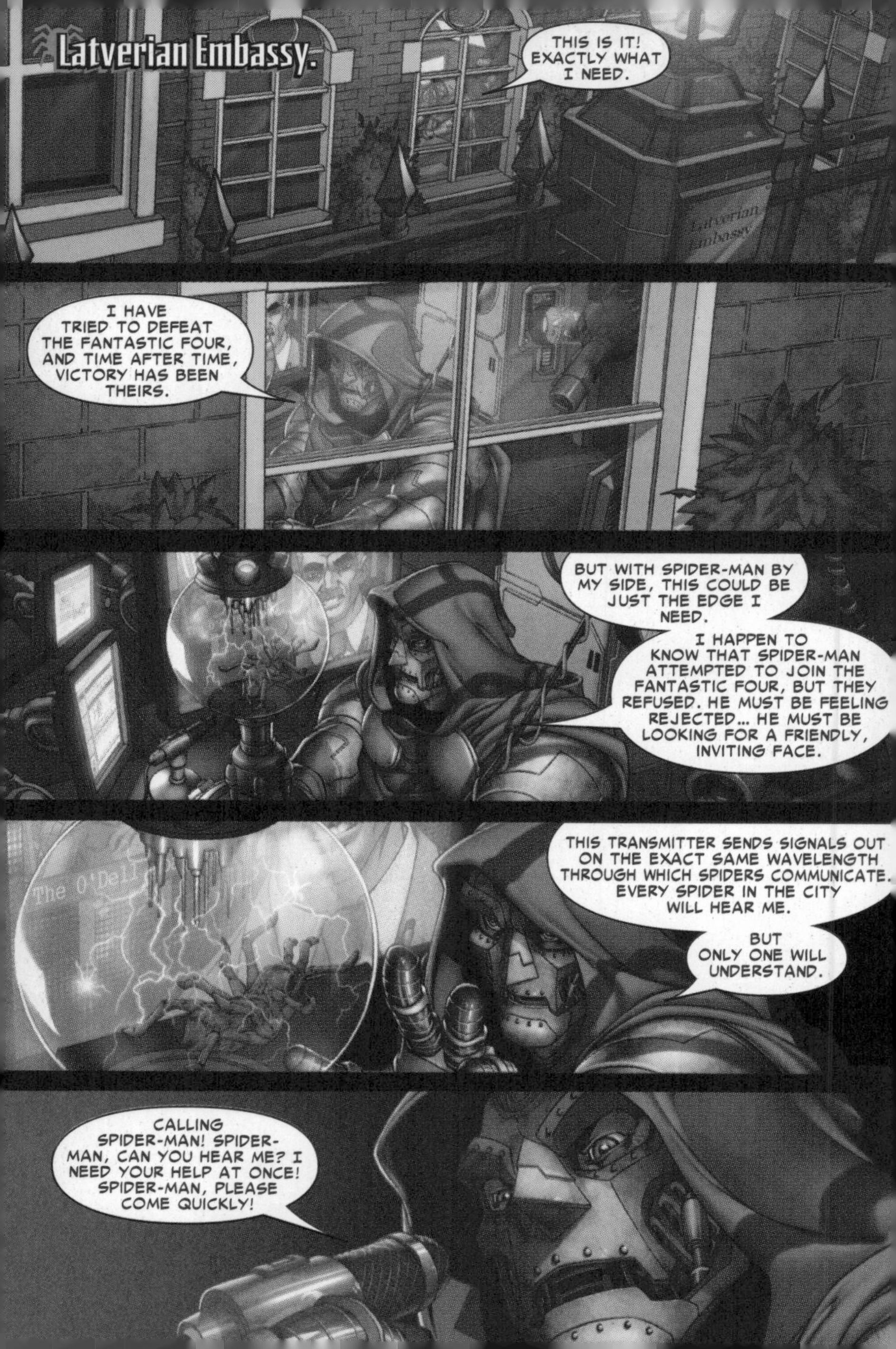
Latverian Embassy.
THIS IS IT! EXACTLY WHAT I NEED.
Latverian Embassy
I HAVE TRIED TO DEFEAT THE FANTASTIC FOUR, AND TIME AFTER TIME, VICTORY HAS BEEN THEIRS.
BUT WITH SPIDER-MAN BY MY SIDE, THIS COULD BE JUST THE EDGE I NEED.
I HAPPEN TO KNOW THAT SPIDER-MAN ATTEMPTED TO JOIN THE FANTASTIC FOUR, BUT THEY REFUSED. HE MUST BE FEELING REJECTED... HE MUST BE LOOKING FOR A FRIENDLY, INVITING FACE.
THIS TRANSMITTER SENDS SIGNALS OUT ON THE EXACT SAME WAVELENGTH THROUGH WHICH SPIDERS COMMUNICATE. EVERY SPIDER IN THE CITY WILL HEAR ME.
BUT ONLY ONE WILL UNDERSTAND.
CALLING SPIDER-MAN! SPIDER-MAN, CAN YOU HEAR ME? I NEED YOUR HELP AT ONCE! SPIDER-MAN, PLEASE COME QUICKLY!

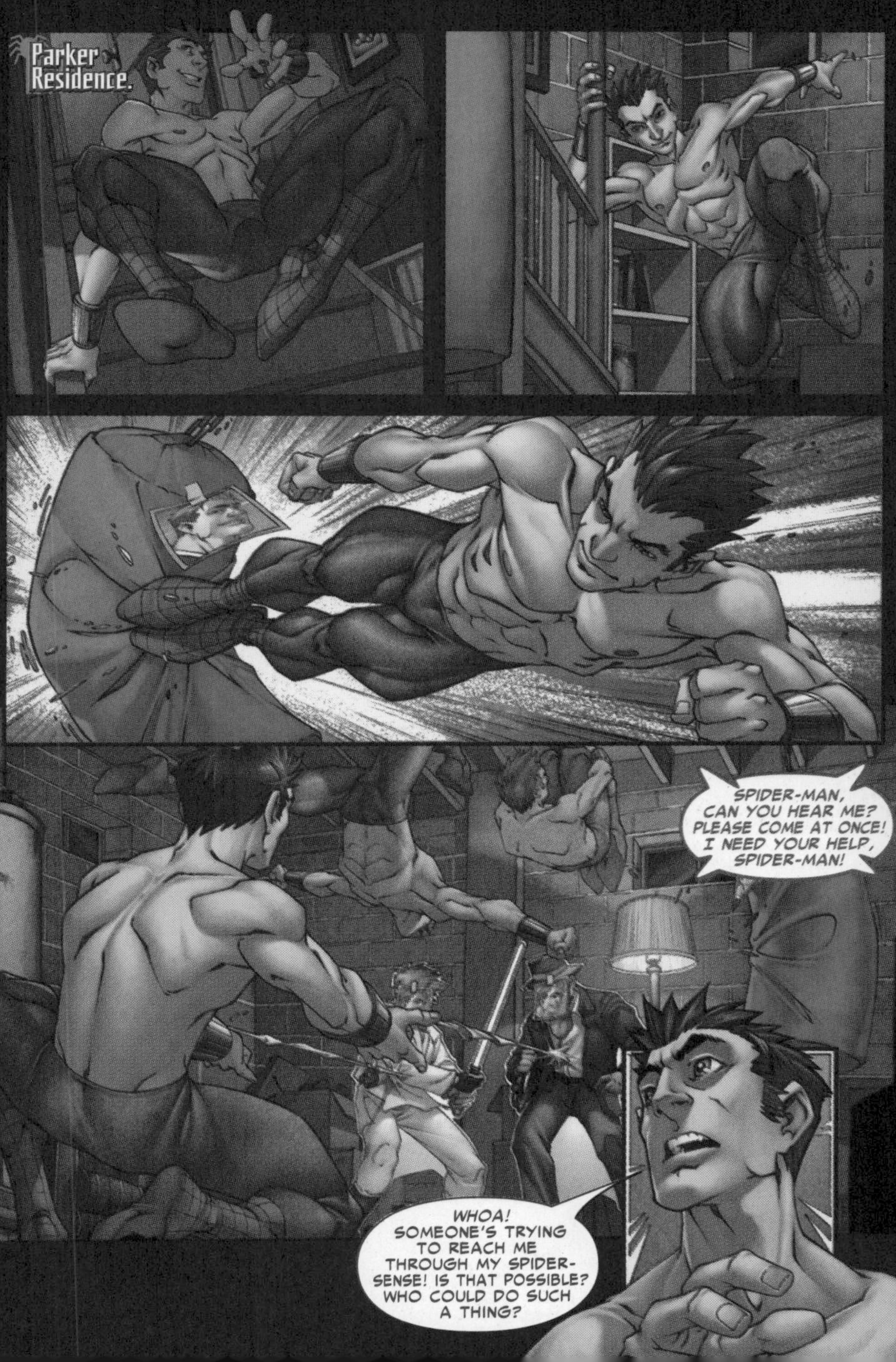
Parker Residence.
SPIDER-MAN, CAN YOU HEAR ME? PLEASE COME AT ONCE! I NEED YOUR HELP, SPIDER-MAN!
WHOA! SOMEONE'S TRYING TO REACH ME THROUGH MY SPIDER-SENSE! IS THAT POSSIBLE? WHO COULD DO SUCH A THING?

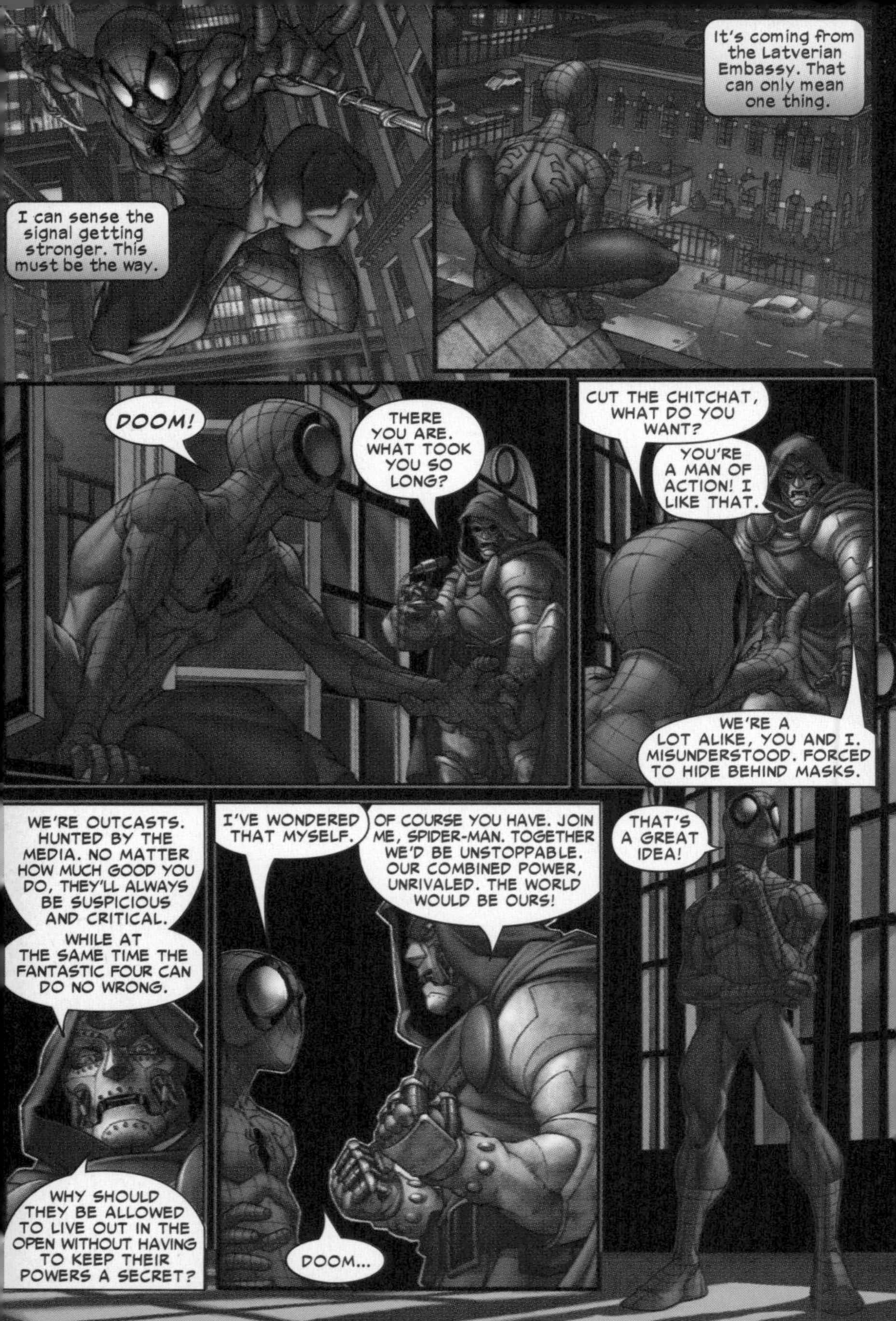
I can sense the signal getting stronger. This must be the way.
It's coming from the Latverian Embassy. That can only mean one thing.
DOOM!
THERE YOU ARE. WHAT TOOK YOU SO LONG?
CUT THE CHITCHAT, WHAT DO YOU WANT?
YOU'RE A MAN OF ACTION! I LIKE THAT.
WE'RE A LOT ALIKE, YOU AND I. MISUNDERSTOOD. FORCED TO HIDE BEHIND MASKS.
WE'RE OUTCASTS. HUNTED BY THE MEDIA. NO MATTER HOW MUCH GOOD YOU DO, THEY'LL ALWAYS BE SUSPICIOUS AND CRITICAL.
WHILE AT THE SAME TIME THE FANTASTIC FOUR CAN DO NO WRONG.
WHY SHOULD THEY BE ALLOWED TO LIVE OUT IN THE OPEN WITHOUT HAVING TO KEEP THEIR POWERS A SECRET?
I'VE WONDERED THAT MYSELF.
DOOM...
OF COURSE YOU HAVE. JOIN ME, SPIDER-MAN. TOGETHER WE'D BE UNSTOPPABLE. OUR COMBINED POWER, UNRIVALED. THE WORLD WOULD BE OURS!
THAT'S A GREAT IDEA!

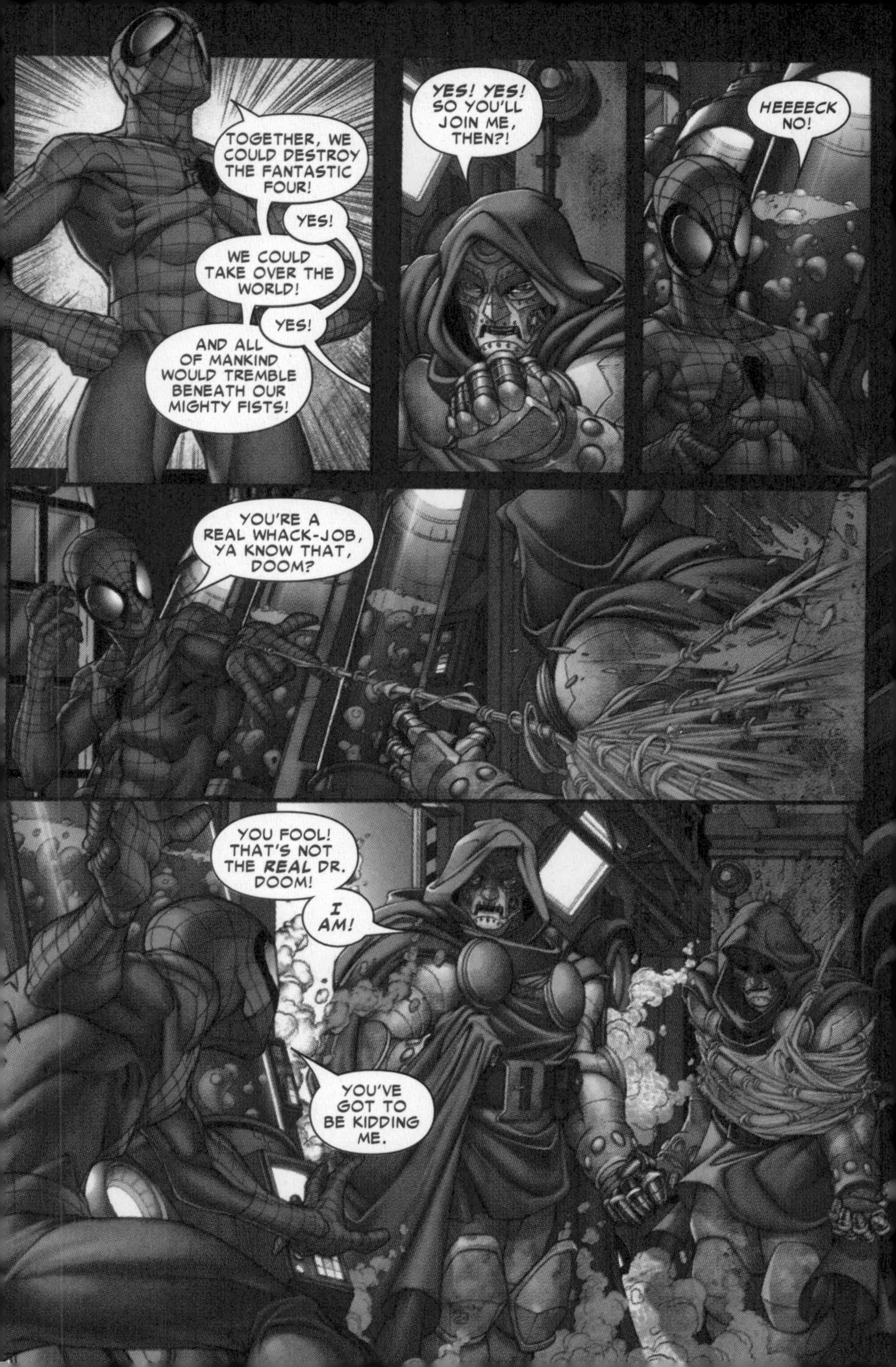
TOGETHER, WE COULD DESTROY THE FANTASTIC FOUR!
YES!
WE COULD TAKE OVER THE WORLD!
YES!
AND ALL OF MANKIND WOULD TREMBLE BENEATH OUR MIGHTY FISTS!
YES! YES! SO YOU'LL JOIN ME, THEN?!
HEEEECK NO!
YOU'RE A REAL WHACK-JOB, YA KNOW THAT, DOOM?
YOU FOOL! THAT'S NOT THE REAL DR. DOOM!
I AM!
YOU'VE GOT TO BE KIDDING ME.

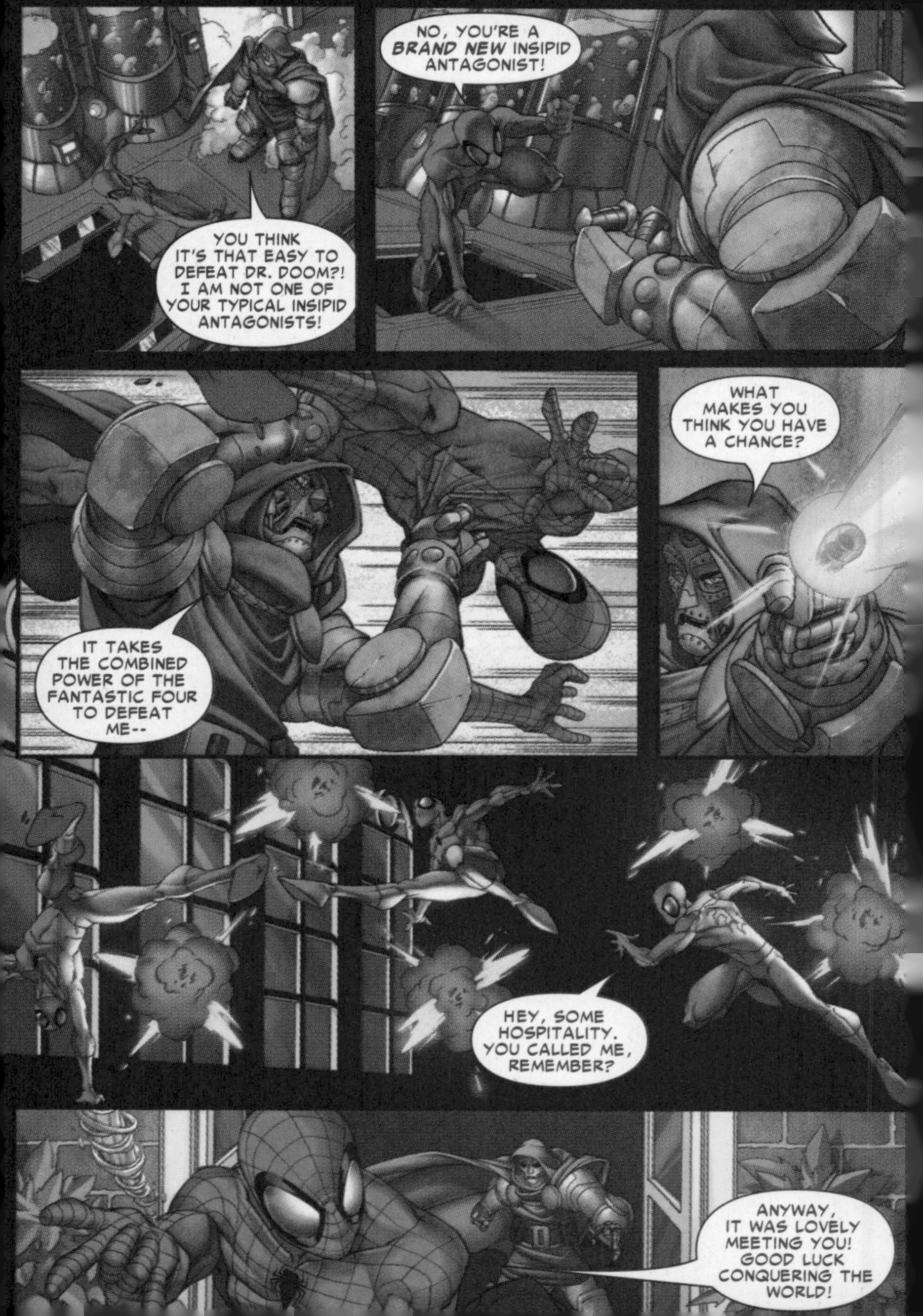
YOU THINK IT'S THAT EASY TO DEFEAT DR. DOOM?! I AM NOT ONE OF YOUR TYPICAL INSIPID ANTAGONISTS!
NO, YOU'RE A BRAND NEW INSIPID ANTAGONIST!
IT TAKES THE COMBINED POWER OF THE FANTASTIC FOUR TO DEFEAT ME--
WHAT MAKES YOU THINK YOU HAVE A CHANCE?
HEY, SOME HOSPITALITY. YOU CALLED ME, REMEMBER?
ANYWAY, IT WAS LOVELY MEETING YOU! GOOD LUCK CONQUERING THE WORLD!

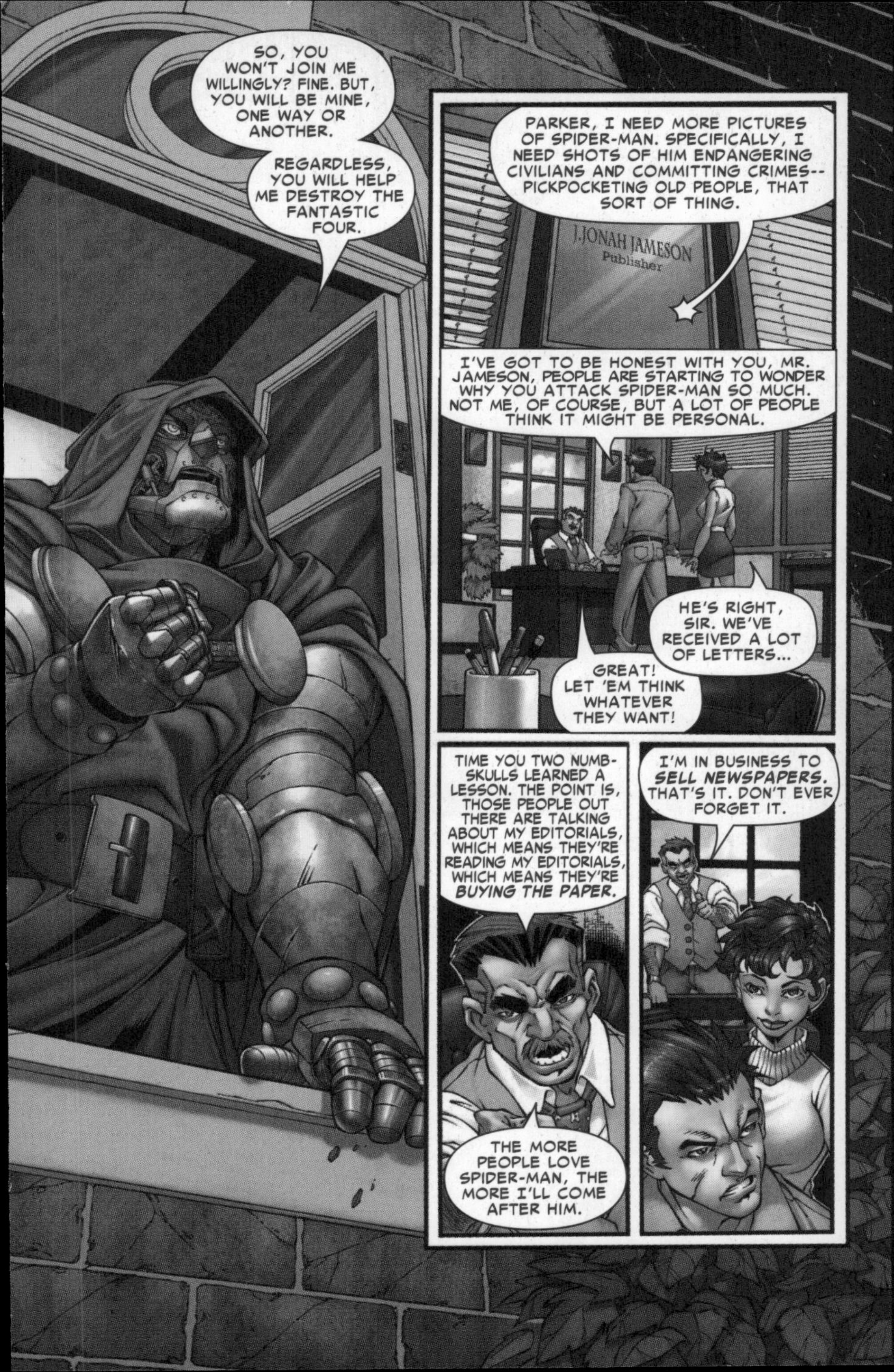
SO, YOU WON'T JOIN ME WILLINGLY? FINE. BUT, YOU WILL BE MINE, ONE WAY OR ANOTHER.
REGARDLESS, YOU WILL HELP ME DESTROY THE FANTASTIC FOUR.
PARKER, I NEED MORE PICTURES OF SPIDER-MAN. SPECIFICALLY, I NEED SHOTS OF HIM ENDANGERING CIVILIANS AND COMMITTING CRIMES--PICKPOCKETING OLD PEOPLE, THAT SORT OF THING.
J. JONAH JAMESON
Publisher
I'VE GOT TO BE HONEST WITH YOU, MR. JAMESON, PEOPLE ARE STARTING TO WONDER WHY YOU ATTACK SPIDER-MAN SO MUCH. NOT ME, OF COURSE, BUT A LOT OF PEOPLE THINK IT MIGHT BE PERSONAL.
HE'S RIGHT, SIR. WE'VE RECEIVED A LOT OF LETTERS...
GREAT! LET 'EM THINK WHATEVER THEY WANT!
TIME YOU TWO NUMB-SKULLS LEARNED A LESSON. THE POINT IS, THOSE PEOPLE OUT THERE ARE TALKING ABOUT MY EDITORIALS, WHICH MEANS THEY'RE READING MY EDITORIALS, WHICH MEANS THEY'RE *BUYING THE PAPER*.
THE MORE PEOPLE LOVE SPIDER-MAN, THE MORE I'LL COME AFTER HIM.
I'M IN BUSINESS TO *SELL NEWSPAPERS*. THAT'S IT. DON'T EVER FORGET IT.

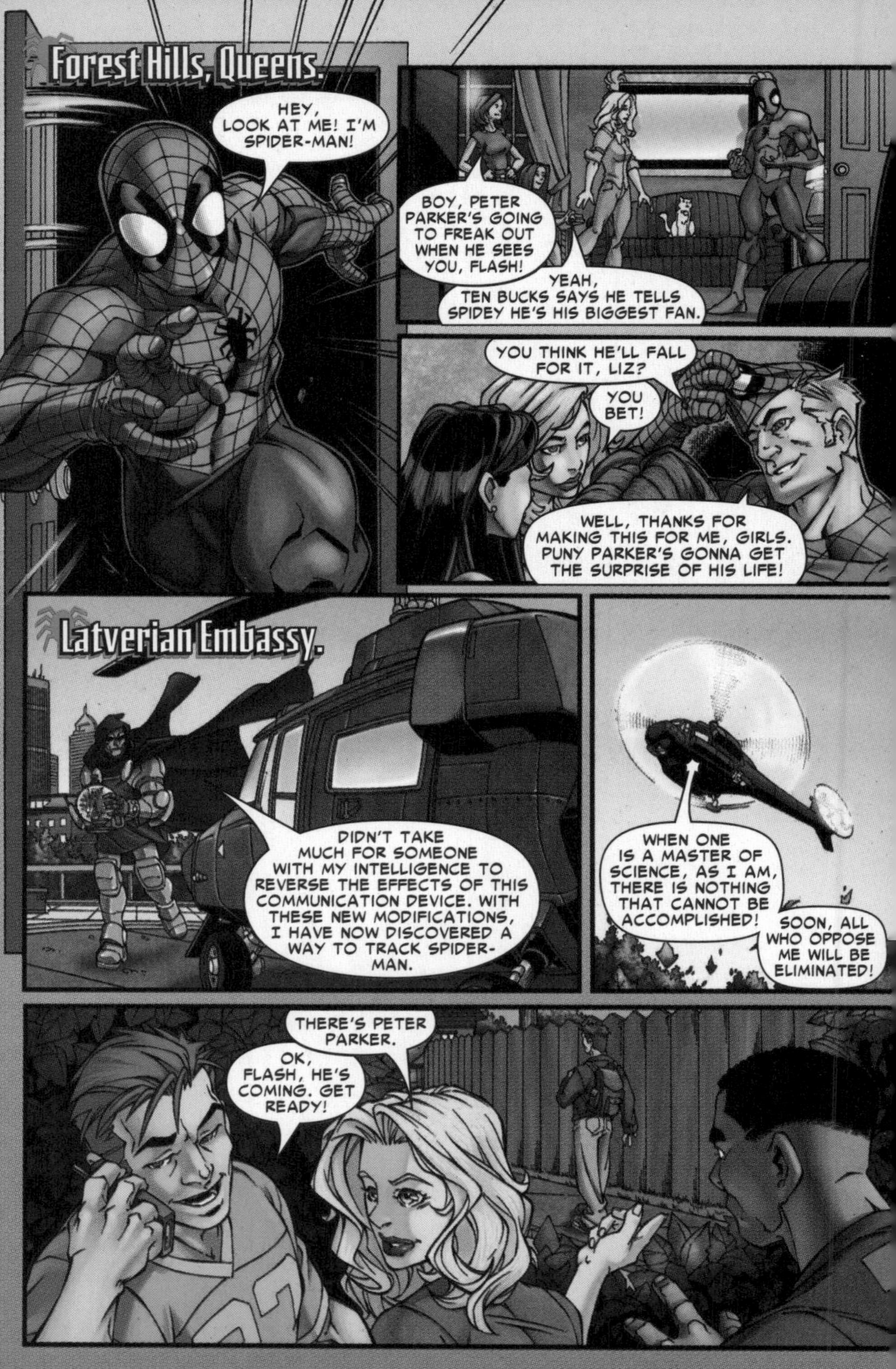
Forest Hills, Queens.
HEY, LOOK AT ME! I'M SPIDER-MAN!
BOY, PETER PARKER'S GOING TO FREAK OUT WHEN HE SEES YOU, FLASH!
YEAH, TEN BUCKS SAYS HE TELLS SPIDEY HE'S HIS BIGGEST FAN.
YOU THINK HE'LL FALL FOR IT, LIZ?
YOU BET!
WELL, THANKS FOR MAKING THIS FOR ME, GIRLS. PUNY PARKER'S GONNA GET THE SURPRISE OF HIS LIFE!
Latverian Embassy.
DIDN'T TAKE MUCH FOR SOMEONE WITH MY INTELLIGENCE TO REVERSE THE EFFECTS OF THIS COMMUNICATION DEVICE. WITH THESE NEW MODIFICATIONS, I HAVE NOW DISCOVERED A WAY TO TRACK SPIDER-MAN.
WHEN ONE IS A MASTER OF SCIENCE, AS I AM, THERE IS NOTHING THAT CANNOT BE ACCOMPLISHED!
SOON, ALL WHO OPPOSE ME WILL BE ELIMINATED!
THERE'S PETER PARKER.
OK, FLASH, HE'S COMING. GET READY!

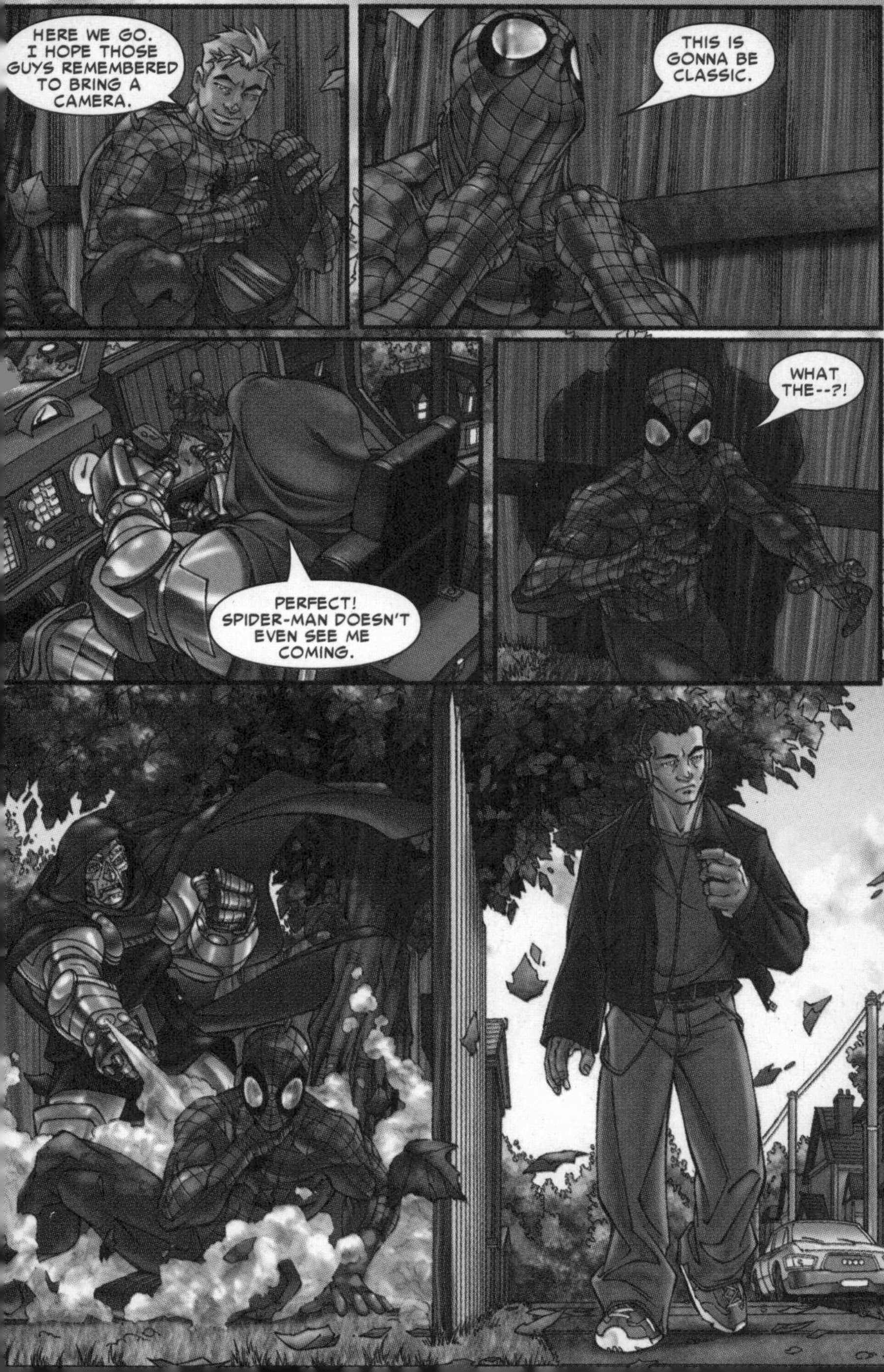
HERE WE GO. I HOPE THOSE GUYS REMEMBERED TO BRING A CAMERA.
THIS IS GONNA BE CLASSIC.
PERFECT! SPIDER-MAN DOESN'T EVEN SEE ME COMING.
WHAT THE--?!

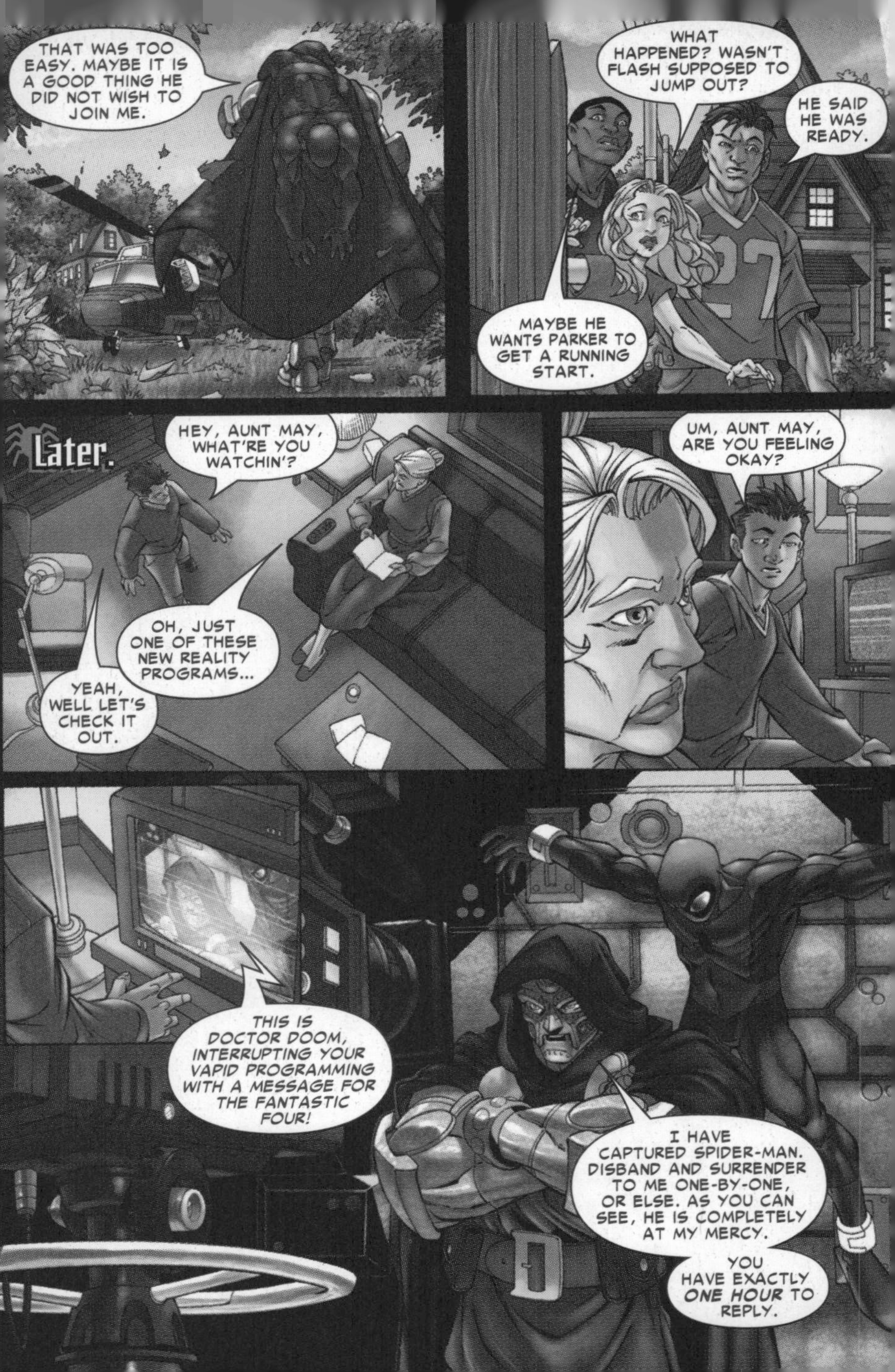
THAT WAS TOO EASY. MAYBE IT IS A GOOD THING HE DID NOT WISH TO JOIN ME.
WHAT HAPPENED? WASN'T FLASH SUPPOSED TO JUMP OUT?
HE SAID HE WAS READY.
MAYBE HE WANTS PARKER TO GET A RUNNING START.
Later.
HEY, AUNT MAY, WHAT'RE YOU WATCHIN'?
OH, JUST ONE OF THESE NEW REALITY PROGRAMS...
YEAH, WELL LET'S CHECK IT OUT.
UM, AUNT MAY, ARE YOU FEELING OKAY?
THIS IS DOCTOR DOOM, INTERRUPTING YOUR VAPID PROGRAMMING WITH A MESSAGE FOR THE FANTASTIC FOUR!
I HAVE CAPTURED SPIDER-MAN. DISBAND AND SURRENDER TO ME ONE-BY-ONE, OR ELSE. AS YOU CAN SEE, HE IS COMPLETELY AT MY MERCY.
YOU HAVE EXACTLY ONE HOUR TO REPLY.

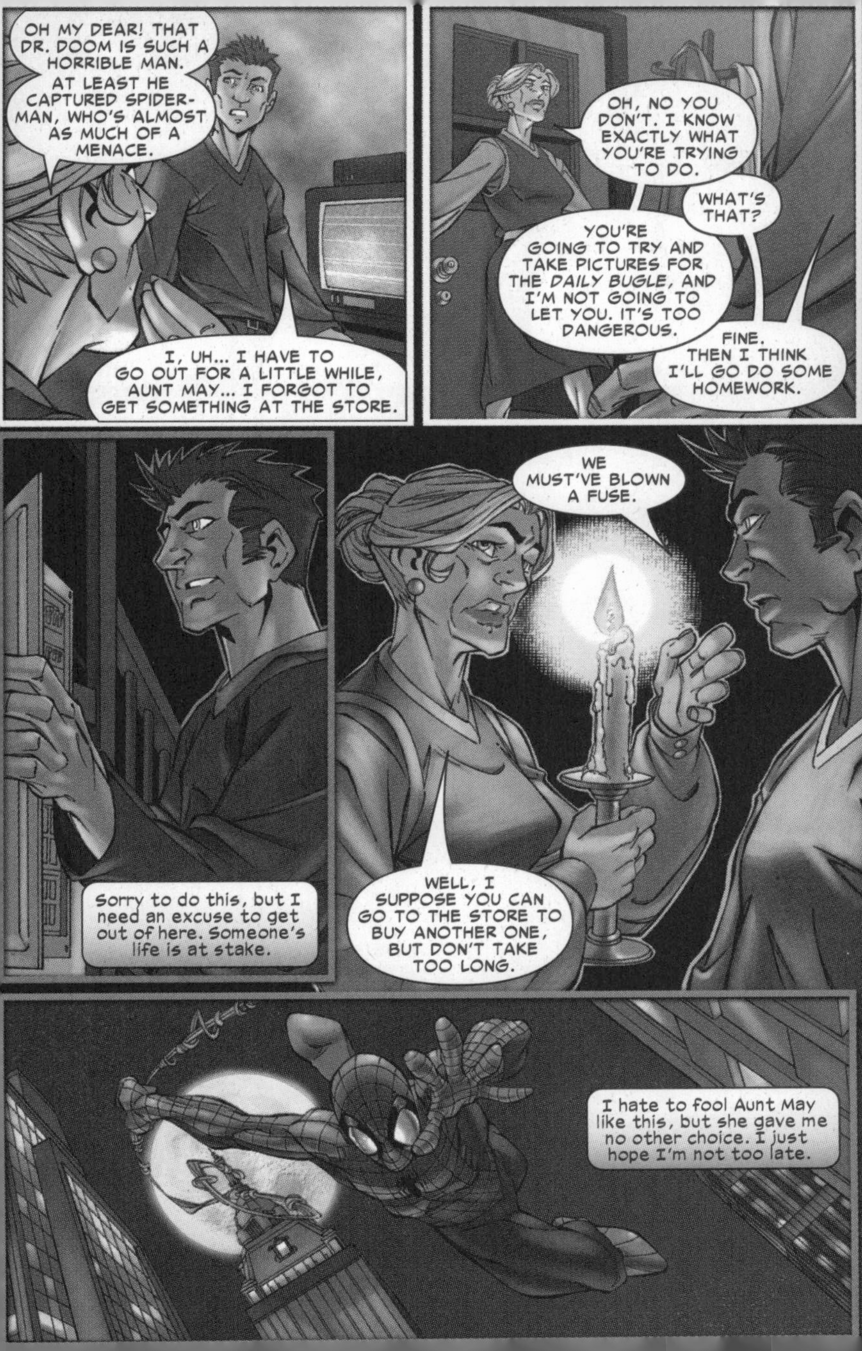
OH MY DEAR! THAT DR. DOOM IS SUCH A HORRIBLE MAN.
AT LEAST HE CAPTURED SPIDER-MAN, WHO'S ALMOST AS MUCH OF A MENACE.
I, UH... I HAVE TO GO OUT FOR A LITTLE WHILE, AUNT MAY... I FORGOT TO GET SOMETHING AT THE STORE.
OH, NO YOU DON'T. I KNOW EXACTLY WHAT YOU'RE TRYING TO DO.
WHAT'S THAT?
YOU'RE GOING TO TRY AND TAKE PICTURES FOR THE *DAILY BUGLE*, AND I'M NOT GOING TO LET YOU. IT'S TOO DANGEROUS.
FINE. THEN I THINK I'LL GO DO SOME HOMEWORK.
Sorry to do this, but I need an excuse to get out of here. Someone's life is at stake.
WE MUST'VE BLOWN A FUSE.
WELL, I SUPPOSE YOU CAN GO TO THE STORE TO BUY ANOTHER ONE, BUT DON'T TAKE TOO LONG.
I hate to fool Aunt May like this, but she gave me no other choice. I just hope I'm not too late.

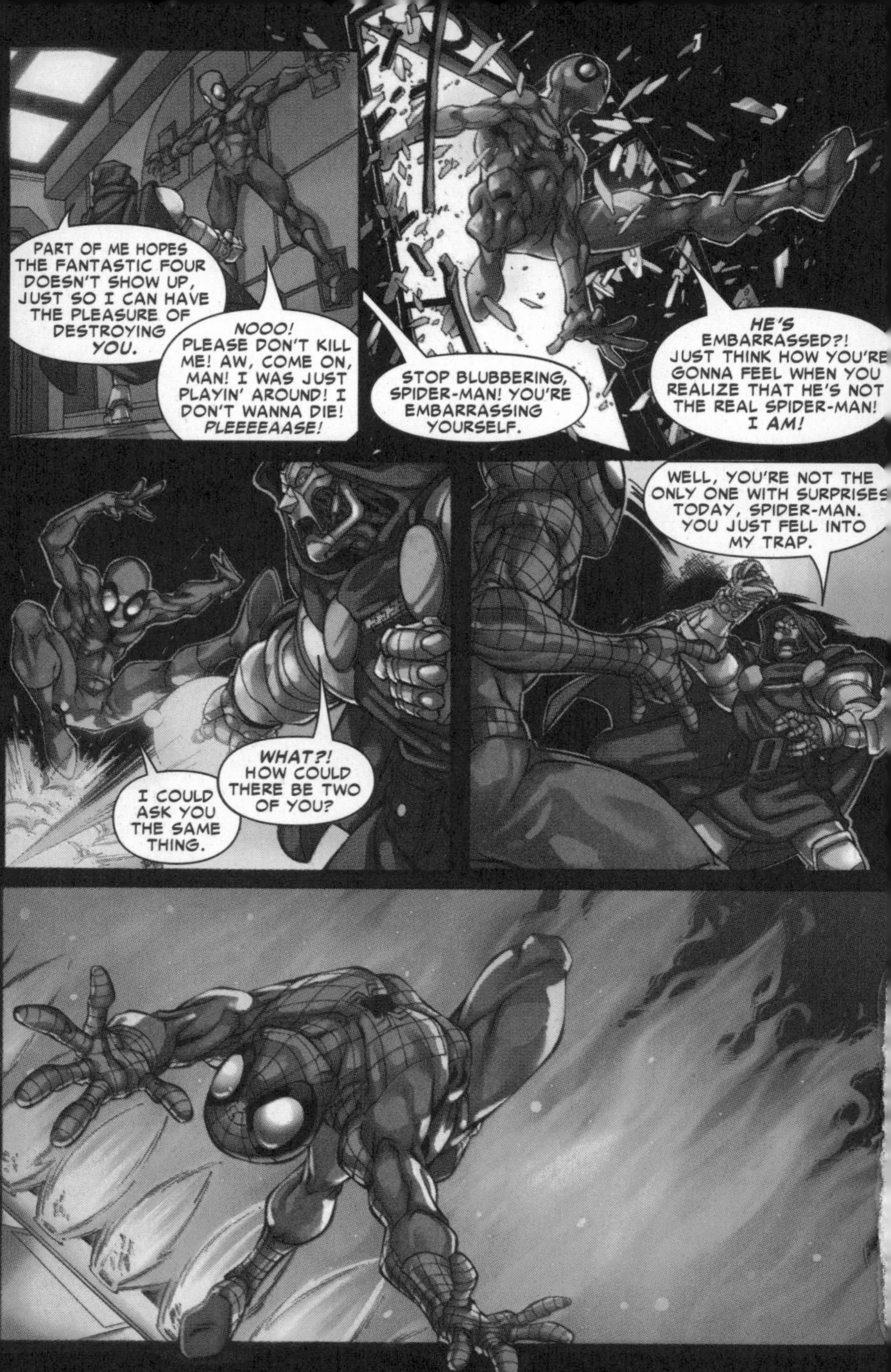
PART OF ME HOPES THE FANTASTIC FOUR DOESN'T SHOW UP, JUST SO I CAN HAVE THE PLEASURE OF DESTROYING *YOU.*
NOOO! PLEASE DON'T KILL ME! AW, COME ON, MAN! I WAS JUST PLAYIN' AROUND! I DON'T WANNA DIE! *PLEEEEAASE!*
STOP BLUBBERING, SPIDER-MAN! YOU'RE EMBARRASSING YOURSELF.
HE'S EMBARRASSED?! JUST THINK HOW YOU'RE GONNA FEEL WHEN YOU REALIZE THAT HE'S NOT THE REAL SPIDER-MAN! *I AM!*
WHAT?! HOW COULD THERE BE TWO OF YOU?
I COULD ASK YOU THE SAME THING.
WELL, YOU'RE NOT THE ONLY ONE WITH SURPRISES TODAY, SPIDER-MAN. YOU JUST FELL INTO MY TRAP.

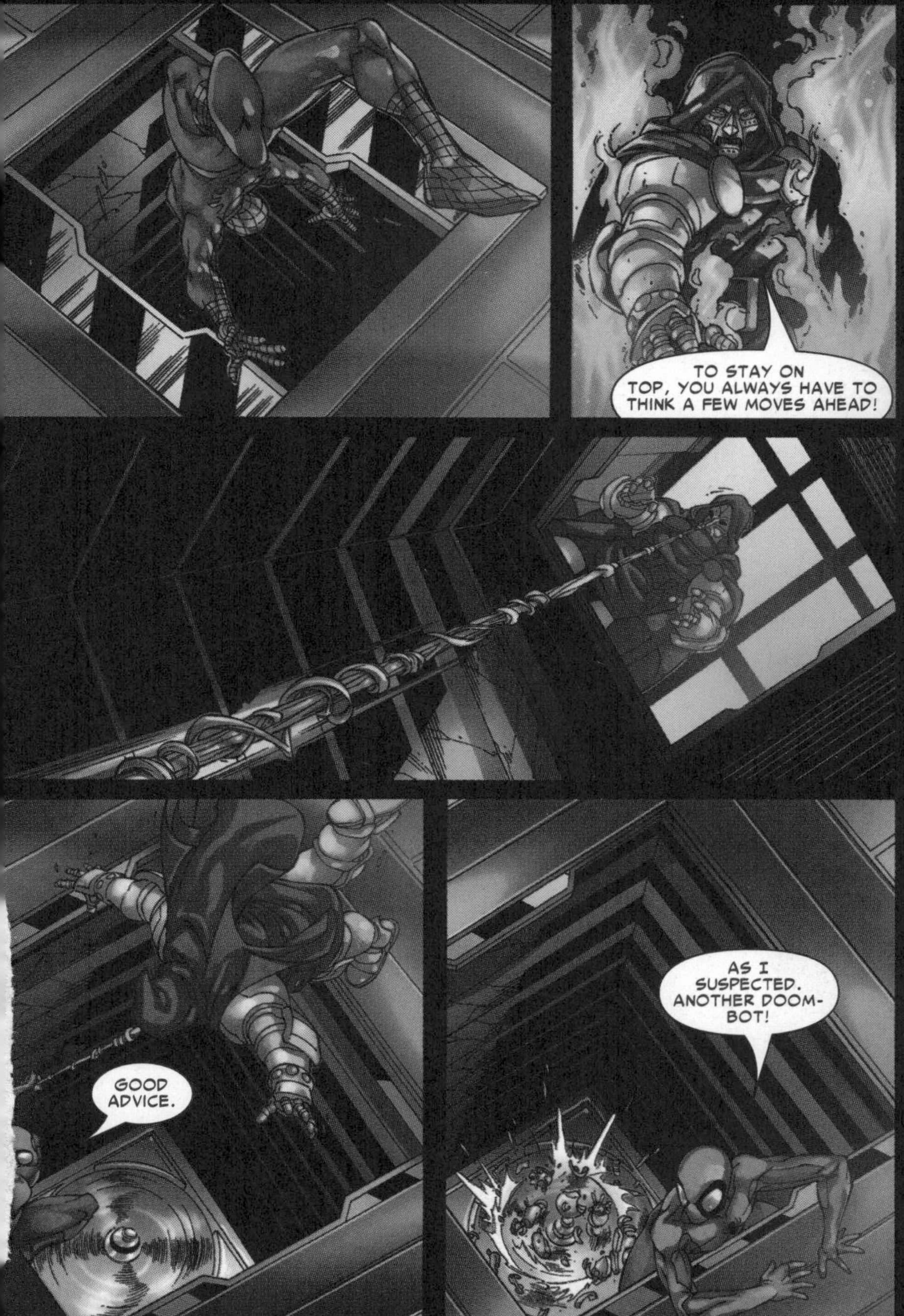
TO STAY ON TOP, YOU ALWAYS HAVE TO THINK A FEW MOVES AHEAD!
GOOD ADVICE.
AS I SUSPECTED. ANOTHER DOOM-BOT!

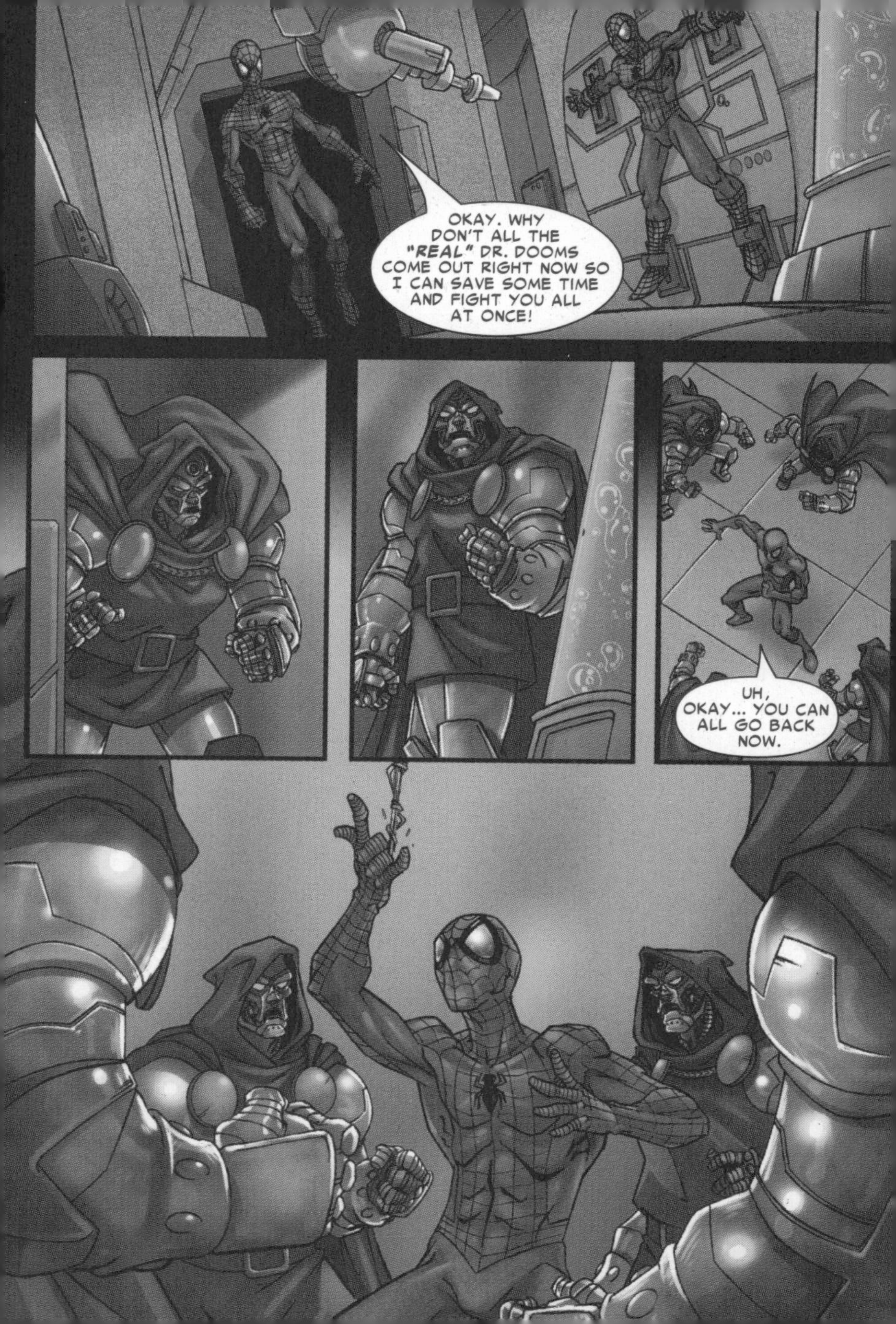
OKAY. WHY DON'T ALL THE "REAL" DR. DOOMS COME OUT RIGHT NOW SO I CAN SAVE SOME TIME AND FIGHT YOU ALL AT ONCE!
UH, OKAY... YOU CAN ALL GO BACK NOW.

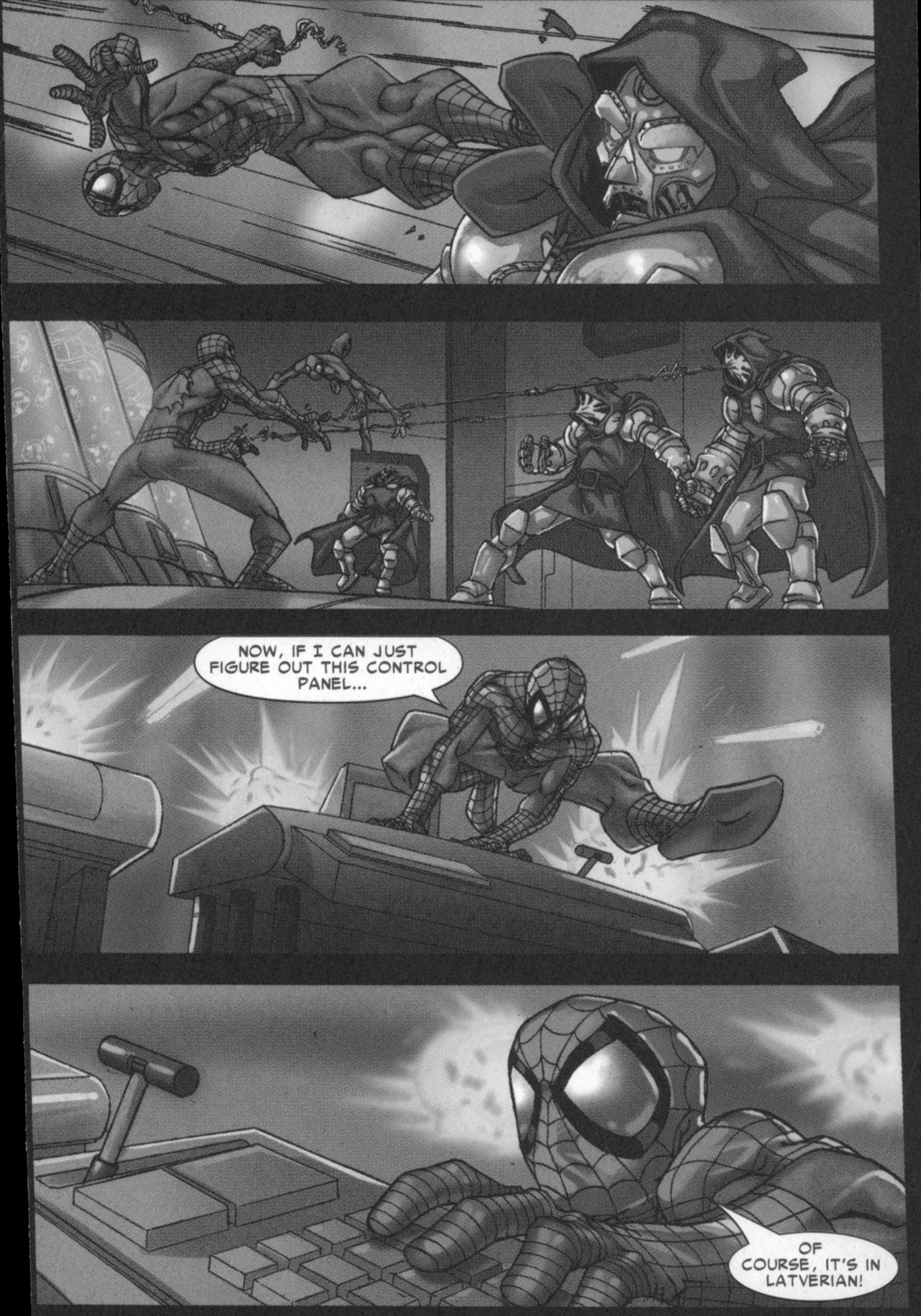

NOW, IF I CAN JUST FIGURE OUT THIS CONTROL PANEL...
OF COURSE, IT'S IN LATVERIAN!

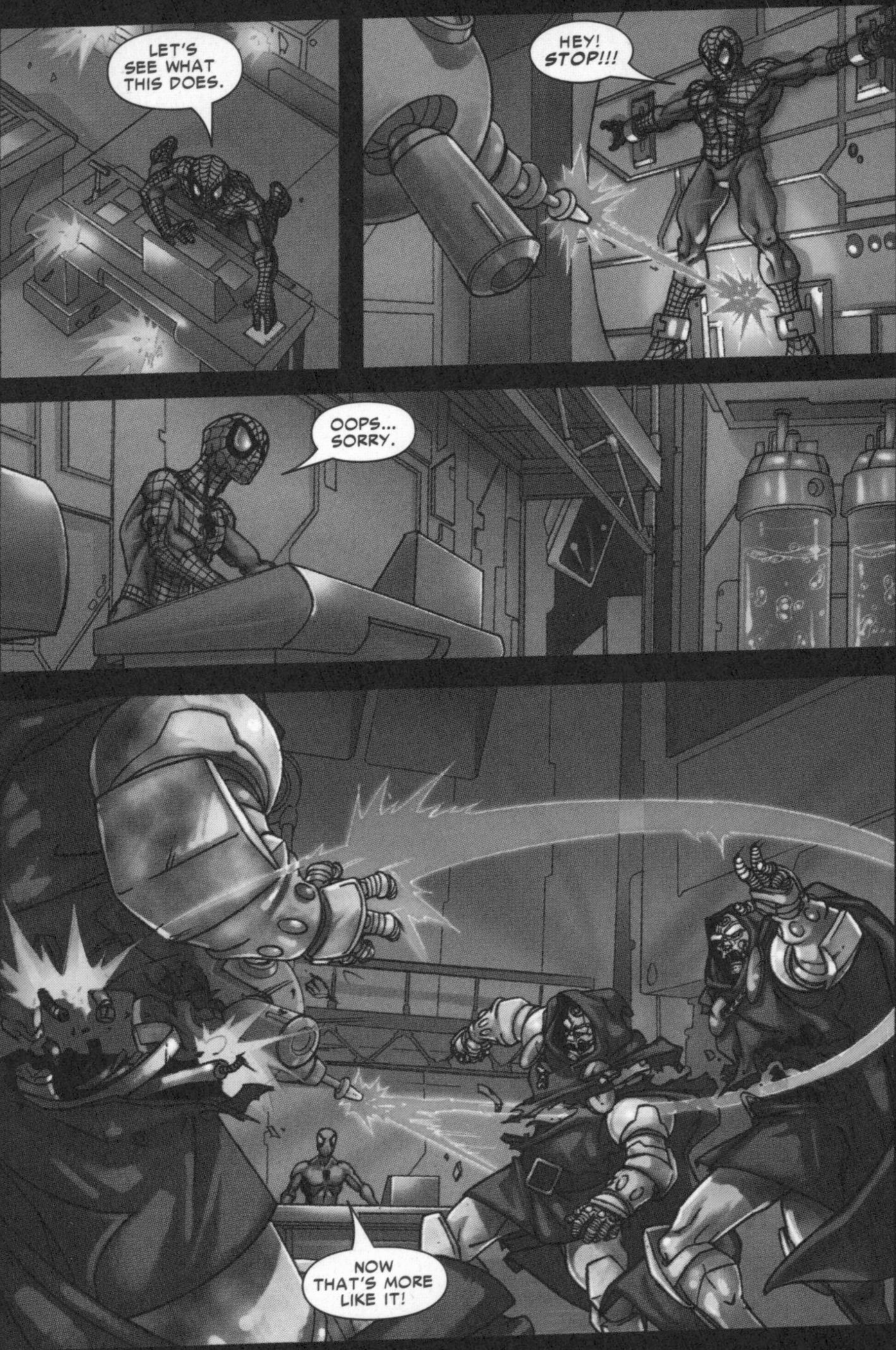
LET'S SEE WHAT THIS DOES.
HEY! STOP!!!
OOPS... SORRY.
NOW THAT'S MORE LIKE IT!

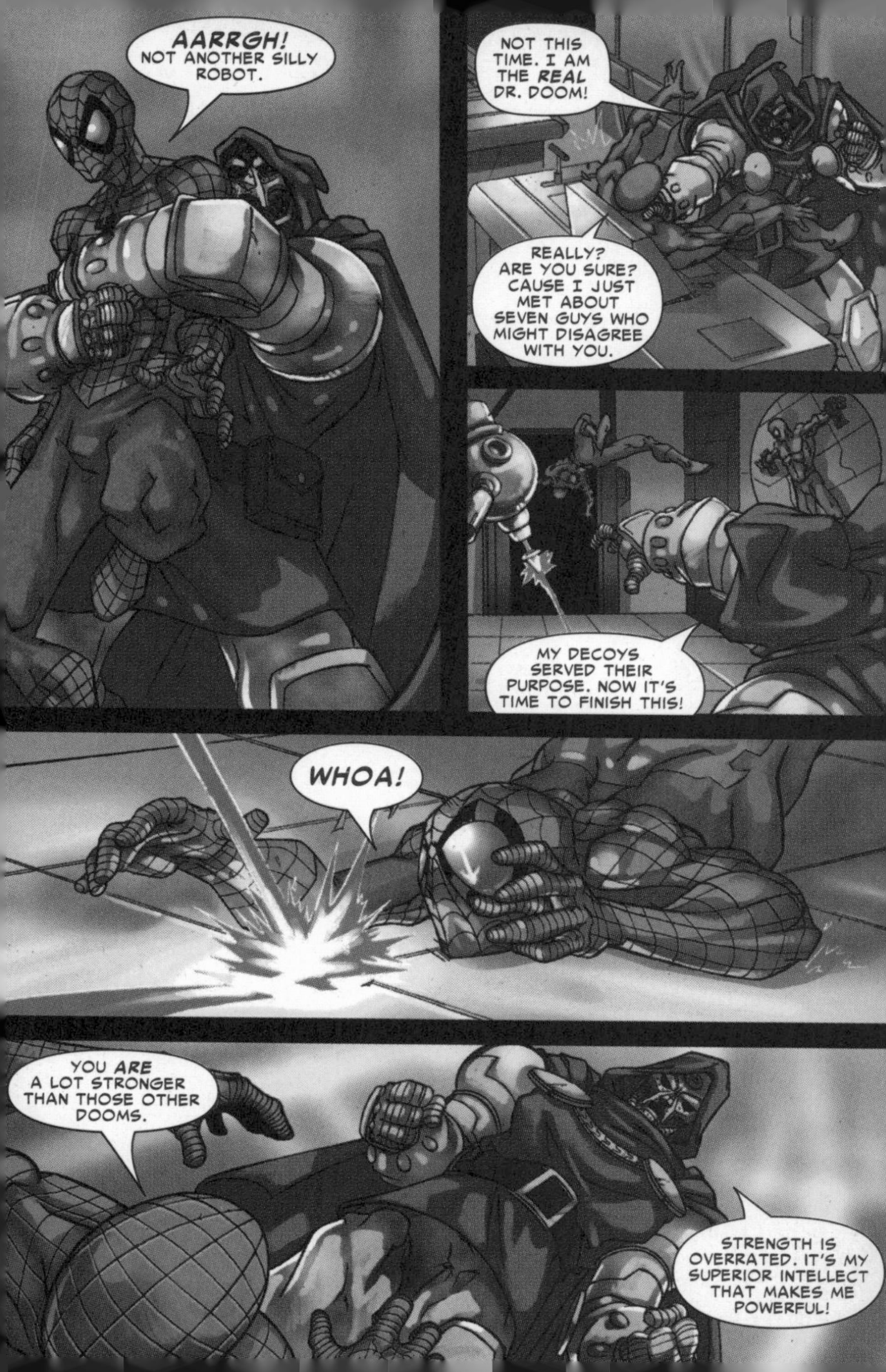
AARRGH! NOT ANOTHER SILLY ROBOT.
NOT THIS TIME. I AM THE REAL DR. DOOM!
REALLY? ARE YOU SURE? CAUSE I JUST MET ABOUT SEVEN GUYS WHO MIGHT DISAGREE WITH YOU.
MY DECOYS SERVED THEIR PURPOSE. NOW IT'S TIME TO FINISH THIS!
WHOA!
YOU ARE A LOT STRONGER THAN THOSE OTHER DOOMS.
STRENGTH IS OVERRATED. IT'S MY SUPERIOR INTELLECT THAT MAKES ME POWERFUL!

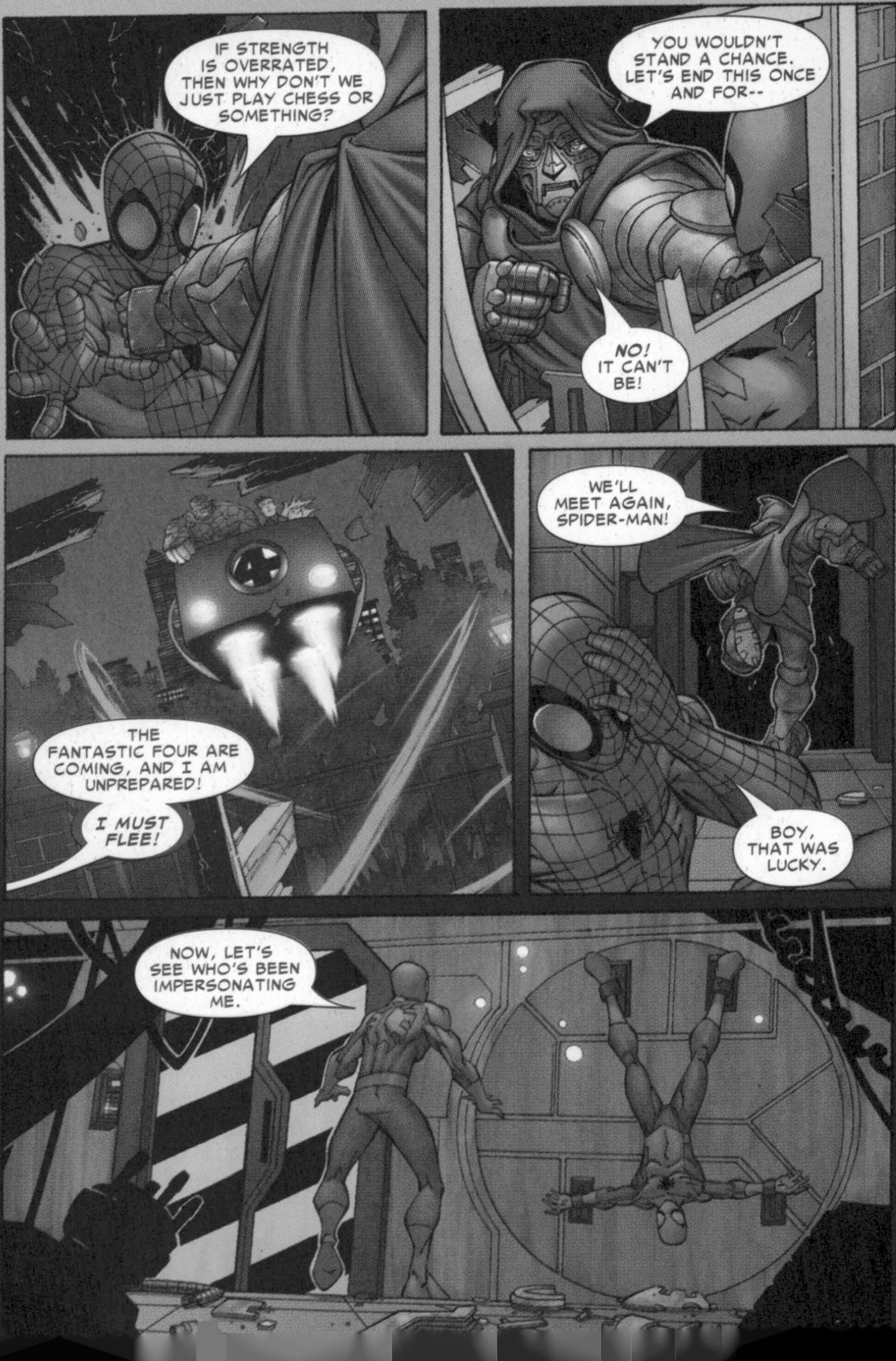
IF STRENGTH IS OVERRATED, THEN WHY DON'T WE JUST PLAY CHESS OR SOMETHING?
YOU WOULDN'T STAND A CHANCE. LET'S END THIS ONCE AND FOR--
NO! IT CAN'T BE!
THE FANTASTIC FOUR ARE COMING, AND I AM UNPREPARED!
I MUST FLEE!
WE'LL MEET AGAIN, SPIDER-MAN!
BOY, THAT WAS LUCKY.
NOW, LET'S SEE WHO'S BEEN IMPERSONATING ME.

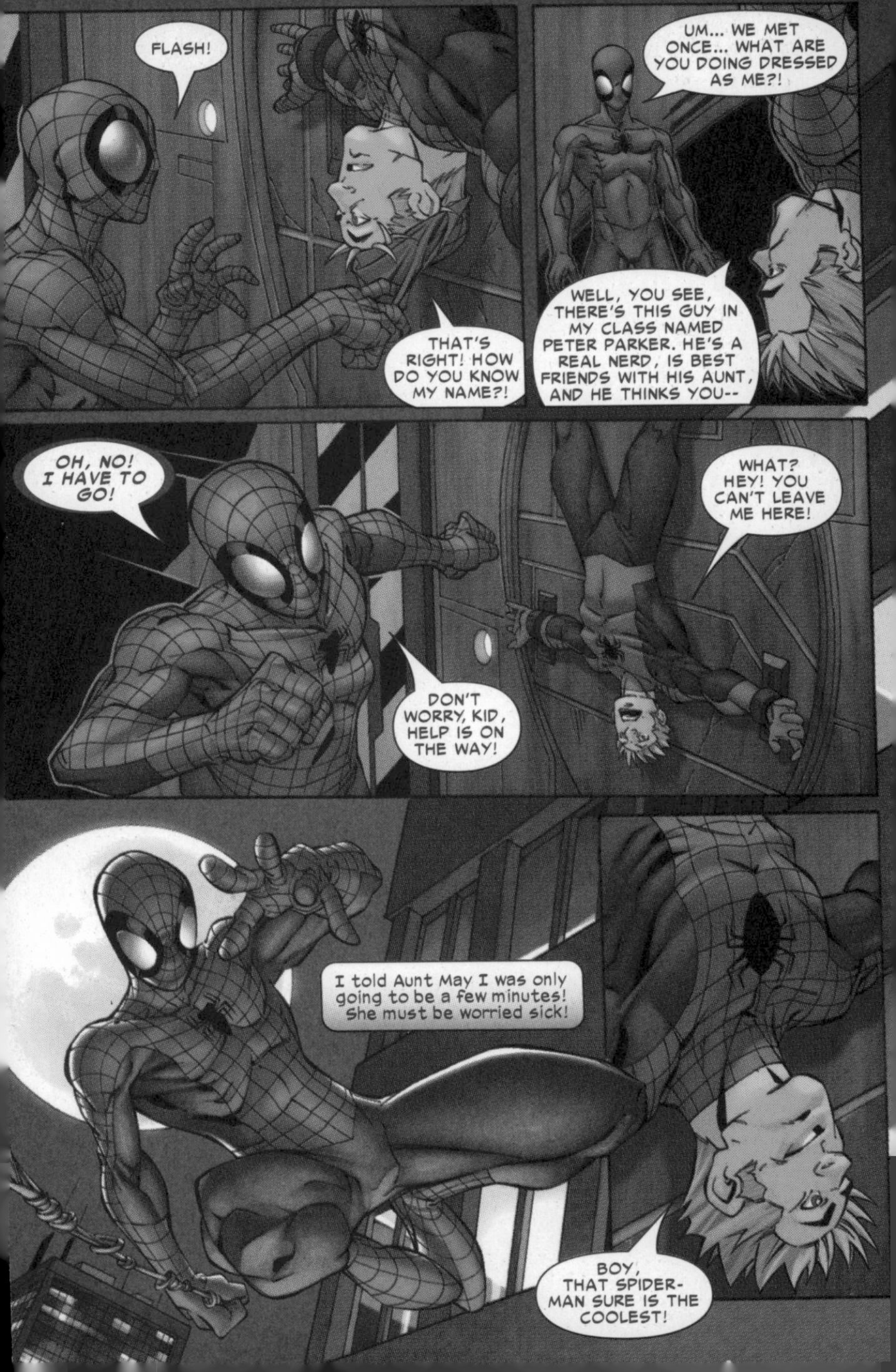
FLASH!
THAT'S RIGHT! HOW DO YOU KNOW MY NAME?!
UM... WE MET ONCE... WHAT ARE YOU DOING DRESSED AS ME?!
WELL, YOU SEE, THERE'S THIS GUY IN MY CLASS NAMED PETER PARKER. HE'S A REAL NERD, IS BEST FRIENDS WITH HIS AUNT, AND HE THINKS YOU--
OH, NO! I HAVE TO GO!
DON'T WORRY, KID, HELP IS ON THE WAY!
WHAT? HEY! YOU CAN'T LEAVE ME HERE!
I told Aunt May I was only going to be a few minutes! She must be worried sick!
BOY, THAT SPIDER-MAN SURE IS THE COOLEST!

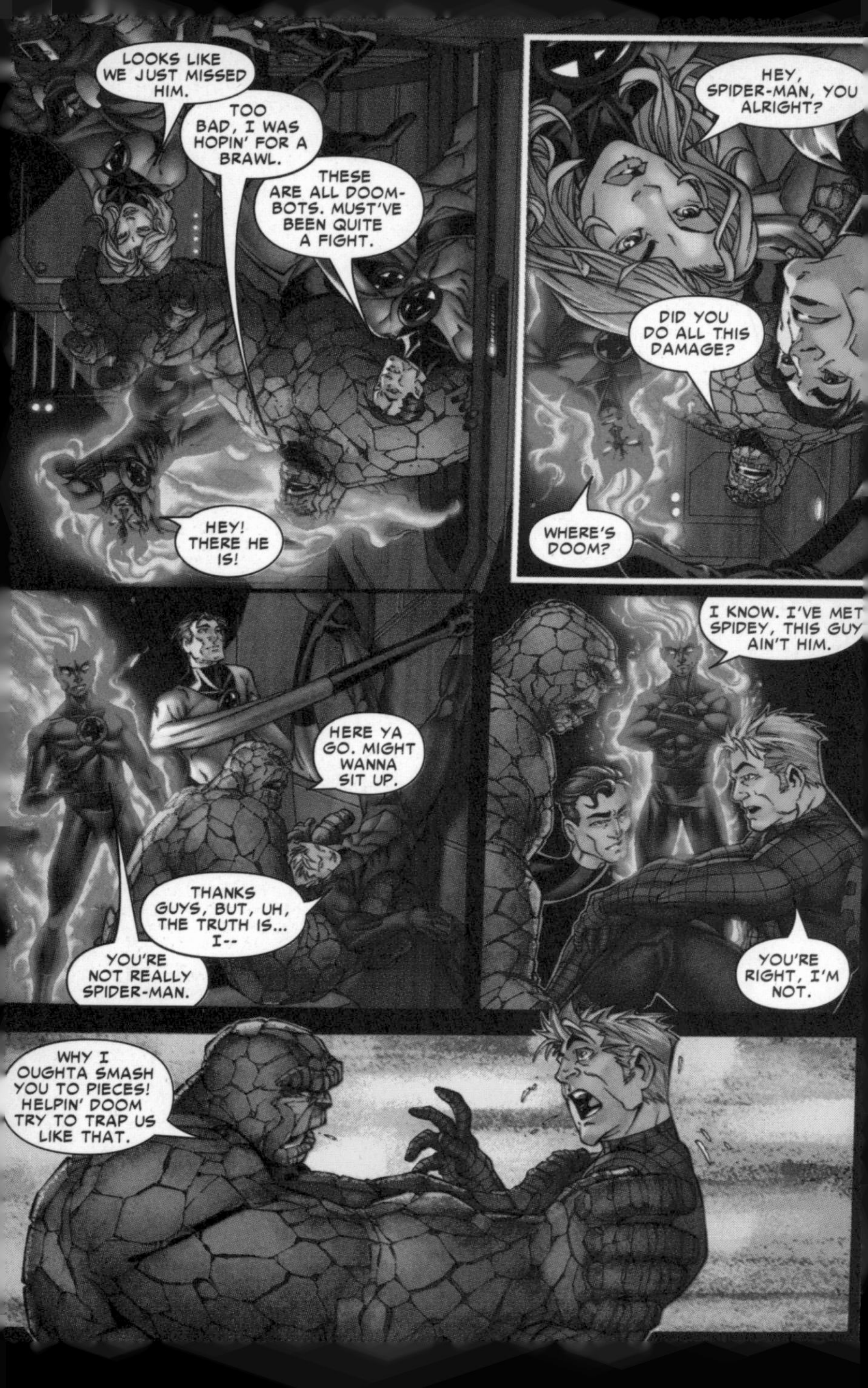
LOOKS LIKE WE JUST MISSED HIM.
TOO BAD, I WAS HOPIN' FOR A BRAWL.
THESE ARE ALL DOOM-BOTS. MUST'VE BEEN QUITE A FIGHT.
HEY! THERE HE IS!
HEY, SPIDER-MAN, YOU ALRIGHT?
DID YOU DO ALL THIS DAMAGE?
WHERE'S DOOM?
HERE YA GO. MIGHT WANNA SIT UP.
THANKS GUYS, BUT, UH, THE TRUTH IS... I--
YOU'RE NOT REALLY SPIDER-MAN.
I KNOW. I'VE MET SPIDEY, THIS GUY AIN'T HIM.
YOU'RE RIGHT, I'M NOT.
WHY I OUGHTA SMASH YOU TO PIECES! HELPIN' DOOM TRY TO TRAP US LIKE THAT.

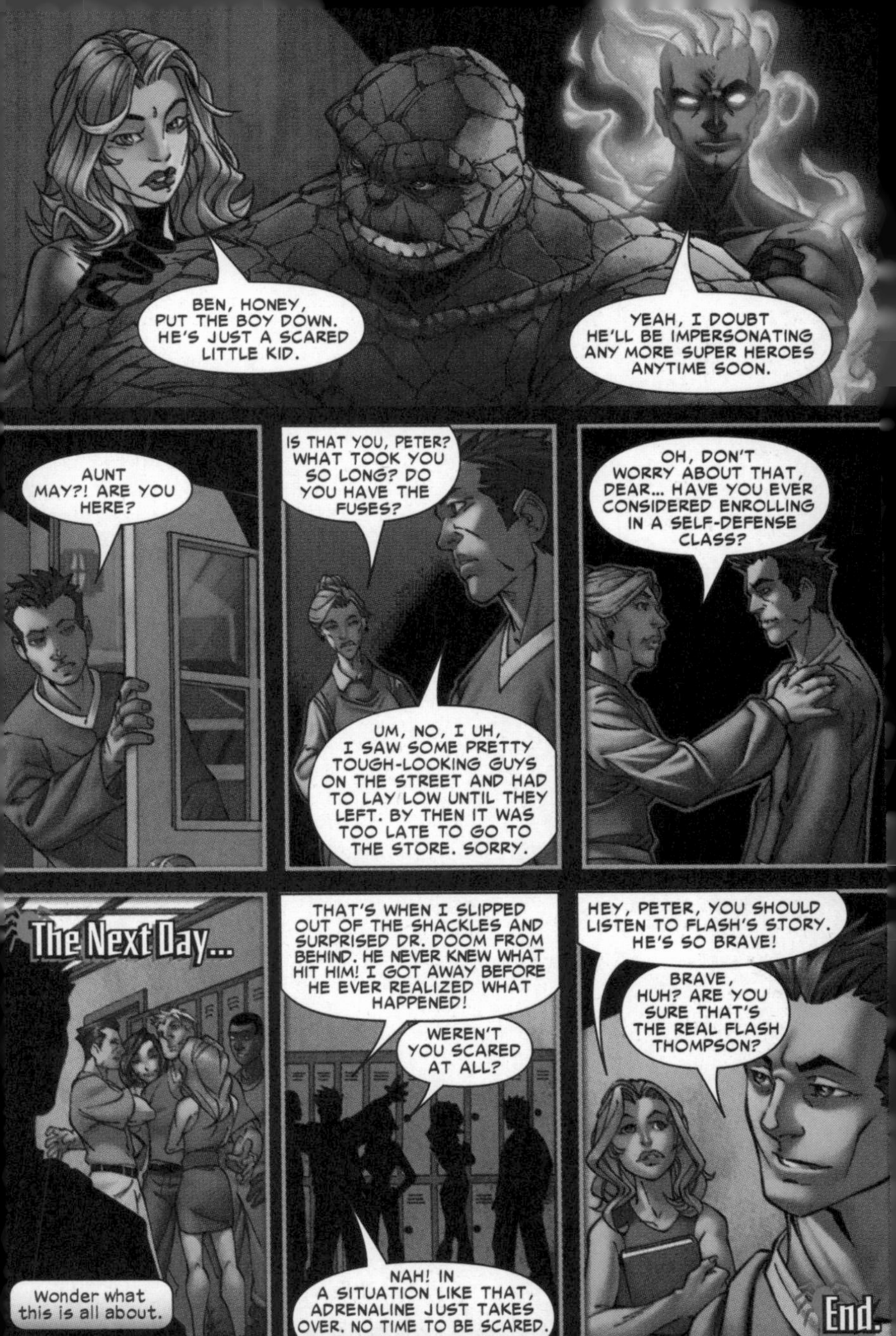
BEN, HONEY, PUT THE BOY DOWN. HE'S JUST A SCARED LITTLE KID.
YEAH, I DOUBT HE'LL BE IMPERSONATING ANY MORE SUPER HEROES ANYTIME SOON.
AUNT MAY?! ARE YOU HERE?
IS THAT YOU, PETER? WHAT TOOK YOU SO LONG? DO YOU HAVE THE FUSES?
UM, NO, I UH, I SAW SOME PRETTY TOUGH-LOOKING GUYS ON THE STREET AND HAD TO LAY LOW UNTIL THEY LEFT. BY THEN IT WAS TOO LATE TO GO TO THE STORE. SORRY.
OH, DON'T WORRY ABOUT THAT, DEAR... HAVE YOU EVER CONSIDERED ENROLLING IN A SELF-DEFENSE CLASS?
The Next Day...
Wonder what this is all about.
THAT'S WHEN I SLIPPED OUT OF THE SHACKLES AND SURPRISED DR. DOOM FROM BEHIND. HE NEVER KNEW WHAT HIT HIM! I GOT AWAY BEFORE HE EVER REALIZED WHAT HAPPENED!
WEREN'T YOU SCARED AT ALL?
NAH! IN A SITUATION LIKE THAT, ADRENALINE JUST TAKES OVER. NO TIME TO BE SCARED.
HEY, PETER, YOU SHOULD LISTEN TO FLASH'S STORY. HE'S SO BRAVE!
BRAVE, HUH? ARE YOU SURE THAT'S THE REAL FLASH THOMPSON?
End.

DOCTOR OCTOPUS

POWERS/WEAPONS

- Four telepathically controlled, super-strong steel tentacles attached to a harness encircling his lower chest and waist
- Brilliant engineer and inventor
- Extraordinary intelligence and concentration, enabling him to perform multiple complex actions simultaneously with his tentacles

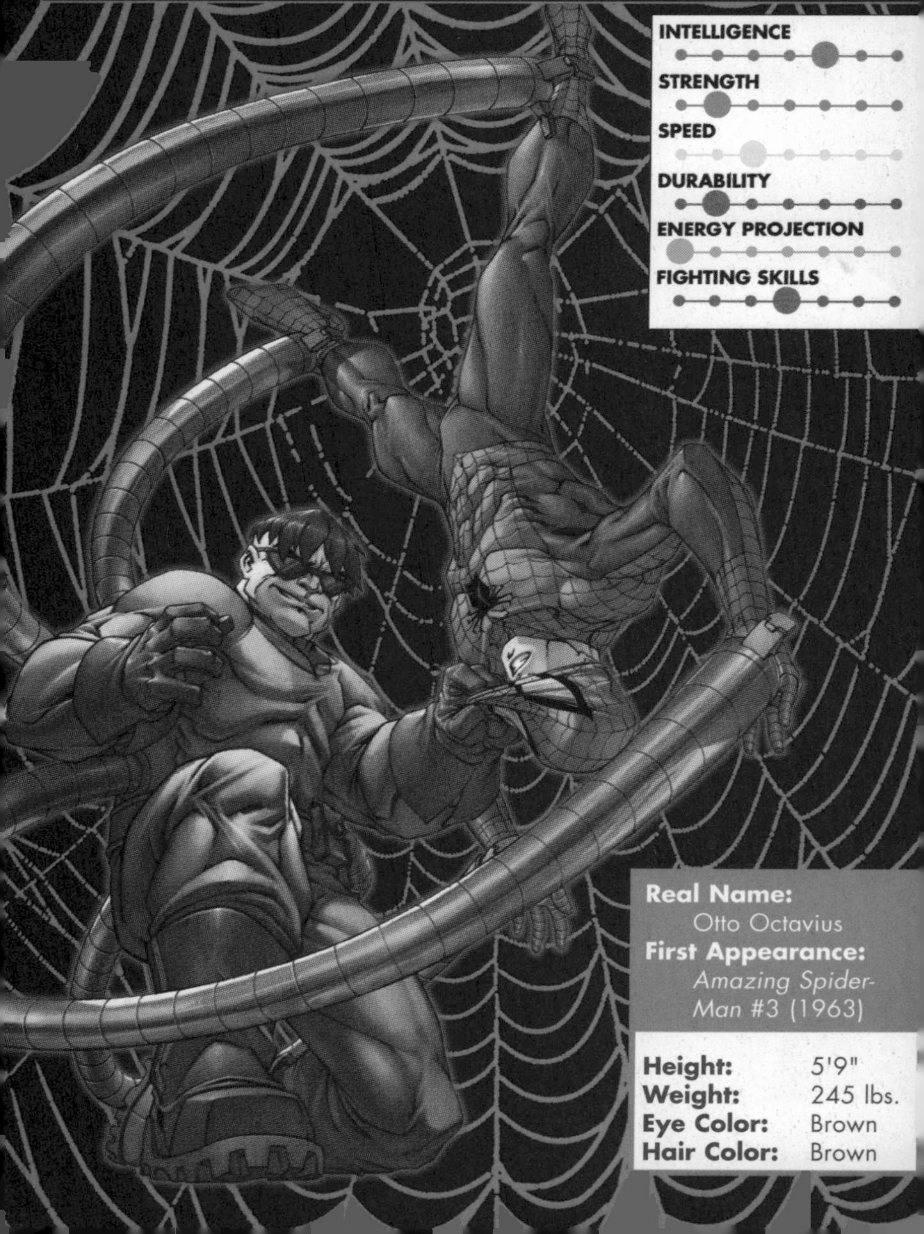

INTELLIGENCE	5 of 7
STRENGTH	2 of 7
SPEED	3 of 7
DURABILITY	2 of 7
ENERGY PROJECTION	1 of 7
FIGHTING SKILLS	4 of 7

Real Name:
Otto Octavius
First Appearance:
Amazing Spider-Man #3 (1963)

Height:	5'9"
Weight:	245 lbs.
Eye Color:	Brown
Hair Color:	Brown

The son of an overbearing mother and a bullying father, Otto Octavius grew up to become a reclusive but brilliant atomic researcher. To help manipulate radioactive substances from a safe distance, Otto constructed a chest harness controlling four mechanical, tentacle-like arms — earning himself the nickname Doctor Octopus. In a freak laboratory accident, volatile liquids exploded — bombarding the scientist with radiation. The substances left him capable of mentally controlling the arms, but the accident also caused irreversible brain damage — transforming the respected scientist into a megalomaniacal criminal. Waking in a hospital, Otto knew this newfound strength — combined with his awesome intellect — could render him supremely powerful. Holding the medical staff hostage, he easily defeated Spider-Man in their first meeting. Doc Ock then took control of a leading nuclear research facility and again squared off with the wall-crawler, who this time defeated him with one punch to the jaw.

After serving time, Doc Ock attempted to raise funds by springing gangster Blackie Gaxton from prison — assisted by Gaxton's lawyer, Bennett Brant. Spider-Man foiled the scheme, but could not save Bennett from being shot in front of his sister, Betty Brant. Octopus then assembled the first Sinister Six to combat Spider-Man. He plotted to take Betty hostage, knowing Spider-Man had previously rescued her and would likely do so again. May Parker, visiting Betty at the time, was also captured. Otto treated May kindly, and she remained blissfully unaware she had been kidnapped by the charming villain.

Following Spider-Man's defeat of the Sinister Six, Ock assembled another group of criminal underlings and established an undersea base. Calling himself the Master Planner, he embarked on a series of thefts of experimental substances — seeking to further expand his mastery of the atomic sciences. His goal: to develop a radiation ray with which he could rule the world. But his path was fated to entwine with Spider-Man's: When May fell sick, Peter provided her with a blood transfusion — not realizing the radioactivity in his plasma would kill her. The only substance capable of saving her was the experimental ISO-36. Peter managed to obtain enough money to fund the operation, but the Master Planner's forces hijacked the shipment for their own deadly research. Spider-Man tracked the Master Planner to his underwater hideout and confronted his foe, revealed to be Doc Ock. After the base was destroyed, Doctor Octopus escaped once more. Spider-Man recovered the ISO-36 and saved Aunt May's life with the aid of Dr. Curt Connors (Lizard).

Doctor Octopus' next scheme involved the theft of a projector that could disable any device. After two failed attempts, Otto finally succeeded on his third. Turning the Nullifier against Spider-Man, he caused the wall-crawler to lose his memory and persuaded him they were allies. He then enlisted Spider-Man's help to steal the remaining components for the device. Though the hero had not regained his memory, his instinctive spider-sense persuaded him not to trust Doc Ock, and he defeated him once more. Now imprisoned, with his arms confiscated, Otto demonstrated that the range of his psionic control over the limbs had increased to a far greater distance than previously believed. The arms freed him from captivity; in the ensuing battle between Doc Ock and Spider-Man, George Stacy was killed while protecting an innocent child.

Free again, Doctor Octopus seized upon the Kingpin's absence to gather his forces and launch an all-out gang war against Hammerhead's thugs. But Spider-Man's involvement quickly resulted in Otto's return to prison. While incarcerated, Doctor Octopus learned May Parker had inherited a small Canadian island containing a commercial nuclear reactor. On his release, he set out to woo and marry May. But Hammerhead interrupted the wedding, and the ensuing chase and brawl led to the destruction of the reactor.

When Doc Ock went to war with the Owl, Spider-Man and the Black Cat attempted to intervene. Devastated that the confrontation had left the Black Cat near death, a cold-hearted Peter said farewell to his friends before entering what he believed to be his final showdown with Doctor Octopus. Spider-Man's victory was remorseless, and Doc Ock developed a morbid fear of his arachnid foe. Imprisoned in a mental institution, Otto struggled with his overwhelming phobia of Spider-Man. Knowing he could not face his foe directly, Ock's next plan involved the use of biological weapons to kill the entire population of New York. Spider-Man was forced to fake a humiliating defeat lest the city be destroyed, restoring Otto's self-confidence.

Still, Otto had clearly changed. As a young scientist, he had fallen in love with a fellow researcher, Mary Alice Burke — but his demanding mother jealously sabotaged the relationship. Learning Mary Alice was dying from AIDS, Otto began a desperate search for a cure — stealing research materials to do so. His attempts failed, Mary Alice died, and the villain meekly surrendered to Spider-Man. A world-weary Otto nonetheless escaped from prison. At the time, Spider-Man was dying from a chemical virus. Hoping to one day kill the hero himself, Doc Ock captured and unmasked his foe. Analyzing the virus, Otto offered him a cure. Daring to trust his enemy, Peter accepted the mixture and was healed.

But having found his own salvation in this act, Doctor Octopus did not live to enjoy it. Intending to protect Peter by killing his enemies, Kaine murdered Doc Ock by snapping his neck. But Dr. Carolyn Trainer, Otto's young assistant, had been working with him in the area of solid holographic projection and mind-to-computer communication. Prior to Peter's unmasking, she had created a backup brain-imprint of Doc Ock. With Otto's passing, the backup of his mind became a software projection known as the Master Programmer, and Carolyn used his tentacles to become the second Doctor Octopus. Meanwhile, the Rose (Jacob Conover) employed a cult, the True Believers, to magically resurrect Doctor Octopus as an empty-minded servant. As soon as he was raised, Carolyn uploaded the Master Programmer persona into Octavius' brain. She returned his tentacles to him, and they fled.

With his memories restored from a past snapshot, Otto has forgotten he once knew Spider-Man's true identity. He remains very much the deadly and manipulative criminal genius he was in his heyday.

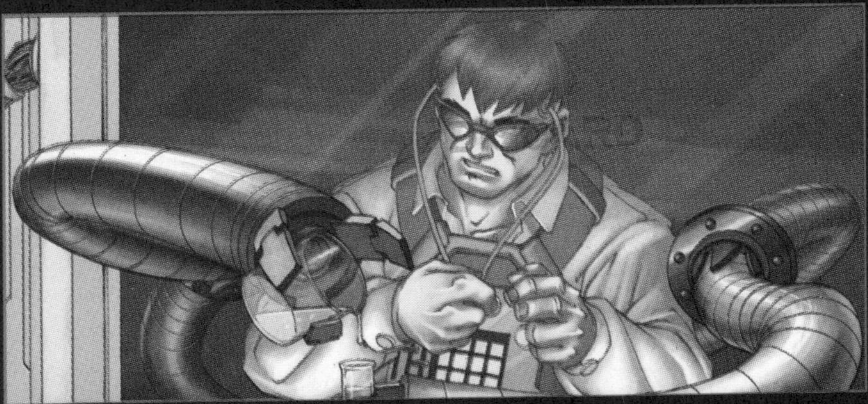